# Our Friend Travis

CSHI Media Publications
2015

# Our Friend Travis

## THE TRAVIS ALEXANDER STORY

*Chris and Sky Hughes*

FIRST EDITION

CSHI Media Productions
P.O. Box 13
Preston, Idaho 83263
(888) 400-6412

ISBN: 0692446613
ISBN 13: 9780692446614
Library of Congress Control Number: 2015940956

Cover design by 2Soph Creative Solution
CSHI Media Publications, Preston, ID

# Table of Contents

# Dedication

This book is dedicated to Detective Esteban Flores of the Mesa Police Department and his family. Thank you, Detective Flores, for your dedication and compassion. Thank you for getting justice for Travis Alexander. To the Flores family for the sacrifices you make daily by allowing your husband and father to protect and serve the rest of us.

# Acknowledgements

To Travis's family: you guys are amazing! We are so sorry for your loss and what you have been forced to endure ever since. Your support and love for Travis has been a beautiful display of devotion. Travis loves you all so much.

To Deanna for always keeping it classy! We love you!

To Juan Martinez for your bulldog style and passion for winning.

To all those who showed such amazing love and support to Travis's family and friends.

To Nora and Elna for their countless hours in seeking justice for Travis while supporting his family and friends.

To Michael, thank you for encouraging us to write this book. Thank you for your example of constant giving and helping. Thank you for your love, support, and friendship. We love you!

To our cute kids, who have dealt with all the craziness surrounding this trial. You guys have been amazingly strong. Thanks for being our kids. We love you!

And most importantly, to Travis Victor Alexander. Thank you for being such an amazing example of kindness, love, and service. Thank you for your friendship. You will continue to change lives and help people. We look forward to the day we meet again. We love you!

In Memory of

Travis Victor Alexander
July 28, 1977 - June 4, 2008

and

Antonio "Tony" Flores
September 9, 1999 - January 24, 2015

Note to the readers: The majority of this book is written in Sky's voice, from her perspective, unless otherwise noted.

# Introduction

CHRIS AND I DIDN'T WRITE this book for a publisher, to win a literary award, or to become best-selling authors. We wrote this book to tell Travis's story and to defend him against the many despicable false-hoods presented as fact in the ten-month murder trial. Further, we want the world to know who Travis really was. We wrote this book to tell the truth and to defend the good name of our friend Travis.

We considered writing this book for many years until we received a call from Shanna Hogan, a true-crime writer and the author of *Dancing with Death*. She informed us that she was in the process of writing a book about Travis titled *Picture Perfect: The Jodi Arias Story*. This came as a great relief to both of us. We wanted to defend Travis, but we didn't want to take on the monumental task of writing a book. We cheered Shanna on in her effort to write her book, and we made ourselves available as often as she needed to give her any additional details.

In the end, Shanna wrote a fantastic book, while the book was favorable to Travis, his full story had not been told, and many of the lies put forward about Travis during the trial were not refuted. What we really hoped was for someone to write a book about the real Travis Alexander—his life, his light, his triumphs, his mistakes, his death, his murderer's trial, and his legacy. As it would turn out, Chris and I were the only ones who could really tell that story. Travis was our best friend. He was our business partner. We were like a big brother and sister to him, perhaps even like a mother and father. We were there the night he met his murderer, and we watched their relationship bloom, wither, and die. Our home became their rendezvous point, a place where they could meet in the middle—Travis coming from Arizona, and Jodi coming from Palm Desert. We had a front-row seat to this drama and tragedy as it unfolded, which provides so much insight into what really happened. After serious consideration, we made a decision to write this book.

Initially, we intended this book only to be about Travis. We did not want to mention his murderer's name, but there were so many lies that needed to be addressed which cannot be accomplished without talking about *her* and all that she did to him.

Anyone who followed the trial knows that Travis, like the rest of us, was far from perfect. That said, he *was* a great guy. So great in fact that the defense could not find one man, woman, or child who would take the witness stand and say anything bad about him. That's pretty impressive. Nonetheless, his private life, his emails, texts, and phone records became a matter of public record. Virtually everyone, if put under this kind of scrutiny, would be embarrassed at best and absolutely mortified at worst. Though not perfect, Travis, more than anyone we know, made a focused effort to become better every day. He was an example to us in so many ways and an amazingly loyal friend. We hope you will be able to get to know Travis Alexander a little better by reading this book. We hope you will be inspired by the amazing person he was and what he had accomplished in his short life. We hope you will realize what a horrible injustice was done, and what a great and powerful spirit was taken from this earth way too soon. We hope you will come to love him, if you haven't already. So many people reached out to us during the trial and said things like, "I know it's weird, but I feel like I knew him." Or, "I feel so close to him." People have told us that he has changed their lives. That is Travis. Those that knew him loved him. They also felt an amazing amount of love from him. It's our hope that by reading this book and getting to know Travis better that you will want to be better and do better. That's what Travis was all about. He was about serving more, forgiving more, being better, being kinder, having more gratitude, loving more, and ultimately fulfilling your divine human potential.

Chris and I have written this book to honor the memory of our friend Travis. Before each chapter, we have included facts about Travis, short stories, or his favorite sayings that we hope will help you get to know Travis a little better.

# Prologue

CHRIS AND I HOSTED A training event for independent associates of Pre-Paid Legal Services, Inc., every Tuesday night at the San Bernardino Hilton Hotel. One Tuesday evening in October 2006, me, Chris, Travis, and our friend Jacob were standing in front of our registration table that was situated in the hallway just outside the banquet room where Travis would be training within the hour. Our friend Hollie was sitting in a chair behind the registration table. Travis, ever the entertainer, had us all laughing at something witty he'd said. Just as our laughter subsided, an attractive blonde-haired woman turned the corner and was walking toward us. She had attended a couple of our Tuesday night trainings. Jacob and Hollie knew *of* her, but didn't really know her.

We watched her for a moment, then Jacob whispered, "Stay away from that chick! She's crazy!" He then told us that he had looked at her Myspace page and thought there was something wrong with her. "She's into Wicca and makes all sorts of crazy posts. I've never seen anyone with so many photos of themselves. She is nuts . . . and I know nuts!"

Jacob didn't know that Travis and the "crazy chick" had been spending time together. Chris and I just looked at each other, squirming, hoping this awkward moment wouldn't last long. Travis was in on the conversation, but he didn't say anything. He just quietly walked away from us and greeted the blonde with a warm embrace and a kiss on the cheek.

Jacob had a stunned look on his face. "Insert foot in mouth," he said.

Hollie gasped and cupped her hand over her mouth to prevent the laughter from roaring out. Travis and the blonde walked toward the banquet room. He opened the door for her, they walked in together, and the door closed behind them.

Hollie, Chris, and I let it all out! We laughed hysterically, partly because it was funny, and partly because it was so outrageously awkward. Jacob stood there quietly, looking at the closed banquet door, realizing just how far he had crammed his foot into his mouth.

"So, uh . . ." Chris said, "they've been hanging out."

Suddenly, Jacob's look of disbelief and bewilderment vanished. Now he looked serious and very concerned. "Remember I said this," Jacob warned. "That woman is going to ruin his business, and ruin his life. I'm not even kidding. You watch."

"Something is not right with her," Hollie chimed in. "I don't trust her, and I don't like her."

Time would soon reveal how prophetic Jacob's words were and how spot-on Hollie was.

# Background

ON THE AFTERNOON OF JUNE 4, 2008, Travis Alexander was savagely murdered by his ex-girlfriend, Jodi Arias, in the bedroom of his home in Mesa, Arizona. Though no one but Jodi knows exactly why she committed such a heinous crime, several theories have been put forward. Some feel it was because Travis had plans to take another woman on a trip to Cancun, Mexico, on June 10, 2008. Others speculate that Jodi decided that if she could no longer have him, no one would. Still, others feel it was the big fight between them, which occurred on May 26, 2008, that ultimately triggered her decision to slaughter him. The fight began with her not wanting to put "incriminating" information about something she had done in writing or on a voicemail. She also told him she would be contacting an attorney. We believe it was all of the above. We feel strongly that each of these stressors contributed to her premeditated decision to end his life, specifically the May 26 blowout. It was in the heat of this fight, via text and Google Chat, where Travis would finally see Jodi for the monster that she really is, and he told her so, saying things like:

"I've never been hurt so badly by someone!" "You don't care! It doesn't serve your evilness!"

"I don't want your apology! I want you to know how evil I think you are!" "You are the worst thing that has ever happened to me!"

"Why did you manipulate me into loving you? Why me? I was a good guy! Why did you have to do it to me? Why do you hate me?"

"I'm just tired of all of this, it's killing me!"

He even called her a sociopath.

Jodi Arias was a twenty-seven-year-old waitress from Yreka, California. She worked incredibly hard to manufacture an image, one that in no way resembled who she really was. She painstakingly and purposefully made Travis's world *her* world—his business, his religion, his friends . . . his life. And all of that was about to go away for her. Travis was her "golden ticket" out of her miserable life. No more jumping from meaningless job to meaningless job. No more moving around. No more struggling to pay the bills. No more living in a tiny, little room in her grandparents' humble home in a small town most people have never heard of, much less ever been to. Yes, all of that was abruptly threatened, including the status she wrongfully assumed she had achieved by being "Travis's girlfriend."

After eighteen months, Travis's eyes had finally been pried open. Jodi was about to be exposed for what she really was. Travis was finally moving on. Jodi was attractive, and she knew how to work it. She could find another successful man to manipulate, but maybe she feared that Travis was going to tell the truth about her, ruining her prospects in the only social circle where she had access to people who could save her from her unhappy, little world. Realizing her predicament, she began to plan what she naïvely thought was the perfect murder.

Following that May 26 fight, Jodi asked Darryl Brewer, an old boyfriend she lived with while she was dating Travis, if she could borrow a couple of gas cans for a "trip she was taking to Mesa." This trip to Mesa, which only Darryl and one other person knew about, would coincide with another trip she had planned to Utah to spend time with Ryan Burns, a rising star in Pre-Paid Legal. Jodi planned this trip to see Ryan after the fight as well. Two days after the May 26 fight, Jodi's grandparents' home, where she was living at the time, was robbed. Everything of value was left untouched in the home except a DVD player, a .25 caliber pistol, and $30 Jodi claimed had been taken from her bedroom. It was *after* the May 26 fight when Jodi evidently decided that her car—a newer, silver Infinity G35—would be too conspicuous to take on her secret trip. She opted to rent a car instead. At first, the rental company offered her a red car. That, too, would be conspicuous, so she refused the car. She wanted something more muted, less conspicuous. Finally, they offered her a white car, which she accepted.

One of her first stops was at Darryl's house to pick up two five-gallon gas cans she had asked to borrow. She also visited Matt McCartney, another former boyfriend. She also met up with a man that said she borrowed money from him. He reported that she was in a rush to get to Mesa to fix things. Later, she stopped at Walmart to buy a third gas can. She stopped in Pasadena, California, for gas, filling up her car and the three gas cans. She turned off her cell phone. She drove to Travis Alexander's house in Mesa, Arizona, arriving around four in the morning on June 4. She left Travis's home in the late afternoon/early evening of June 4. She arrived in Utah on the morning of June 5, and was making out with Ryan Burns before the end of the day.

No one had heard from Travis in days. His mutilated body was found on June 9, 2008, crumpled up on the floor of the shower in his master bedroom. He had been stabbed twenty-nine times, and his throat was slit from ear to ear. He had been nearly decapitated. He had been shot in the face with a .25 caliber pistol. The bathroom and the hallway leading to the bathroom from his master bedroom were covered in blood . . . a lot of blood. When the police began asking questions, many of Travis's friends immediately implicated Jodi Arias.

After initially denying a request for an interview because she was "too busy," Jodi finally agreed to be questioned by the Mesa Police Department on June 19. She was emphatic that she was nowhere near Mesa, and that she had not seen Travis since April. She even gave the investigator the name of someone she felt might have had a motive for killing Travis.

On July 9, 2008 Jodi's twenty-eighth birthday, she was indicted on first-degree murder charges. On July 15, she was arrested on suspicion of first-degree murder. After spending one night in jail, her story changed. She admitted that she actually had been in Mesa, Arizona, with Travis on the day of his death. She further reported that she barely escaped with her life. She told a farfetched tale of two masked intruders, a man and a woman, claiming that *they* were the ones who had killed Travis. She could not be clear about exactly what happened because one of the intruders had knocked her unconscious. When she "came to," she saw blood and heard Travis moaning. While trying to help Travis, the female intruder approached her. Jodi attacked her and a struggle ensued. Then, the man came into the room, put the gun to Jodi's head, and pulled the trigger. Miraculously, the gun misfired, and Jodi was able to flee from the house. This was not before the intruders reached into Jodi's purse, pulled out her vehicle registration, and told her they now knew where she lived and that they were going to kill her and her family.

According to Jodi, she had just endured a horrific attack and witnessed Travis struggling for his life. She never called the police. She never called Travis to see if he survived. She never told anyone about the alleged attack. She drove to Utah, spent a romantic evening with Ryan Burns, and then drove back to Yreka, California, settling back into work and her room at her grandparents' house. She told and retold this story for two years, including in front of national news cameras.

If our memory is correct, it was around May 2010 when Jodi revealed a new tale. According to her, the truth of the matter was that *she* killed Travis in self-defense. Travis was in the shower. Jodi, using Travis's new camera, was squatting, taking "tasteful pictures" of him, when she dropped his camera onto the bathmat from about two feet in the air. Outraged, Travis allegedly exploded out of the shower, picked her up, and body-slammed her on the hard bathroom floor. Scared for her life, she got up, ran into his oversized bedroom closet, climbed up the shelving, and grabbed "Travis's gun" (Travis did not own a gun). Jodi claimed Travis came at her like "a linebacker," and the gun must have gone off because she did not remember shooting him. She described a "fog" that prevented her from recalling critical moments of her tall tale. The next thing she knew, she was driving in the desert. She noticed that her hands were covered in blood, and she "knew something bad had happened."

Realizing the depth of her troubles, and in a desperate effort of self-preservation, Jodi got creative. Not only did she claim that Travis body-slammed her just prior to her killing him, but she also claimed that he'd beaten her on many occasions throughout their relationship. But she did not stop there. She went on to claim that this man, who was "the man of her dreams" and would be "an amazing father" to her children, raped little boys. Her vile slander has no bounds. Her version of the story ended with her as both victim and hero. She did the world a favor, by doing the "pedophile" in. A jury of twelve of her peers, the national media, and the rest of the world saw it differently. They completely rejected Jodi and her ridiculous tales.

It the State of Arizona vs Jodi Arias, Juan Martinez was the prosecutor. The defense team consisted of two attorneys, Kirk Nurmi and Jennifer Willmott. Also a part of the defense team was Maria De La Rosa, a mitigation specialist. The death-penalty trial, held in the Maricopa County Court in Phoenix, Arizona, began on January 2, 2013. The guilt phase lasted more than four months. Jodi was on the witness stand for an astounding eighteen days. On May 8, 2013, Jodi was found guilty of first-degree premeditated murder. Within minutes of her conviction, Jodi was providing a pre-arranged media interview. On May 23, 2013, the jury came back hung for the penalty phase of the trial. Four jurors wanted her to have life in prison. Eight jurors wanted her to have the death penalty. In Arizona, when there is a hung jury in a death penalty case, the Prosecutor's office can choose to retry the penalty portion of the case. The penalty phase retrial began October 21, 2014.

# CHAPTER 1

# Travis Alexander's Early Life

Written with the help of Deanna Reid.

*Travis would often repeat several of his*
*funny sayings and movie quotes.*
*Here are a few of our favorites:*
*"Word to Big Bird, ya big nerd!"*
*"Is a ten-pound robin fat?"*
*"San-dee-ah-go!" - Ron Burgundy, Anchorman*

TRAVIS VICTOR ALEXANDER WAS BORN on July 28, 1977, to Gary and Pamela Alexander in Riverside, California. He had two older brothers, Gary and Greg, and five younger siblings, Tanisha, Samantha, Hillary, Steven, and Allie. He was an adorable child, with green eyes and full lips. He had the look of a king's son, but his life was far from that of a prince. The following is an excerpt from his blog recalling his life as a small boy in his own words. We did not edit his writing. (http://travisalexander.blogspot.com)

> *My childhood, unfortunately, was very much like any child's that*
> *had drug addict parents. My father was never around, which left my*
> *siblings and I to the fate given by my mother, a good woman, with*
> *the intent at an early age to be a loving mom. A few poor decisions*

*changed that. As she progressively got more involved in drugs, she progressively got less capable of raising children. Most commonly was a beating for waking her up. It hurt, but we got used to it. I learned how to turn so that when she hit me she would strike my back and arms. The pain was less there. If it was just that, I think it would have been relatively manageable. It was not, however. You see, when you are high on meth for a week, when you eventually come down there is a lot of sleep to catch up on. When you sleep for four days with a house full of kids, there isn't any food cooked. We would eat what was there, but before long what was edible would be eaten or rot, and then what was rotten would be eaten too. I don't remember much of this. I can only think of one instance where I found a piece of moldy bread on the side of the fridge which represented the last thing we could eat. I remember being teased by canned food, knowing full well what was in the can but not knowing how to use a can opener.*

*I remember the filth, admittedly caused by us kids, that compounded on itself for weeks and months at a time. With that came thousands and thousands of roaches. My sisters and I found some amusement in the fact that an entire colony of albino roaches had broken out so that house looked like a bunch of moving salt and pepper crawling on everything. To this day, I only have one phobia, roaches. There was nothing more disgusting to me than to wake up to feel roaches crawling on my body. The good news is that we finally lost that house. The bad news is, our next option was to live in a camper shell in my Aunt's back yard. We kept it next to the Garage where the washer and dryer were. The washer wasn't hooked up to plumbing so the dirty water would drain into the back yard and stagnate there. We were there for more than a year our home four feet tall, five feet wide and six feet long, my mother, my three sisters and I. We didn't have the convenience of bathing every day, so we tended to stink. I didn't mind going without a bath that much really. I was a boy, and like most, didn't have a problem being dirty. But I was scared of*

*bathing because I once got the bathroom floor wet and my mother ac-*
*cused of me of urinating on the floor and threw me half way through*
*a wall. School wasn't much better, when your clothes are as dirty as*
*the rest of you, and you stink, and have lice, you don't make a ton of*
*friends. Sadly, as you could imagine, I was mocked for my appear-*
*ance. Nothing too harsh, nowhere close to what was said at home. I*
*will not give much detail on that as I feel it is inappropriate to state.*
*I will say though, I have never heard in any movie, on any street cor-*
*ner, or amongst the vilest of men any string of words so offensive and*
*hateful, said with such disgust as were the words that my mother said*
*to my sisters and I. I remember my mother emptying a revolver on the*
*car my father was driving and my father subsequently taking an axe*
*to my mother's belongings and destroying them. I remember being on*
*the other side of the front door when my father kicked it down. The*
*police were called that time along with many others, but I knew what*
*had to be said, and knew they would leave us to more of the same. I*
*remember the day I came to the conclusion there was a God. I was 6.*
*I screamed as loud as I could all day long for my nearby grandmother*
*to get me and take me for the weekend. I screamed so long and loud*
*that I actually woke up my comatose mother long enough to beat me*
*for waking her up. When she went back to bed, I went back to scream-*
*ing to God. Sure enough that evening, my grandmother came and*
*picked me up, while my mother slept. I could go on and tell you more*
*of mine, and worse stories of my siblings, but I think enough has been*
*said. I will say that this is nothing, nothing at all compared to the*
*whole of it. This continued until I was ten, when I ran away and I*
*never came back.*

*During this time, I could think of two fond memories of my child-*
*hood. The first was Sesame Street. My Sisters and I watched it ev-*
*ery day and it took our minds to Sesame street where kids were happy*
*and learning. It took our minds away from Allwood Dr. where we got*
*the hell beat out of us. The other was visiting the home of my Great-*
*Grandfather, Vic.*

*My Mother didn't have very much family, and even less that she got along with, but she adored my Grandfather Vic. He only lived about an hour away from our family in southern California, but it was rare that she was in any condition that she'd let Vic see her in. About twice a year, my Mother would fix herself and us up enough for a visit with my Grandfather. For the most part, our visits would be stereotypical. He'd take us out for pizza, to walk his dogs, play checkers and with other toys he kept for us, and taught me how to write the alphabet.*

*However, there was one thing that was out of the ordinary about our visits. Every time before my Mother, siblings and I would leave, I would go to hug my Grandfather goodbye. Without exception, before I received my coveted hug, the cheery casual countenance of my Grandfather would change to something very serious. He would then grab me by my shoulders and shake me, then would follow these words, these words that alter every aspect of my life, "Travis, you need to know that you are special, that there is not anything that you can't do. There is something great inside you. You're special Travis, don't you ever forget it." That was quickly followed by a rigid hug that would squeeze the breath out of me.*

*Now there is an easy explanation for why my life has been, in my opinion, amazing. It is the same reason I have had success financially and otherwise. It is the same reason I feel that every facet of my life has been blessed and continues to be more and more every day. The reason is that the words my Grandfather said were spoken with such conviction that I believed him. You see, what I wasn't aware of then, that I have since figured out was my Grandfather was savvy to the way Mother was raising her children. She would often make remarks while coming down from drugs about how miserable we all were, that we ruined her life, that we were worthless. Although those words hurt very deeply, as you could imagine, every time she would scream those words I would hear his words instead. Every time I would feel her fist sink into my back, I could feel my Grandfather's hands on my shoulders, and I knew she couldn't reach what was great inside of me. And*

*again I'd hear the words "You're special Travis, don't ever forget it."*
*Then in my mind I would think, "This woman has no idea what she is*
*talking about, she doesn't know that I am special." No matter how loud*
*she'd yell those colorful words, she could never top the conviction of my*
*Great-Grandfather Vic. Since then I have come to realize two things.*
*First, my Great-Grandfather was right, I am special. I took his advice;*
*I never forgot it and I never will. Second, I have learned I am no better*
*than anyone else.*

Travis moved in with his grandparents, Jim and Norma Sarvey, when
he was ten years old. Travis used to quote Abraham Lincoln when referring to his grandmother. Changing the quote slightly, he would say,
"All I am, or can be, I owe to my angel (grand) mother."

When Travis first started high school, he was very shy. He went
to Rubidoux High in Rubidoux, California, and most of the time, he
would eat lunch alone in the library. School was very difficult for him.
One experience caused him a lot of trauma, but perhaps it also inspired him to be the kind and compassionate person that he became.
Travis was a little chubby, and he had a large rear-end and thighs. He
had a pair of white Levi jeans that were too small and very tight. While
he walked down the hallway at school, kids would follow behind him
and chant, "Up, down, up, down," making fun of the fact that his jeans
would ride up his rear-end as he walked. Travis shared this story with
us, and others, on multiple occasions. Travis carried an incredible
burden, just trying to survive his home life, and that burden was made
worse by some of the cruelty and bullying he experienced in school.
Those experiences made Travis a defender of the less fortunate, the
underdog, and those who could not protect themselves.

Travis considered himself to be an introvert, but he started to
break out of his shell after he became active in the Church of Jesus
Christ of Latter-day Saints (the Mormon church) when he was sixteen
years old. Church was a place of solace and safety for him. He was accepted there, and he began to thrive. He developed friendships that

would last a lifetime, but he also developed a burning desire to serve God, as a missionary, and to preach the Gospel of Jesus Christ on a full-time basis.

After high school, Travis worked to save money in an effort to pay for his mission-related expenses. He was assigned to serve in Denver, Colorado, and surrounding areas. He served from 1996 to 1998. During his mission, on July 28, 1997, Travis's father, Gary, was killed in a motorcycle accident. It was Travis's birthday. Gary had cleaned up in the latter years of his life and was working on mending relationships with his children. Gary made a video for Travis just shortly before his death, telling Travis that he was proud of him and that he loved him. In this video, Gary was getting ready for church while looking into the camera asking Travis if he was proud of him for going to church.

Travis went home just long enough to lay his father to rest, and then he immediately returned to complete his two-year mission. He returned from his mission in 1998 and began attending a singles-only congregation (referred to as singles wards) in Riverside, California, shortly after. Singles' wards in the Mormon Church are for single members of the church between the ages of eighteen and thirty-one. Travis loved attending and serving in his singles' ward. He loved to be social, hang out, and date, and he went out of his way to make friends with everyone.

His church and spiritual life were very important to him. Long after his full-time missionary service had concluded and until his death, Travis remained a missionary. He was always striving to find those who were searching for something more, so he could share his knowledge of the Gospel with them. Mormons are prolific record keepers and lead the world in genealogical efforts. Mormons have the largest genealogical library in the world. Doing his family's genealogy was very important to Travis. It was exciting for Travis to locate the records of his deceased family members and link his family tree together. This was a passion of his and brought him great joy.

Travis worked many different jobs in search of a career, but none of them seemed to work out. He prayed that he would find something, and while he was praying, he felt an impression to "talk to Chris Hughes." Meanwhile, Chris had been praying for someone who could be a leader in his developing business with Pre-Paid Legal—someone with the same vision he had.

CHAPTER 2

# How We Met Travis

*Travis would often randomly break into song, frequently accompanied*
*by dancing, head banging, etc. The messages he left on voicemail*
*were often sung. His favorites were anything by Neil Diamond, the*
*Ramones, the Smiths, Morrissey, Jack Johnson, Outkast, and old ska*
*bands like the Hippos and the Aquabats. Travis would sometimes*
*enter the room singing at the top of his lungs, doing high kicks . . .*
*it was quite a sight. Sadly, Travis had tickets to a Neil Diamond*
*concert in October 2008. This was three months after he died.*


CHRIS:

MY PARENTS DIVORCED IN 1986. Two of my brothers, my dad, and I moved
from Benbrook, Texas, where I'd lived for most of my life, to Ft. Worth,
Texas. I started high school as a five-foot-two-inch, ninety-five-pound
fourteen-year-old who, with my long, bleached-blonde hair, and hair-
less, acne free face, looked like a little girl. Other than my twin brothers, who were a year ahead of me, I only knew one or two other people
in the entire school.

I prayed that I would find a friend quickly so I could better inte-
grate into my new school, but my hopes were dashed on the very first
day. I was sitting at my desk, pretending to be looking through my
backpack for something, when a long haired, tough guy sat down next
to me and yelled, "Who's this prepubescent-looking motherf*****?"
Everyone started to laugh. *Prepubescent*, I thought. *What's that?*

It sounded a little like puberty and I knew "pre" meant "before," so I deduced that he was suggesting I was before puberty or hadn't yet hit puberty. He was right, and now everyone in my class knew it too. I sat there feeling like a fool, counting the minutes before class would be over, hoping I would have better luck at finding a friend in my next class.

I did end up making some good friends that year and every year I was there. Four years later, on graduation day, I watched many of those friends graduate. I was up in the stands looking down on the class of 1990. They were all there except me. I'd failed my senior year and would be doing it all over again in 1991. As I sat there pathetically sad, embarrassed, and humiliated, I made a feeble attempt to console myself. *Hey, it's okay. These are my good friends. They will be going off to college soon, but they will stay in touch. They will write me letters and call me from time to time.*

A year later, I found myself up in the stands again, watching all of my friends from the class of 1991 walk the graduation walk and get their diploma. I failed my senior year . . . again. A deep sense of sadness came over me as I watched some of my very best friends walking the stage. I thought, *That's okay. These are my good friends. They will stay in touch and come to see me from time to time . . .* And then everything stopped. It was as if the entire gym went silent and even ceased to exist. I felt sick. One year previous, I had been sitting in that exact same spot watching my class and my friends graduate without me. A full year had passed, and none of my friends from 1990 had ever called, written, or come to see me. Not one.

A few months later, I started school again. I would be entering my senior year for the third time, a total of six years in high school. Six years in high school seemed terribly excessive. It still does. It was like the movie *Groundhog Day*, but rather than having to relive the same day, I was reliving the same year, year after year. I couldn't believe it. *Who goes to high school for six years?* I wondered. Then I answered my own question. *I do.*

Though I had reached near-legend status at school, and I had more friends than I had time to hang out with, I was different. I had changed. My friends were fun, but they were no longer my priority. I had to graduate. And I did. In 1992, I walked my own graduation walk. I gave my principal a bear hug as he handed me my hard-earned diploma. The crowd went wild. It was pandemonium. I didn't stop crying for hours.

Although I stayed in touch with a few friends from the classes of 1991 and 1992, I no longer put an emphasis on friendship like I did as a vulnerable freshman. Friends would come and go in my life, but all the while, I was emotionally guarded. I didn't want to invest too heavily in a friend, and I didn't want to let anyone in, perhaps for fear of being hurt, abandoned, and forgotten as I had experienced so many times before. But all of that would change when I met Travis.

I graduated from high school in 1992. From 1992 to 1994, I served a two-year mission for the Church of Jesus Christ of Latter-day Saints. After my mission, I attended Utah Valley State College for a couple of years before dropping out and moving back to Texas. I bounced around from job to job, and college to college, before finally dropping out for good. Knowing I wasn't going back to college, I felt the pressure to get something going in my life.

At one of my previous jobs, I was introduced to the concept of personal development and a book entitled, *Think and Grow Rich* by Napoleon Hill. As a young man, Napoleon was commissioned by the steel magnate, Andrew Carnegie, the richest man in the world at the time, to dedicate twenty years of his life to interviewing the world's most successful people and then write a book on the philosophy of success. Napoleon accepted the challenge, did the research, and wrote the book, *Think and Grow Rich*.

I was intrigued with the title of the book, and I devoured it. One of the success strategies taught in the book was the concept of the mastermind. Napoleon defined the mastermind as, "Coordination of knowledge and effort, in a spirit of harmony, between two or more people, for the attainment of a definite purpose." Said another way, it is when two or more minds come together for a positive purpose which creates a third and more powerful mind. This was all new to me, but it sounded like a good idea, so I talked to my brothers and their wives about the idea of having a weekly "mastermind meeting" where we could come together and support each other for the purpose of becoming more successful in our lives. Everyone liked the idea, so we moved forward.

Our second mastermind meeting was held in my brother Mike's government-subsidized apartment in Valley Ranch, Texas, right across the street from the Dallas Cowboys practice field. When there was a short gap in the conversation, my sister-in-law Cindy nervously said there was something she and her husband, my brother Jeff, wanted to share with us. She pulled out a VHS tape and put it in the VCR. I will never forget the first sentence of that video: "Pre-Paid Legal Services, Inc., the #1 performing company on the American Stock Exchange!" It got my attention, and when the video ended twelve minutes later, I made a decision to change careers.

Pre-Paid Legal Services, Inc. (known as LegalShield as of the writing of this book) offers a membership which gives individuals, families, and businesses access to some of the best attorneys in the country for as little as $20 a month. I thought the concept was phenomenal and bought the service for myself right away. Additionally, Pre-Paid Legal allows their independent associates to recruit other people to share the service. Jeff and Cindy recruited me into Pre-Paid Legal on September 15, 1999, and I had a new lease on life. I had been praying to God for an opportunity to better my life, and I felt like this was it.

Like starting any new job or business, the first few months were awkward and clumsy, but really fun and exciting. I was earning a few hundred dollars per month right out of the gate, and by the end of my first year, I was earning thousands of dollars a month . . . more money than I had ever earned in my life.

In April of 2001, my brothers, Mike and David, and I moved to Riverside, California. We'd heard business was booming in Southern California, and we wanted to see if we could tap into some of the momentum. One of the first things I did when I got to Riverside was to find the local singles' ward. I discovered there was a ward in Riverside and began attending each Sunday, as well as participating in the many social activities.

A couple of weeks after I began attending that ward, the congregational leader, called a bishop (similar to a pastor), asked to see me. After getting acquainted, he asked me if I would be willing to teach one of the Sunday School classes. I enthusiastically accepted the opportunity. During one of the lessons I taught, I read the following poem by W. Livingston Larned, as quoted by Dale Carnegie in the book, *How to Win Friends and Influence People.*

*Listen, son; I am saying this as you lie asleep, one little paw crumpled under your cheek and the blond curls stickily wet on your damp forehead. I have stolen into your room alone. Just a few minutes ago, as I sat reading my paper in the library, a stifling wave of remorse swept over me. Guiltily I came to your bedside.*

*There are things I was thinking, son: I had been cross to you. I scolded you as you were dressing for school because you gave your face merely a dab with a towel. I took you to task for not cleaning your shoes. I called out angrily when you threw some of your things on the floor.*

*At breakfast I found fault, too. You spilled things. You gulped down your food. You put your elbows on the table. You spread butter too thick on your bread. And as you started off to play and I made for my train, you turned and waved a hand and called, "Goodbye, Daddy!" and I frowned, and said in reply, "Hold your shoulders back!"*

*Then it began all over again in the late afternoon. As I came up the road, I spied you, down on your knees, playing marbles. There were holes in your stockings. I humiliated you before your boyfriends by marching you ahead of me to the house. Stockings were expensive - and if you had to buy them you would be more careful! Imagine that, son, from a father!*

*Do you remember, later, when I was reading in the library, how you came in timidly, with a sort of hurt look in your eyes? When I glanced up over my paper, impatient at the interruption, you hesitated at the door. "What is it you want?" I snapped.*

*You said nothing, but ran across in one tempestuous plunge, and threw your arms around my neck and kissed me, and your small arms tightened with an affection that God had set blooming in your heart and which even neglect could not wither. And then you were gone, pattering up the stairs.*

*Well, son, it was shortly afterwards that my paper slipped from my hands and a terrible sickening fear came over me. What has habit been doing to me? The habit of finding fault, of reprimanding - this was my reward to you for being a boy. It was not that I did not love you; it was that I expected too much of youth. I was measuring you by the yardstick of my own years.*

*And there was so much that was good and fine and true in your char-acter. The little heart of you was as big as the dawn itself over the wide hills. This was shown by your spontaneous impulse to rush in and kiss me good night. Nothing else matters tonight, son. I have come to your bedside in the darkness, and I have knelt there, ashamed!*

*It is a feeble atonement; I know you would not understand these things if I told them to you during your waking hours. But tomorrow I will be a real daddy! I will chum with you, and suffer when you suffer, and laugh when you laugh. I will bite my tongue when impatient words come. I will keep saying as if it were a ritual: "He is nothing but a boy - a little boy!"*

*I am afraid I have visualized you as a man. Yet as I see you now, son, crumpled and weary in your cot, I see that you are still a baby. Yesterday you were in your mother's arms, your head on her shoulder. I have asked too much, too much.*

After I finished reading the poem, I ended my lesson for the day. Then a nice-looking, stocky, dark-haired, green-eyed guy I had seen in church a couple of times, and perhaps shared a "hello" or two with, walked right up to me and enthusiastically exclaimed, "*Father Forgets* from *How to Win Friends and Influence People!*"

I was surprised he knew the book! It was written in 1936. "You read that stuff?" I blurted out with excitement.

"Absolutely!" he said. "I friggin love that stuff!"

"Me too, man," I said. "That stuff has changed my life!"

Then he put out his hand and said, "Travis Alexander."

We shook hands as I thought to myself, *I like this guy.*

## A GOD THING

The weeks before I met Travis were among the worst weeks of my life. I was living with my brother David and his family in an apartment in Riverside, California. Both of us were in a serious slump in our businesses, and because we didn't have jobs and were doing the business full time, we had fallen behind on our bills. We were sharing a car until the repo man came and took it, and there was a three-day notice hanging on our apartment door. We split rent fifty-fifty, and both of our rent checks bounced. We had three days to pay rent, plus late fees, or move out. Dave came up with his half somehow, and at the very last moment, a friend of mine came to my rescue and lent me $600, my half of the rent.

I had been living below the poverty line for the better part of a decade before I started my Pre-Paid Legal business, but I had never experienced financial stress like I was enduring at that time. I had been self-employed for nearly two years, but things weren't going well, and I was considering getting a job.

One Friday afternoon, I called a friend who worked for a mortgage company in Riverside, the same friend who'd lent me the money, and asked him if his company was hiring. He said they were, and expressed that he felt confident I could get the job. He gave me his manager's number, and I called him immediately. He hired me over the phone and told me to start my training the following Monday.

That weekend, I agonized over this decision. I needed the income badly, but the hours I would be required to work would prevent me from attending my weekly Pre-Paid Legal meetings. On Saturday, I began fasting.

In the Mormon Church, fasting is a regular practice. One day per month, typically on the first Sunday of every month, practicing members will go without any food or drink for a twenty-four-hour period of time. During this time, they remain spiritually, emotionally, and mentally focused on a particular desire, and pray for that desire during their fast. For example, one might fast to overcome a personal weakness, or perhaps for a friend or family member who is sick. Mormons fast for virtually any reason, and they donate the money saved on the meals they didn't eat to the poor and needy of the church. On this occasion, I fasted specifically for a leader to come into my business who would help me turn things around. I spent much of that Saturday evening in prayer asking God to bless me with a leader.

While I didn't know it at the time, another man was praying over his financial stress that same Saturday night when I was praying for a leader for my business. He was praying for an opportunity.

Travis Alexander found himself at a dead-end in life. He felt distraught and helpless, so he reached out to God for help. As he was pouring his heart out to God, he said he heard a voice say, "Talk to Chris Hughes."

Travis was the Sunday School president at the singles' ward we both attended, and I was a Sunday School teacher. One of Travis's duties as the Sunday School president was to attend each of the Sunday School classes to see how they were going and to offer feedback, suggestions, and to help any teachers who needed it. That Sunday, Travis attended my Sunday School class, the class where I read the poem, *Father Forgets*. It was a God thing. As Travis used to say, "God answered two prayers that night." As a result, Travis and I would bless each other's lives in special and unique ways, and we would become best of friends, business partners, and brothers.

Hear Travis tell this story at www.ourfriendtravis.com/god-thing

Travis Alexander and Chris Hughes

Travis Alexander and Chris Hughes

SKY:

I met Travis at church in 2001. He was great! He was so friendly and so funny. He would say hello to everyone, and he always tried to make sure that everyone was included. It seemed like Travis was loved by everyone, and he was involved in everything. So many people considered Travis their "best friend" and many considered him "family." Women loved Travis's charm. Naturally, this made him unpopular with some of the guys. Even the guys who didn't want to like him always liked him when they got to know him. My friend Shari and I would often try to leave church a little early, only to be met in the parking lot by an overzealous Travis, encouraging us to stay a little longer. Fortunately for Shari and I, he succeeded more than he failed.

Travis Alexander on a cruise. (This is one of my favorite pictures of
Travis. I love that Travis was just Travis. He didn't care if people stared.)

After Travis joined Pre-Paid Legal, he would come to mine and
Shari's apartment while we were at work. He would study the scriptures,
read personal-development books, set goals, make phone calls, and often wash any dishes we might have left in the sink. He would often
leave funny notes or pictures he had drawn, or an inspirational quote
on the counter before he left. Chris and Travis had become really good
friends. They spent a lot of time together, goofing off, chasing women,
and working on their businesses. I began hanging out with him and
Chris. Chris and I lived in the same apartment complex, which was
interesting, because we met originally while living in the same apartment complex in Provo, Utah, when we were going to college. We were
"friends" in college (well, more like frienemies), but had since lost

touch with one another. It was wild that we ended up moving into the same apartment complex again, in another state, seven years later.

I had a boyfriend and Chris had many girlfriends, but for some reason, Chris, Travis, and their friends decided that Chris and I were destined to be married. I would spend all day at work only to be barraged by a dozen or more messages on my cell phone from complete strangers. Some of the messages were singing, made-up poems, and raps about how I should dump my boyfriend and marry their friend Chris. Chris left all sorts of messages and would leave poems, notes, gifts—some strange, some cute—on my car every day. I had already broken up with my boyfriend, but I wasn't going to tell them that! It became overwhelming.

Finally, I had had enough. Chris called me from a party, and I asked if I could talk to Travis, who was also there. I told Travis that Chris and I would never get married and he needed to tell him to cool it! Travis tried to talk me out of my resistance to the whole idea, but to no avail. He was at my house the first thing the next morning trying to convince me that Chris was the guy for me and that I should give it a chance. It worked. Chris and I began dating and were soon married. I owe it all to Travis that Chris and I are married.

Even after we married, Travis was still a wonderful friend. He was often at our house or on a trip with us. We sat together at Pre-Paid Legal leadership banquets and at our conventions. Travis made everything fun. He was part of our family, and our two boys, Ryell and Zion, loved him! When they knew he was coming for a visit, the kids would sit and stare out the window waiting for the "T-Dogg" to show up, which was how Travis would refer to himself, always in the third person. Chris and Travis would talk business, and Travis and I would talk about his social and romantic life.

Travis was excellent at acknowledging his weaknesses and working on them. He never became offended if someone talked with him about a character weakness they had observed in him. He would want to discuss it in great detail and decide on ways he could improve and become a better person. He always asked me what I thought about the girl he was dating, "because you are gonna have to hang out with her," he often reminded me. He talked about the vacations and adventures we would all take together when he finally found the right woman to marry.

I was really hard on Travis, especially when it came to women. I am sure I drove him nuts most of the time. I never told him what he wanted to hear. I always told him how I really felt, even if it took him by surprise or hurt his feelings. Looking back, I can't figure out why he kept calling me for dating advice. I hope it was because he knew that I loved him and wanted what was best for him. I worried about him constantly, and I pestered him all the time. He was like a little brother. My siblings know I am obnoxious, and I can even be a real jerk sometimes. Travis was right. I was going to have to hang out with whomever he married, so I would facetiously remind him that this meant I had a say in who he dated. I know I bugged him and frustrated him to no end, but he was always sweet and never got upset with me—except once, and I deserved it.

One of the many things I admired about Travis was his desire and ability to always find opportunities to serve. One of my favorite stories was before he started his business with Pre-Paid Legal. He worked at the Tyler Mall in Riverside, California. Each day, as he drove to work, he would pass the same homeless man on the off-ramp. He would often strike up a conversation with him while waiting at the light, and they became friends. One day, Travis brought him home, let him shower, and gave him some of his clothes and a pair of shoes. Then they headed out to find the man a job, which they did, at a Subway restaurant. That was Travis. While many others looked away from this man and his troubles, driving right by him in the comfort of their cars, Travis engaged him, befriended him, and changed his life. I imagine he will never forget Travis, ever.

Travis always thought he would die young, and he talked about this on more than one occasion. The last time I remember him talking about it was in our living room in early 2007. I wonder if the thought of him dying young pushed him to do more and to be better.

I feel like I have done an injustice describing Travis. It's like I don't have the words to do him justice. As I sat up late, staring at the computer and thinking about how I could fix this, I realized that Travis was someone who had to be experienced. He was special because the way he made people feel. When you left Travis's presence, you always felt loved and that you were a better person than you were before spending time with him.

Sometimes, people tend to aggrandize those who have passed on, but I hope you will realize that this is not the case with Travis. Most people, myself included, just *blend* in. We can go through life without a second glance from those we come in contact with. But Travis was different. He stood out. He stood out everywhere and in everything he did. He made a positive difference wherever he went. We are not saying he was a wonderful person because he is no longer with us. He really was a wonderful person. Certainly not average, and I would even venture to say that he was *one of a kind*. How many single thirty-year-old guys do you know who make hygiene kits for the homeless, and then deliver the packages while engaging in deep conversations with people who are shunned by society? What single twenty-something-year-old do you know who has brought a homeless man to his house, then feeds, showers, and clothes this man and takes him job-hunting? Travis was the guy Hallmark movies are made about! He really did exist! Travis was the guy who asked the lonely girl who was standing in the corner to dance, and he would dance with her and compliment her. He was the guy who would go into a cafeteria and find the kid who was eating alone, and he would sit down, get to know him, and let him know he was important and loved. He was the guy who paid for the toll or the food for the person in line behind him. This was Travis Alexander.

# CHAPTER 3

# Who Travis Was and What He Stood For

*TRAVIS LOVED CHRISTMAS! HE ENJOYED getting presents for people, and he took time to make them meaningful. The Christmas before Travis was killed, he gave our family gifts that we still cherish. He gave the kids three books (all of them great and highly recommended): The Giving Tree by Shel Silverstein (Travis really liked Shel Silverstein), Martin's Big Words by Doreen Rappaport and Bryan Collier, and The Tale of Three Trees by Angela Elwell Hunt. He gave us a dozen or more reusable grocery bags and The Live Earth Global Warming Survival Handbook by David De Rotshchild.*

The following is Travis's bio from his Myspace page at the time he was killed. I remember him reading it to me before he posted it, and I laughed so hard that I cried, which was a common occurrence with Travis around.

*I'm a simple man, really. Smart, successful, smashing good looks, a real suitor. I love nature, helping the homeless, and cooking with my grandmother just to create memories.*

*Do I work out you ask? Well I'd like to be modest, but can you say triathlete, and if you can't say that, well, simply say 16 1/2 inch biceps. If I look familiar, you are probably an avid reader of GQ or Mens Health.*

*Anyway, I enjoy going to Church, teaching foreign children English, and gourmet cooking. You might say to yourself, yes but what are Travis' talents. Well if I must answer, poetry, playing the Spanish guitar (or what I like to call the strings of Love) and understanding more than just peoples' voices, but understanding peoples' hearts. At least that's what Maya Angelou said at the awards ceremony when I was nominated for my first Nobel Peace prize.*

*If you'd like to know more. Don't be shy, go ahead and drop Travis a line. Unless of course a common phrase you use is "Thanks for the add," in which case, you are wasting your life on MySpace, you should probably go do something more productive like read a book, or build an ant farm. Ciao*

*Music:*
*Jack Johnson, Ben Harper, Pete Yorn, OutKast, Saves The Day, The Huxtables, Wedgekase, The Siren Six, The Adventures of Jet, The Huntingtons, The Ramones, Darlington, The Young Hasselhoffs, Me first and the Gimme Gimmes, Aqua Bats, The Hippos, Unsteady, Jem, Jurassic 5, Swollen Members, The Smiths and Morrissey*

*Movies:*
*The Secret, Zoolander, Dumb and Dumber, Life Aquatic, The Royal Tennnbaums, Ferris Buellers day off, and most old movies*

*Television:*
*TV is for the weak. But if you have Tivo... Lost and The Office.*

*Books:*
*Think and Grow Rich, How to Win Friends and Influence People, Slight Edge, Richest Man in Babylon, You were Born Rich, The Greatest Salesman in the World, Atlas Shrugged.*
*Heroes:*
*Gordon Hinckley, Harland Stonecipher, Killer Kane, Jeff Olsen, Travis Alexander, Darnell Self, and Adam (for getting this party started).*

Travis was a single, good-looking, charismatic, and absolutely hilarious young man. He wanted to change the world and save the world. Travis loved to help people. He was on his way in life. His income and notoriety was continually moving up. People loved to hear him speak. He had an incredible gift to motivate and inspire others. He would have them laughing one moment and crying the next. I am smiling through tears as I write this. Just thinking about Travis brings on an array of emotions, such joy and happiness of who he was, where he came from, what he had accomplished and his ambitions, followed by sadness and heartache for how his life was so pointlessly taken by evil. Travis woke up every day with one purpose in mind—become better.

Travis had a black pug, Napoleon, whom he called "Naps" for short. Naps was Travis's child. He absolutely loved that dog. He knew pugs had issues with weight, so Napoleon had an exercise program. Travis took him running, and he even had Napoleon running on his treadmill. He took him everywhere and pampered him in ways that bordered on ridiculous.

After Travis was murdered, many people shared their thoughts about him. One person talked about how he was always the first to volunteer for service projects and would encourage others to do the same. Another shared how they saw Travis emptying the trashcans throughout the church building every Sunday not because someone had asked him to, but because he knew it needed to be done. Tanisha, one of his sisters, recalled the last time she hung out with Travis. He put together hygiene kits for the homeless, and they drove around town delivering them. He was all about improving himself and helping other people.

One of Travis's dreams was to teach kids about who they are, per-haps more accurately stated, "whose" they are. The belief his Grandpa Vic instilled in him, that *he* was special, completely altered the course of his life. He wanted to instill that same belief and confidence in other underprivileged kids. He wanted to make the world a better place simply because he was in it. Because of his premature death, he wasn't able to affect it on the level he had hoped, but he has changed this world for the better, and the ripple effect of who he was and his example will continue to serve those in need.

Travis loved animals and nature. He enjoyed hiking and spending time outdoors. Travis loved the planet. He retired his BMW and bought a Toyota Prius. He joined in cleanup efforts, planted trees, and was an activist for being more responsible with our resources. He spoke to everyone he knew about taking care of our world and leaving a smaller "footprint." One of the last email exchanges between Chris and Travis was about this very topic. Chris enjoyed pushing Travis's buttons. Travis was passionately telling Chris the importance of doing his part in preserving the earth, and Chris began spouting off all sorts of anti-global-warming statistics. Travis got so frustrated, while Chris sat in our kitchen on the desktop typing anything he could to further egg Travis on. Chris typed as he laughed at Travis's emotion-filled responses. Finally, after my encouraging, Chris told Travis he was kidding and agreed he needed to do more to preserve our earth. To make amends, for Travis's birthday in 2013, Chris bought a Prius. The license plate said, "4TDogg."

One of my favorite things about Travis was his shameless flirting. He wasn't a Rico Suave, "let me get you into my bed" type of flirt. When people hear us talking about what a flirt he was, they view it as negative, but it wasn't. Travis flirted to entertain people and to make those he flirted with feel good. It was harmless. He didn't flirt in an attempt to lead women on. Sometimes it was so ridiculous and over the top it bordered on embarrassing, but it always left the woman, or women, laughing or with a big smile on their face. He would flirt with old women, attractive women, women who some would say weren't so attractive, thin women, and heavy women. He would flirt with married women with their husband standing right there, and the husband would always be laughing or smiling! It didn't matter what a woman looked like, and it didn't matter if he could physically see them. He would flirt through the intercom while ordering fast food. Our friend, D'Ann, happily married, smiled as she told us what she missed most about Travis: the instant messages he would send her on the computer. He would say things like, "Good morning, beautiful! Make it a wonderful day!" He didn't want anything from her other than for her to feel good about herself, to know she was loved, and to have a great day!

Travis loved to entertain people and make people smile. He had a contagious laugh; we called it his "hyena laugh." He would lose complete control, and his laugh would get louder and crazier. Often, when putting his name on the list at a restaurant, after the hostess told him how long the wait was, he would pull up his sleeve exposing his bicep, flex, and ask, "How 'bout now?" If the hostess was quick on her feet and responded, "Still twenty minutes," he would hike up both sleeves, flash her a double flex, and ask, "And now?" He would have everyone in the waiting area laughing. Travis wasn't just funny; he was also very deep and an amazing friend to so many people.

Travis loved life and he loved making others happy, smile, and laugh. He looked for opportunities to comfort and console—to lift people up and to lighten their burdens. He made the world a better place. Travis was a friend you could call in the middle of the night, tell him you needed him to drive five hours, and he would do it without asking questions or complaining. You could talk on the phone and think you had been talking for fifteen minutes, only to discover you had been on the phone for well over an hour. He was genuinely concerned for others and not because he felt like he "should" be, but because that is who he was.

CHAPTER 4

# Travis Finds a New Direction in Life

*Travis loved the hit television show, The Office. He often wore*
*a Dunder Mifflin Paper Company T-shirt (Dunder Mifflin is*
*the name of the paper company in the show.) He was always*
*looking for a chance to quote Michael, the character played by*
*Steve Carell, saying, "That's what she said!" It was uncanny how*
*often he would say that phrase for so many different occasions.*

CHRIS:

THE DAY TRAVIS AND I first connected at church, he asked, "By the way, what do you do for work?"

Not wanting to talk business at church, and wanting to break the ice a bit, I smiled and said, "I dance. Have you ever heard of Chippendales?"

He laughed. "Seriously, bro, I know you do something with attorneys. What is it?"

Again, not wanting to get into it at church, I said, "Why don't we go to lunch this week and we can talk about it?"

The following Tuesday, we met at Chevy's Mexican restaurant outside the Ontario Mills Mall in Ontario, California. Mostly, we just got acquainted. We talked a little bit about business, but not much. After about an hour, Travis said he needed to get back to work, so I gave him a DVD with a video that explained how he could earn money working part time with Pre-Paid Legal. I also invited him to attend a business opportunity meeting that would happen later that evening at the Hilton Hotel in Ontario. He agreed to watch the DVD and meet me that night at the meeting.

True to his word, Travis met me at the Hilton Hotel. The speaker for the night was Russell Peden, a Pre-Paid Legal legend and a good friend of mine. He and I were in our early thirties at the time. He was the regional vice president for California, and was earning about $400,000 a year with Pre-Paid Legal. He's also one of the funniest guys in the business. I was excited for Travis to see Russell's presentation. I thought for sure he would love it.

Travis showed up on time, dressed sharp, as usual. I introduced him to several of the leaders, and we sat down next to each other when the presentation started. It was one of the best presentations I had seen up to that point in my career. Russell had me laughing, but every time I looked over at Travis, he was stone-faced. *Uh-oh,* I thought. *This ain't good.*

When the presentation was over, I tried to appear confident and unmoved by Travis's lack of enthusiasm. "So what did you like best?" I asked.

His response surprised me. "Everything!" he said.

*What?* I wondered. I didn't expect that. He seemed disinterested throughout the entire presentation. Months later, when recounting the events of that night, Travis remembered it differently. He recalled laughing through the presentation and thought Russell was fantastic. Regardless, he signed up that night.

The doors had been opened to the ride of his life. It was Tuesday, September 16, 2001. He bought the legal plan and became an independent associate on my team. Within a matter of days, he had gotten his first promotion and pay raise. Then another and then another. Within just a few months, he reached the top permanent position in our compensation plan, and by his seventh month, he reached the level of executive director, which had six- and seven-figure annual income potential. Travis went through the ranks faster than any of the tens of thousands of associates who have joined my team.

In those days, in order to qualify for the executive director position, you and/or your team of independent associates had to market at least seventy-five memberships in a calendar month. Prior to recruiting Travis, one of my team leaders in Texas quit the business, and my team was no longer producing enough memberships in the right places in order for me to qualify for executive director. At the time, I was living with my brother and our rent checks bounced; we were a day from being homeless. However, since recruiting Travis, and to this day, I never missed qualifying for executive director again. Travis was a superstar and more. He was in large part responsible for helping me earn my first million dollars with Pre-Paid Legal. I will forever be grateful to him and to God for putting him in my life. Travis was, for me, a physical embodiment of the fact that God hears and answers prayers.

At his peak, Travis had worked his way up to nearly $100,000 in annual income, though he had an air about him that led many to think he was earning much more than that. He developed a love for custom-made shirts and suits and had a closet full of them. There were nearly four hundred thousand distributors in the company, hundreds of whom were earning $100,000 a year up to more than $2 million per year. Travis was soon to be among that elite group of leaders. He was on an incredibly aggressive trajectory and was making a name for himself company-wide.

# I QUIT!

Travis was twenty-three when I met him. He had two jobs. He was working as a "substance abuse professional," which was his way of saying he tested peoples' urine for drugs. He was also working at a Franklin-Covey store in the mall. Eventually, he quit the drug-testing job and was only working part-time in the mall.

Within a couple of months, Travis was earning thousands of dollars per month building his Pre-Paid Legal business part-time from his home. This early success with his Pre-Paid Legal business, had an adverse affect on his attitude about his job at Franklin-Covey. There were a couple of times when he had arrived late to his job and had even received a verbal warning from his boss. One day just before leaving his home for his job, Travis was enrolling a new Pre-Paid Legal member. He knew he might be late for his shift at his job, but he also knew he would earn twice as much money from enrolling a new Pre-Paid Legal member than he would earn working all day at the mall. So, he took his time, enrolled the new member, and made $207 in commissions!

He was only a few minutes late for work, but his boss was outraged. With a crazed look on his face, his boss stormed up to Travis. "You are four minutes late, Travis!"

Without hesitating, Travis shot back, "Yeah? Well, you better get used to it, because I'm gonna be ten minutes late tomorrow."

"You're fired!" his boss yelled.

"You can't fire me, because I quit!" Travis yelled back.

That was the last day on the last job Travis Alexander would ever have.

## BONDING AND BUSINESS

In that first year working with Travis, we became really close. We were together all the time. During that time, I opened up to allow him to get to know the real me, and he did the same. In many ways, we were both a mess, but in many other ways, we had a lot to offer this world, and we intended to do it together.

In the gaps of our business-building activities, we shared the tragedies and the triumphs of our lives. We shared a love for Jesus, business, helping people, public speaking, personal development, telling stories, making people laugh, and laughing really, really hard. Travis could make me laugh like no one else. He was such an interesting guy. He could be so deep, spiritual, intelligent, and refined, but he could also be silly, goofy, crude, and flat out offensive. But even in his crudest moments, he could get away with it. It was him, and people loved everything that made him, *him*. Like all the rest of God's children, but in his own special way, Travis was flawed perfection.

Over the next several years, Pre-Paid Legal was Travis, and Travis was Pre-Paid Legal. They became inseparable in my mind. He was like the mascot for my business. He was my business partner, my workout partner, my confidant, and he was always the life of the party.

Over the years, Travis attended every company convention and never missed one. He understood that eighty percent of success is just showing up. Each convention ended the same way, with Travis and his top one or two leaders hanging out in our suite until nearly dawn. We would talk the night away as though it were our last. We never ran out of things to talk about and never tired of each other's company.

Later, when Travis moved from Southern California to Arizona, I looked forward to conventions even more. Sky was equally fond of him, and we always loved staying up late at conventions hanging out with the T-Dogg. He would often come to California and stay with us for days at a time, and we always enjoyed these visits.

Travis and I were more than friends. We had become brothers. And he was every bit as close to Sky as he was to me. In fact, toward the end of his life, he and Sky would talk on the phone every week and have long conversations about his relationship issues. He was a glutton for punishment, because Sky always busted his chops and told him the truth even when it hurt his feelings. She was like a big sister to him, and he loved her for it.

## A Speaker is Born

One of mine and Travis's favorite aspects of being Pre-Paid Legal independent associates is the many speaking opportunities it avails. Before starting my business, I wanted to be an author and motivational speaker, but I couldn't get past my limiting beliefs. I didn't believe anyone would want to buy a book from a guy like me: a college dropout, who had never experienced any real success up to that point in my life. I often visualized writing a book, but I would get stuck on the back cover. *What am I going to put on the back cover about the author?* In those days, I had no credentials, no degree, no successes, and I believed that should disqualify me from writing a book and becoming a speaker. Travis was in the same boat.

Though I had no formal credentials and no documented success, I had stumbled onto a very unique education that I would call the "secrets" to success. When I started my business, I did so with this thought in mind: *I am going to experiment with these "secrets" in the laboratory of my own life and business, and when they work, and when I become successful, I will write about it and speak about it.* And that's exactly what has happened and exactly what I have done.

Even though I was off to a slow start, I reached the executive director position in Pre-Paid Legal in less than a year. This put me on the map and on the speaking circuit. I began to get regular invitations to speak all over the country. I absolutely love to speak, and I was just hitting my stride about the time I recruited Travis.

Travis was also attracted to the opportunity to speak. He, too, dropped out of college and saw Pre-Paid Legal as his vehicle to become successful, and then to become an author and motivational speaker as well. He learned to love public speaking when he was a full-time missionary. He would speak regularly there, and there were always opportunities to speak in church before and after his mission.

After starting his business, Travis began speaking regularly at in-home meetings he would do for his team of independent associates. He did several of these each week, but he had never spoken at a large hotel meeting.

Before Sky and I were married, my brother David and I hosted a weekly business opportunity meeting for Pre-Paid Legal every Thursday night at the Hilton Hotel in San Bernardino, which was where Travis attended every week with his team before he moved to Arizona. At that time, we had about two hundred Pre-Paid Legal associates and their guests attend this event each week. Southern California has always been the number-one market for Pre-Paid Legal, and some of the best speakers in the company lived there and rotated as guest speakers at all the meetings in the area, including ours. So, Travis got to see and learn from the best of the best, but for whatever reason, he just didn't feel comfortable getting on stage.

Dave and I both had to leave town for a business trip, so I asked Travis and our good friend and business partner, Mike Chapman, if they would be willing to set up the hotel and get everything ready for the meeting. I told them I would find someone to speak for the evening, but I needed them to manage everything else, which they agreed to do.

Thursday, the day of our meeting, I realized I had never arranged to have someone speak. I was out of town and I could not reach any of our regular speakers, so I called Travis.

"What up, T-Dogg?" I said. "I've got good news and bad news. The bad news is that I didn't get a speaker for the meeting tonight."

"*Okay* . . ." Travis said hesitantly. "So what's the good news?"

"The good news is that I didn't get a speaker for tonight's meeting, so you're it!"

Before I could finish my sentence, he was backpedaling. "No way, bro! No! Way! I am not speaking!" he shouted defiantly.

I aggressively tried to convince him that he was ready and that it was his time to shine. He aggressively rejected the notion. Travis hung up the phone and immediately called Mike Chapman to ask if he would be the speaker for the night. Like Travis, as a former full-time missionary, Mike had significant public speaking experience, but he had never spoken at one of our large hotel meetings. Mike said they went back and forth all day trying to convince the other why he was more equipped and qualified to speak that night. Mike told me that Travis was a wreck all day, but in the end, he was left with no alternative. Mike prevailed and convinced Travis it was his time.

The compromise they agreed to was that Mike would be the host and Travis would do the sixty-minute Pre-Paid Legal presentation. Mike welcomed everyone out to the event and introduced "Pre-Paid Legal's rising star, Mr. Travis Alexander," and in that moment, a star was born!

Mike told me that Travis was absolutely fantastic and everyone loved him on stage! He also shared with me how important that day was for both he and Travis. Mike had an important breakthrough watching his friend come into his own on stage that night. He said, "I realized if Travis could do it, I could do it."

Within a matter of weeks, Mike began to speak regularly as well. Both Mike and Travis were in high demand as speakers in Southern California and later in Arizona, where both of them would eventually relocate. From that frightful day forward, Travis was a speaker. Eventually, he would speak at Pre-Paid Legal events all over the country and was on the path to becoming a world-class speaker.

That evening, after Travis's first big hotel presentation, I called him to congratulate him on a job well done. He was trying to be mad at me, but I wasn't having it.

"It was destiny, Travis!" I said. "My forgetting to get a speaker was part of the grand plan for your life. You have come out of your shell, and you're going to be unstoppable."

"Cut the crap!" he barked.

I laughed. "What do you mean?"

"You know exactly what I mean. You and I both know you didn't 'forget to get a speaker.' You did it on purpose, so you could make me speak, and I don't appreciate it," he said.

I laughed uncontrollably. "Dude, I promise it wasn't intentional. It was an honest oversight, I swear."

We bantered back and forth for ten minutes or so, but he never bought my story. He always believed I did it on purpose, but I didn't. It was an oversight. Either way, a speaker was born! Travis dazzled audiences inside and out of Pre-Paid Legal until the very end of his life.

Travis Alexander, Chris Hughes, and Mike Chapman

The last training Travis ever did for me in San Bernardino was captured on audio (and a few minutes of video). Watch and listen at www.ourfriendtravis.com/sb.

As far as we know, the last public training Travis did before he was murdered was at my brother's Pre-Paid Legal training seminar in Ft. Collins, Colorado, on April 24, 2008. Sadly, this was his first and last training ever captured on video from start to finish. You can view it at www.ourfriendtravis.com/fc.

## LEAVING THE NEST

In 2003, I was a trainer for Pre-Paid Legal during the time Travis's business was moving into momentum. Pre-Paid Legal paid me to train all the new independent associates who were recruited in San Bernardino and Riverside counties. A majority of Travis's team was living in these two counties. In other words, I was earning notable income training Travis's team.

Travis called me one day and said there was something he and Mike Chapman wanted to talk to me about. We agreed to meet at a local restaurant to discuss it. The core of the conversation was that Travis and Mike wanted to run all of the events I was running, including the weekly trainings Pre-Paid Legal was paying me to conduct. Since most of the people at the trainings were on his team, he felt he should be the one to train them and benefit financially.

I understood where he was coming from, but it wasn't up to me to make that decision. At that time, I was an area coordinator, and I worked under the regional vice president of the state, Russell Peden. If Travis wanted my position, he would have to convince the regional vice president to let me go and put Travis in my place. This wasn't going to happen. Russell was a friend of mine, and I was getting incredible results. Our training was one of the largest and most effective in the company.

This was the first time since becoming friends that I'd ever felt any strain in our friendship, but it wasn't a personal thing. This happened with almost every developing leader. There comes a time in every business leader's life where they want to spread their leadership wings and find ways to bring additional value to the marketplace. Travis was no exception. He was developing into a very talented leader, and he wanted his own domain.

I experienced this same thing about sixteen months into my business. My brother Jeff and his wife, Cindy, ran all the events in the Ft. Worth area. They were the leaders, and I was under their wing. I was ready to leave the nest, and that was one of the things that prompted my move to Southern California.

I never discussed it with Travis, and have no way of knowing for sure, but I feel fairly confident this experience was an indicator that Travis was ready to leave the nest. We worked together daily for several months. As his team began to grow and expand in Southern California and across the country, we began working together less on a daily basis. But we continued to see each other at our weekly meetings and continued to build our friendship.

A couple of months after our meeting where we discussed Travis's desire to take over the events in the area, I heard a rumor that Russell would be resigning from the regional vice president position and moving to Virginia. I sent my résumé to the president of Pre-Paid Legal, indicating that I wanted the regional vice president position. In a matter of days, I had the job.

In May 2003, upon accepting the regional vice president position, I resigned as area coordinator. As the regional vice president, I was responsible for selecting and training the trainers in my region. My first order of business was to offer Travis the area coordinator position, but it was more than he was prepared to take on. Accepting this position entailed much more than the possibility of increased income. He would now be responsible to pay $1,200–$1,400 a month to rent the hotel for all the events we did there each month. He would have to pay to get the fliers designed and printed, to bring in guest speakers, to purchase name tags, markers, clip-boards, signage, and other needed office supplies. He would also need to inventory marketing tools for other associates to purchase, which was hundreds of dollars per month in additional overhead. He would need a laptop and a projector, and he would need to send two to three emails a week to communicate with other associates in his market. It was overwhelming for him to even think about, much less commit to. Mike Chapman, on the other hand, was married with children and owned his own Allstate Insurance business. Mike and Travis agreed that Mike might be in a better and more stable position to take on the responsibilities of an area coordinator. Mike and Travis agreed to a partnership when it came to running the marketplace and doing trainings and other events. Neither Mike nor I can recall the specific details of the deal, but we know it worked out great for everyone. But, most importantly, it gave Travis a little more time to take his business to the next level.

Travis had wanted to purchase a home for quite some time. Southern California real estate prices were exploding, which led him to look for a home in Arizona. In 2004, he found the perfect home—a brand new, large, luxury home for an incredible price. He worked out the financing, packed up all his stuff, and moved to Mesa, Arizona.

No one could have expected what would happen in Travis's life as he made the transition from California to Arizona. In California, he was the up-and-comer. In Arizona, he was a superstar, not only in Pre-Paid Legal, but in all areas of his life.

He immediately found a singles' ward to attend in Mesa. He was a little older than most of the people there, and so he was looked up to by many. He had an excellent command and recall of the scriptures and was a very knowledgeable and spiritual guy. He drove a nice BMW, wore custom-made suits, and earned an incredible income. His confidence was soaring. Add all of that to the fact that he was funny, charming, good-looking, charismatic, and the life of every party. He had it made! His home became a hub for his friends from church, and later, his Pre-Paid Legal team. It was very common for him to have a houseful of people hanging out, partying (like Mormons do), or watching movies or UFC fights in his upstairs loft that he had converted to a theater. He offset the cost of his mortgage payments by renting rooms to his friends, so there were always other people in his home, and he loved it.

He had a treadmill and some free weights in his oversized bedroom. He was incredibly regimented and worked out daily. Both his mother and father were overweight, and he struggled with his weight as well. Do to his exercise regimen, he was able to control his weight and got into great shape.

Travis's business boomed in Arizona. When he first arrived, he attended the weekly meetings led by other Pre-Paid Legal leaders. He found them all to be good but lacking that special something we all enjoyed in Southern California. One night, he called to tell me his plan to dominate Arizona by starting his own meeting. He said he really liked all the people there and the state leadership but "they don't do it like we did it in So Cal." He wanted the meetings to be magical.

Travis Alexander at an Executive Director Banquet

Over the course of a couple of weeks, we created a plan of attack. He found a nice hotel to hold his meetings. He networked with other leaders who wanted what they referred to as "So Cal style leadership." He had also began recruiting new associates from his singles' ward, as well as other people he had met since arriving in Arizona. When he was ready, he and his team launched their own Pre-Paid Legal weekly meeting and training system. It was a huge and immediate success! His meeting was so exciting, so full of energy, and became so large so quickly, the other meetings in the area shut down and joined Travis and his leadership team. Travis welcomed everyone with open arms, whether they were on his team or not, and everyone loved him for it.

Everything Travis learned in the early years of his business in California was paying off. His patience, while waiting in the wings, was now being rewarded. He was no longer known as a kid hoping to be successful. Travis was now known as a serious and successful entrepreneur. He was a man on a mission, and people were attracted to his vision and his leadership. He had audacious goals in business and in life, one of which was to be on the cover of *Time* magazine. One of his friends, Aaron, photoshopped a *Time* magazine cover with Travis on it. It was one of his favorite pictures. Travis had such passion, vision, focus, and energy, and there was no doubt in anyone's mind he would have accomplished his *Time* goal and every other goal he set for himself. Were it not for a terrible force of darkness that would soon enter his life, he truly would have been unstoppable.

## EDDIE SNELL

Pre-Paid Legal is made up of teams of independent associates. Many of the larger teams have their own team websites where they post team announcements, training, and recognition. One day, my brother Dave was bored and decided to post a picture of a fictitious person in the recognition section of our website: Eddie Snell from Alabama. The photo of Eddie was just a random picture Dave had grabbed from the Internet of a man, wife, and child, all rockin' extreme mullets. The man, who Dave named Eddie, looked like someone who was lost in the 1980s and split his time between singing Ozzy Osbourne songs way too seriously at the local bar on Karaoke nights and frequenting monster truck rallies, while smoking bags of weed. We left the profile up for years and were amused that no one ever asked us about it.

While planning our annual team-training event to be held at Daniels Summit, Utah, in 2006, we asked Travis to train on our business system, the 10 Core Commitments. He accepted. "It will be unlike any training you have ever seen," he promised. He became Eddie Snell.

Travis took this assignment very seriously. It was his opportunity to do one of the things he loved most: make people laugh. He acquired the perfect mullet wig (short in the front, long in the back). He cut a pair of old blue jeans and made them into shorts—*very* short. They were so short, he was fortunate to have kept everything contained in his nether region. He found the perfect shirt at a thrift store that said, "Who wants to marry a hundredaire?" He cut the sleeves and the sides off, and with some dark black sunglasses, his outfit was complete.

His assignment was to train on the 10 Core Commitments. He ran with it! The 10 Core Commitments is the business system for success in Pre-Paid Legal. It is a list of simple things anyone can do each day, week, month, and year to build a successful business. Some of the things on the list are sharing third-party marketing tools with prospects every day, attending a meeting a week and a training a month, sending out long-distance packages every week to share Pre-Paid Legal with people in other states, etc. Travis trained on the 10 "Poor" Commitments, mocking the actual 10 Core Commitments.

His skit was a wild success and incredibly funny. His introduction set the stage. He was introduced as someone who had, "trained literally dozens of people all over the United States, made hundreds of dollars in this business, and knows at least thirty-two percent of the facts of how to do the business." He was Eddie Snell from Alabama!

The audience rose to their feet, as a loud shrill was heard from the back of the room. It was Eddie in full effect! He ran to the front of the room, rockin' out to "Pour Some Sugar on Me" by Def Leppard. For a full minute before he started talking, he worked the crowd like a pro. He clapped his hands to the beat of the music, banged his head, threw his mullet around, and flicked his tongue repulsively at the people on the front row. He lip-synced the song, gyrated and contorted his body, screamed randomly, jumped around, rubbed his nipples, dirty danced with a giant balloon, and risked it all by doing high kicks in his short-short shorts. It was the most repugnant, foul, and offensive thing, but we loved it! He was in his element.

He started his training by yelling out, "I freakin' love that song," followed by a beastly grunt. So much of what he said would only be funny to Pre-Paid Legal associates, but what he did can be appreciated by anyone.

"Ladies and gentlemen, I'm excited to be here this mornin'. I've got some good crap to talk about. Can we keep it real? Everybody say, 'Keep it real!'"

The audience repeated, "Keep it real!"

"I keep it real. All right, ladies and gentlemen, my name is Eddie Snizz-ell, Eddie Snell. I've been in the business for five years and I'm a senior associate." (Senior associate was the lowest level you could advance to then. Many people became senior associates in their first month or even in their first week or day.)

"Speaking of good crap to talk about . . ." Travis continued. He reached into his back pocket and pulled out his notes that were written on a long piece of toilet paper.

He went through the 10 "Poor" Commitments, one by one, and hilarity ensued. For the most part, he kept the crowd laughing, but there were a few awkward moments that would make your skin crawl and your spine itch, but Travis got away with it. He had that ability. One of my favorite moments from the Eddie Snell skit was when he said, "Everyone always wants to know, 'How much money are you makin'? How much money are you makin'?' Now, some people call it lyin', but I call it, 'selective times to share your affirmation.' 'How much money are you makin'?' *I am* a $100,000 earner! *I am* a Millionaire Club Member. They can take it how they want."

I just watched the recording of this performance and laughed until I cried. Travis was such a funny, unique, and special guy. Not only had he found a new career and a place to shine, but he also found his confidence and a place to give back for all the good he had in his life.

To watch Travis as Eddie Snell, visit: www.ourfriendtravis.com/eddie

# CHAPTER 5

# Travis's Serious Girlfriends and Dating

*Travis loved the French fries at Red Robin, maybe because they were unlimited. He always battled his weight and would often be on a diet that allowed one "cheat day" a week. Cheat days were interesting, almost wrong in a way. Travis would consume an inhumane amount of food. They often consisted of a trip to Red Robin and a trip, or two, to Cold Stone Creamery. One cheat day, while on a cruise with the top executives on our team, everyone was sitting in the Jacuzzi. Travis suddenly got up and walked away. He came back with five ice cream cones, overflowing with soft-serve ice cream. People began to thank him. He furrowed his brow and said, "These are mine!" Then he laughed like a hyena and handed out the five ice cream cones. He left again, came back with five more, and ate every one of them.*

SKY:

IN THE TIME THAT I knew Travis, there were only three girls he was serious about: Deanna Reid, Linda Ballard, and Lisa Andrews. Travis returned from his mission in Colorado in the late summer of 1998. Shortly after, Travis and Deanna met at the home of a mutual friend and hit it off! Travis soon wanted to get married, but Deanna strongly felt that she was supposed to go on a mission, so she did. This left Travis heartbroken. He wrote Deanna often on her mission. He expressed to her how much he loved and missed her. Toward the end of Deanna's mission, he met Linda and they began dating. This was in the Summer of 2001. Travis wrote Deanna and told her he had met someone and that they were dating.

I never knew Linda, but I knew about her. Travis and Linda talked about getting married. Linda knew he was going to propose to her. He had just spent his life savings to purchase an engagement ring, but she was having doubts about whether or not she wanted to continue the relationship. Travis told Chris she wasn't a fan of Pre-Paid Legal and didn't want to live a life married to an entrepreneur. According to Travis, she valued traditional education and the predictability of a job over the greater earnings potential of an entrepreneur. Knowing Travis dropped out of college and had no intentions to go back was a problem for her. That, and the fact that he was so passionate about Pre-Paid Legal, was a deal breaker. She wouldn't budge, and Travis wouldn't give up his business and his new life. Pre-Paid Legal came as an answer to prayer. Travis knew he was supposed to continue on that course. Linda broke up with him before he had the opportunity to propose. She said she was "very in love with Travis," and breaking up with him was one of the hardest things she ever had to do.

She said, "I was praying a lot about whether or not I should marry him and I just didn't feel like it was right. I didn't feel like he was the right man for me, even though he was a wonderful man and I loved him. I was also very young at the time. I was only twenty-one years old. The Travis I knew was kind and loving. He treated me very kindly. He was always doing nice things for me. He gave me flowers and would sometimes pick flowers for me, and he even wrote me a beautiful poem after we broke up, but were still dating on and off.

*All the Best* by Travis Alexander

*Although we are uncertain,*
*as to what you and I will be.*
*I wish you all the best,*
*and through time I guess we'll see.*
*Although we don't know what tomorrow brings,*
*Of our future, we are unaware.*
*I wish you all the best,*
*even if tomorrow I'm not there.*
*May your life be filled with happiness,*
*and all of your dreams come true.*
*May your heart never feel sorrow,*
*and may your countenance never be blue.*
*May all of your goals be accomplished,*
*and in all that you do you succeed.*
*May your heart never be left wanting,*
*and your soul never left in need.*
*May the strength of the Lord be with you,*
*and the Holy Ghost always be near.*
*May his love burn from within you,*
*and radiate to all you hold dear.*
*Why? Because you deserve it,*
*all this and much more too.*
*I wish you all the best,*
*and only all the best will do.*
*This is the life I know you will have,*
*I'm certain, I know that you can.*
*This is the life I pray for me,*
*and so I will finish as I began.*
*Although we are uncertain,*
*as to what you and I will be.*
*I wish you all the best,*
*and hope all the best is me.*

Deanna returned from her mission in November 2001. After Linda and Travis broke up, she and Travis began dating again in January of 2002. They got really serious and often discussed marriage. They were amazing together. They made each other very happy, but eventually they caused one another a lot of heartache. Over time, Deanna and Travis's relationship would become an issue between Travis and me, one that surfaced often. Travis loved and trusted Deanna, and I think this terrified him. He was vulnerable because of his deep love for her, and this scared him. I think it was this vulnerability that drove Travis to sabotage their relationship, leading to their break up. Travis had a difficult time letting people love him, and loving and trusting someone made him vulnerable, which took him back to his childhood where vulnerability led to pain and heartache. I think this is more common than we think, especially when someone has been raised in an abusive home. Love, or the lack of it, becomes a painful thing, a very scary thing. Most of us are not aware of how much our subconscious mind affects our daily lives and relationships.

Even after they broke up, Travis and Deanna told each other that they loved one another every time they ended a phone call. Deanna meant everything to Travis. They even got back together again for a little while, then broke up again, prior to his meeting Jodi, but they remained friends through it all. Deanna and Travis's final break up was in 2005. They continued their friendship until he was murdered. Travis told me that no matter whom he married, she would have to accept that Deanna was a part of his life and would always be his friend. They were best friends. Travis and I argued about this all the time. I told him it wasn't fair to Deanna or his future wife. I felt if he didn't completely separate from Deanna, and Deanna from him, neither of them would ever move on, and this concerned me for both of their sakes. Deanna was one of the best things that ever happened to Travis. He knew it, and he didn't want to let her go. I think Deanna was the first person that Travis ever let love him, and the first time he ever felt deeply loved was by Deanna. This was also the first time he ever deeply loved someone. It was this love that would make Jodi resent Deanna . . . and Travis.

Deanna Reid and Travis Alexander

If you followed the trial in 2013 and again in 2015, chances are you fell in love with Deanna. Get to know her, and it is easy to see why she meant so much to Travis. Deanna is just good. She is kind, laid back, loves people, a great friend, funny, honest . . . she is just wonderful. She is just incredibly kind and good, while also being strong, confident, and courageous. Chris and I adore her. Travis loved her a great deal. He wasn't able to get over her, and she meant the world to him. She knew him better than any of us. When it came to Deanna, Travis felt so safe and loved. Ironically, this made him feel unsafe. In other words, the fact that she was so good and he was so comfortable with her made him uneasy, because he knew that she was someone he wanted to marry. He wasn't able to commit, and this left him in a quandary.

It was the above "issues" that would become the topic of an email exchange between Travis, Chris, and myself. I told him he needed to seek counseling for these "issues." Because Travis was in love with Deanna and not emotionally available to anyone else, I told him it wasn't fair for him to date other women. I also told him it wasn't fair what he was doing to Deanna by not letting her go. Deanna was not willing to let go either. Both were needing to move on. They needed to let go of their friendship for them to really be able to move on, but neither one of them were letting go. He had a really difficult time committing, and this was also the topic of many of our conversations. Travis met Jodi in 2006 after Deanna and Travis decided to "just be friends." Jodi and Travis's relationship will be discussed in detail in the next chapter.

Travis and Lisa met in August 2007, and he was smitten! Lisa was several years younger than Travis. During the murder trial, the defense team postulated that Lisa was young and weak, but she wasn't weak, and she certainly wasn't someone whom Travis could control. They began dating in August 2007 after Jodi and Travis had broken things off in June, 2007 (there is no evidence that Jodi and Travis had ever been in a "committed" relationship). Travis was so excited about the potential of this relationship. They eventually broke up, because Lisa felt like things were getting too serious, too fast. Lisa really liked Travis, and Travis liked Lisa, so they got back together. After dating for a while, they began talking about marriage. Travis was really excited. He called Chris to figure out a budget and how he could make it happen financially. Travis spent a lot of time and money traveling with Jodi and had neglected his growing business. As a result, his business began to deteriorate, and with it, his income. He was still making decent money, but certainly not what he was used to.

At some point in the relationship, Jodi made sure a friend of Lisa's sister knew that Jodi and Travis were still messing around, and that friend told Lisa's sister, who told Lisa. Lisa was heartbroken. Travis lied to Lisa and said it wasn't true. Lisa believed him. Unfortunately, it was true. Travis was messing around with Jodi. Jodi claimed during her interrogation and the trial that she did not know about Lisa. She lied. She knew all about Lisa and everything else in Travis's life.

While Travis was dating Lisa, he called me and told me he wanted to bring Lisa to our house for a few days and take her to Disneyland, to which I responded, "Good, then I can tell her you are cheating on her with Jodi." During the trial, the defense wanted the jury to believe that Jodi was Travis's "dirty little secret." The whole idea that Jodi was ever a "dirty little secret" is such a ridiculous prevarication. Jodi and Travis were together all the time. When Chris told his brother, Tony, who lived in Arizona and worked with Travis and Jodi (Jodi was also in Pre-Paid Legal), that Travis was going to get married, Tony's response was, "Travis is marrying Jodi?" Tony assumed Jodi and Travis were dating because they were always together. Many people thought they were together.

I know saying that Travis really cared about Lisa may sound crazy to some, but he did. Before he was killed, he was in agony because he knew how badly he had messed up with Lisa and how deeply he had hurt her. He was a jerk for cheating on her. He knew it, and he felt awful. I have said more than once that Travis had "commitment issues." This may sound weird considering he wanted to marry Deanna, then Linda, then Deanna, then Lisa. He wanted to get married, but he was scared to commit. This plagued him until the very end of his life. Travis suffered from self-sabotage. Many of us do. It may be in relationships, career, health, or parenting. It could be anything. Most of us don't even realize we are doing it. Travis had mastered so much in his life, but he struggled with romantic relationships. If things were going well, he would do something to mess them up. He would do this subconsciously, completely unaware of what he was doing to himself and others.

# CHAPTER 6

# Meeting Jodi Arias: Early Relationship

*Travis was a hugger. It didn't matter if he knew you or*
*not. He would turn any handshake into a hug.*

CHRIS AND I ARRIVED IN Las Vegas on Wednesday, September 13, 2006, for our bi-annual Pre-Paid Legal convention. On Thursday, Travis sent me a text telling me about a girl he had just met who was also a Pre-Paid Legal associate attending the convention. I didn't think much of it, because Travis was always meeting new people. We planned to see him later that night at the Executive Director Banquet, a formal dinner that would be held that evening at 7:00 p.m.

Travis arrived at the banquet twenty minutes early. He was on the phone, and when he finished his phone call, he seemed disappointed. I asked him what was wrong. He said that he had asked the woman he'd met to be his date for the banquet. She had agreed to go if she could find a dress. Travis told Chris and I that she had been out for the last few hours looking for a dress, but with no luck. I had packed an extra dress and shoes, so I asked Travis what size she was. His face lit up, and he said, "I think it will work!" I handed him our room key and he called her immediately. As he rushed from the table, I heard him say, "I found a dress for you!" Twenty minutes later, Travis returned with a pretty woman with platinum-blonde hair.

Travis introduced us to Jodi Arias. During our conversation, we learned that she lived in Palm Desert, California, about eighty minutes from where we were living in Murrieta, California. We also learned that she was an artist and photographer. She made great eye contact, had a firm handshake, and was a great conversationalist. She seemed just as into Travis as he was into her.

The next morning, when getting an update from Travis about how his night went, he told me that he and Jodi were up until four in the morning talking. He also told me she had a boyfriend, Darryl Brewer, she had been with for four years, and they lived together in Palm Desert. I flipped out and scolded him for spending so much time with someone who was in a committed relationship. He took my rebuke in stride and assured me, just as Jodi had him, that the relationship was over. She wanted to get married and have children, but Darryl didn't. He was a divorced father of a young son, and, according to Jodi, swore he would never marry again and did not want any more children.

The week after our convention in Las Vegas, Travis was planning to come stay with us, as he often did. He asked us if it was okay if Jodi came over too. We thought it was a great idea. We decided to have a Pre-Paid Legal team party at our house, since so many people on our team were on Travis's team or had become friends with him over the years. Travis called Jodi and extended an invitation for her to meet him at our house and network at the party. He would be staying with us for a few days, so he invited her to join him at our house. She accepted his invitation and planned to meet him at our house.

Travis was running a little late, as he was driving from his home in Mesa, Arizona. Jodi arrived before he did, which gave us an opportunity to get to know her a little better. We liked her. Chris and I talked about how there seemed to be a little something askew or different about her, but we wrote it off as nothing more than an artist's vibe. Two hours after the party started, Travis finally arrived. The party ended late, and Chris, Travis, Jodi, and I stayed up even later, talking. Finally, we went to bed. Chris and I went up to our room, Jodi went to hers, and Travis went to his.

The next morning, Travis came into the living room with the cheesiest smile on his face. I started laughing. "What did you do?" I asked.

Still smiling, he said, "The T-Dogg left her wanting."

"What is that supposed to mean?" I asked.

He told me how he went into her room after we'd all gone to bed and they started kissing. "It got pretty heated, and it was clear she really wanted the T-Dogg," he said.

"What'd you do?" I asked.

"I stopped her," he said. "I told her I respected her and that I wanted her to know I respected her. Then I kissed her on the forehead, said goodnight, and left the room."

He looked smug. He was so proud of himself. He said he really liked her, respected her, and didn't want to move too fast.

Jodi started spending a lot of time at our house. At first, she only came over when Travis was in town. But before long, she just started showing up by herself, often, and sometimes unannounced. We thought it was weird, but her life was in transition. Even though we didn't know her that well, she told us things about her life. She told us that she didn't have a good relationship with her parents. Jodi was learning about "Mormonism," which would require a major lifestyle change. She had recently broken up with her long-term boyfriend, Darryl, even though she was still living with him. (However, when Darryl testified during the trial, he made it clear that they were still together at this time. Jodi was cheating on Darryl, and Travis had no idea.) We thought she just needed to get away and needed a friend. We spent quite a bit of time together, and we were always kind to her, but I was really surprised when Travis told me I was her "best friend."

A few months after we met Jodi for the first time, Travis was sitting at the counter while I was doing dishes after dinner. Travis gushed about Jodi. He went on and on about how much he liked her and how amazing she was. He said she was the nicest person he had ever met, and raved about all of her amazing qualities. Then he said, "She says you are her best friend, and she really likes you."

This caught me off guard, "Best friend?" I asked. "I don't even know her that well. I don't call her—"

"Sky," Travis interrupted. "She has no family and no friends. We are all that she has."

I stopped what I was doing and turned to him. "Travis, is she really that nice, or is she a psychopath?" (I might have said sociopath.)

"She is really that nice," he replied with confidence.

"She says I am her best friend, and I don't even know her. Don't you find it disturbing that she has no friends, yet she is the nicest person you have ever met?"

A little irritated that I would doubt her wonderfulness, he said, "She has one guy friend, an ex-boyfriend. She said she has no girl-friends, because they are all jealous of her and guys just want to sleep with her, so she has no friends."

"I have a lot of really pretty friends, Travis, and they are really nice, and they have lots of guy and girlfriends. I just think it's weird that she doesn't have any."

I should have listened more carefully to my gut, because something was clearly off. But Travis really liked her, which made me want to like her, so I blew off my instinct.

Jodi knew how much the Mormon faith meant to Travis, so when he asked her if she would be interested in meeting with the mission-aries to learn more about what Mormons believe, she jumped on the opportunity. Jodi wanted to get married, have babies, and play house, and she knew that was not going to happen with Travis if she wasn't Mormon. She knew Travis would never marry outside of the church, so she started meeting with the Mormon missionaries in Palm Desert in the fall of 2006 in an effort to learn more about the Church of Jesus Christ of Latter-day Saints, so she could then be baptized.

As an interesting side note, during the trial, Darryl was adamant that she had begun meeting with the missionaries in May or June of 2006. When asked if he was sure, he said it could have been June or July (as opposed to the fall when Travis sent them over). If he were right, that would mean that she was meeting with the Mormon missionaries before she ever met Travis. Was Jodi more calculating than we ever gave her credit for? Was she targeting a Mormon guy because she wanted to get married so badly and had learned that Mormons valued families? Darryl also said that she stopped paying bills in the summer of 2006. Again, this was before she met Travis.

The missionaries taught her the basic tenants of the Mormon faith, including specific commitments she would be expected to make. In addition to *their* teaching her, I had several detailed discussions with her, specifically about the law of chastity, the moral code within Mormonism. Mormonism, like most other Christian denominations, teaches abstinence before marriage, and that any sexual relations outside of marriage are violations of God's law. This included heavy make-out sessions, oral sex . . . pretty much everything. I warned her it was going to be tough, and that it was a big commitment. On more than one occasion, we talked about what was included in this commitment and what was taboo. Travis made it very clear to Jodi that he didn't want her to be baptized for him or for any other reason. He only wanted her to be baptized if she believed it was true. Chris and I also told Jodi that she should only do it for her and not for Travis.

It didn't take long for her to make the decision to be baptized. We think the decision was made long before she even met with the missionaries. It was a means to an end. She announced that she would be baptized and invited us to attend. On November 26, 2006, she was baptized in Palm Desert, California, and became an official member of the Church of Jesus Christ of Latter-day Saints. Travis performed the baptism. Chris and my brother, Zion, gave talks. Normally, baptismal services are special, spirit-filled events. But this one was an exception. It didn't feel right. Chris and I both felt it was awkward. We were convinced she did it for the wrong reasons, and in the end, we were right.

Our friend Debbie knew there was something off about Jodi the first time she'd met her. She did not like her and knew that she could not be trusted. She was worried that Jodi had a thing for my little brother, Zion. After Jodi was baptized, Debbie casually asked her, "Did you get baptized for Zion?"

Without hesitation, Jodi said, "No, for Travis." This was a pretty big slip-up on Jodi's part. This was disheartening to us, and we added it to the "something isn't right" list. We shared with Travis what Jodi had told Debbie, and he told us that she told him she would have gotten baptized even if Travis never spoke to her again.

Jodi and Travis were staying with us for a few days in December 2006, just a couple of weeks after her baptism. I needed to go to the mall, and Jodi wanted to tag along. I remember it perfectly, as if it happened yesterday. We were in Ann Taylor, and I was looking at skirts. She started talking about her relationship with Travis. She expressed that she felt they were at the point in their relationship where Travis should invite her to move to Arizona so they could take the relationship to the next level. Travis liked Jodi, but I knew he wasn't even close to a place where he would ask Jodi to move closer to him. They were still dating other people. They lived in two different states—Jodi was still living with Darryl in Palm Desert, California, and Travis didn't feel like he knew her well enough to make that type of commitment. Further, he was not over Deanna.

Jodi kept talking about how Travis would be the perfect husband and perfect father to her children. Just as I pulled into our garage, Jodi told me that she had what can only be described as a "vision." She had *seen* her and Travis's marriage. She said she *knew* she was going to marry Travis, and she described her vision. I was definitely weirded out, but I had no idea that a dangerous obsession had begun, an obsession that would change all of us—forever.

Once Jodi got the idea that she was going to marry Travis, things got even stranger. It seemed like every time we spoke, she brought up Travis taking the next step and asking her to move to Arizona. When I brought it up to Travis, he toed the same line. He was not ready for that, which was totally understandable. He thought she was really cool, but he was not ready for a committed relationship. They had only known each other for a few months, and Jodi was ready to get married. He did not feel it would be right of him to ask her to move to Arizona if he was not absolutely sure that the relationship was going somewhere.

It was around this time that I began to have strong feelings that something was very wrong and that I needed to protect my family. I only got this feeling when Jodi was around, but I blew it off for about a month before I finally brought it up to Chris.

CHAPTER 7

# The Emails

*Travis named his black pug, Napoleon, after Napoleon Hill, who*
*was the author of one of his favorite books, Think and Grow Rich.*
*Travis's grandmother always had pugs while he was growing up.*
*His favorite was a black pug named Jasper. He was Travis's buddy.*
*One morning before school, Jasper was hit by a car and killed.*
*Travis was devastated. He cried at school. When his teacher asked*
*why he was crying, he told his teacher what had happened, but*
*she didn't believe him. Deanna said this pained Travis years later.*
*Travis knew that when he grew up, he would have a black pug.*

IN LATE JANUARY 2007, JODI came to our house and stayed for a couple days (without Travis). It was a Saturday night, and Chris and I were getting ready to go to bed when Jodi said she wanted to talk to us about some concerns she had about Travis. She felt it was time that they take their relationship to the "next level." She felt that Travis should commit to her. It bothered her terribly that he wouldn't stamp "official" on their relationship. We reminded her that they lived in two different states, and that the sheer distance would slow the progression of a relationship. For two people living four hours apart, they actually spent quite a bit of time together, but nothing in comparison to the time a couple would spend together if they lived in close proximity to one another. She just did not seem to get it. Thinking we did our best to soothe her, we said goodnight and were off to bed, but she stopped us. She said there was more she wanted to share with us, but she was hesitant, because we were Travis's good friends and she "did not want to cause problems." (We later realized that this was exactly what she was trying to do.)

She told us that Travis had called her a "skank." We were both surprised by that. That didn't sound like Travis. In disbelief, I asked her, "He called you a skank?" She confirmed that he had, but then decided to clarify and told me what really happened. Travis's roommate, Josh, is a really sweet guy. Josh was in the room while Travis was talking to Jodi, and Jodi told Travis she wanted to talk to Josh, or say hi to Josh, and Travis, more to embarrass Josh than insult Jodi, said, "He says you're a skank," and started laughing. Josh, of course embarrassed, yelled that he didn't say that, and Travis told Jodi he was just kidding.

She complained that he only called her late at night and she felt like he was using her. She said she was aware that he still loved Deanna, and that he told Deanna he loved her all the time. This really shocked me. *Why would Travis tell her that?* I wondered. Then she started crying, and we sincerely felt bad for her. She really liked Travis, and from what she was telling us, it didn't sound like he was very interested in her. (We would realize later that at this point in their relationship, she didn't just like him; she was completely obsessed with him.)

She went on and on, and by the time she was done, it was clear to Chris and me that this was not a good relationship for either of them. We advised her to talk to him—tell him exactly how she felt, and where she was at emotionally. She said she had already done that and nothing changed. (We later found out that she had never talked to him about any of this. She lied to us. She lied about a lot of things, and distorted and manipulated much of the truth she conveyed that night. She used this situation, and us, to try to get him to commit to her.)

We did our best to go over each of her grievances. I told her that he never should have called her a skank and she needed to let him know that it bothered her. In regards to Deanna, I told her that Travis made it clear to me that Deanna would always be a part of his life, and that if she wanted a life with Travis, she was going to have to be okay with them being friends. I also told her that Travis was aware that he had difficulty committing, and it was something he was working on. I suggested that if she wasn't okay with that, or if she felt Travis was emotionally unavailable or otherwise unable to give her what she wanted, she should move on. Neither Chris nor myself felt we were disloyal to Travis at any point during this discussion. We would give this same advice to anyone representing similar relationship dynamics.

She brought up a bunch of other minor issues, but mostly rehashed things we had already discussed. We talked for more than three hours until well past midnight. We needed to get some sleep, but before Chris and I went to bed, I asked her to let me talk to Travis about all of this before she did. I didn't want him to feel like I was talking about him behind his back. I wanted him to hear what I said from me. She agreed not to talk to him until after I did the following day. Chris and I went upstairs to our bedroom, and Jodi went to her room.

I don't recall exactly why, but I woke up a little later, perhaps to feed my baby, and noticed the lights were on downstairs. While downstairs to turn them off, I checked to make sure all the doors were locked and noticed the door leading into the garage was unlocked. I knew I'd locked it before going to bed, so I opened it to make sure no one was out there before locking it again. I opened the door to find Jodi on the phone talking to Travis . . . about our conversation. *Nice,* I thought. I couldn't believe she did that. I was upset she had lied to me. She had agreed to let me talk to him first, but I wasn't too worried. I would just call Travis the following day and everything would be fine. Everything wasn't fine.

Jodi went home the following morning. That afternoon, we got an email from Travis, and he was really upset. We went back and forth between emails and phone calls. I've included all the emails we have access to below. However, it may seem like some of the emails are missing parts, because some of what was discussed took place over the phone. Also, these are not all the emails included in the exchange, but I am pretty sure these are the worst of them. These are the parts of the emails that were "leaked" to the media, including Michael Keifer who is a court and legal writer for the *Arizona Republic*, pro-Jodi websites, and who knows who else.

While reading these emails during the trial, and considering all the new information discovered leading up to the trial and the information revealed during the trial, I had the sickening realization that Jodi was manipulating all of us. Her plan all along was to drive a wedge between us and Travis, pushing Travis closer to her. It worked. I also realized that she had been reading his texts and emails and eavesdropping on his conversations from the very beginning. She knew too much. She knew about Travis and Deanna's conversations, and the nature of their relationship. She knew what girls Travis was talking to and his schedule.

Not knowing what kind of monster we were dealing with, I incredulously assumed Travis told her these things. Travis thought I was the one who'd told her. Now it's clear why he was so upset at Chris and me, but mostly me. He thought I had completely betrayed him. Nothing made sense, and we both thought the other was lying. It did not cross any of our minds that Jodi had gotten all the information she needed by violating Travis's privacy. Mystery solved. She had been snooping almost since day one!

She lied to him about the late-night conversation she had with Chris and I. She told him that we brought up all these things to "brainwash her." You will see from the emails that she told him that it was three days of "ripping on Travis." Not true. It was one conversation. It was more about how the relationship was affecting her and much less about Travis. She was a mess, but that had less to do with Travis and his normal behavior, and more to do with her and whatever was going on in her head. She was completely obsessed with him and fixated on marrying him. We were watching this girl completely melt down over this relationship, under the guise that Travis had done this to her.

As we got to know Jodi better, it became increasingly clear that something was off about her. It wouldn't have mattered what Travis was doing or not doing; her world was crumbling if he wasn't ready to marry her. But at the time, we were unaware of what we were dealing with. I think anyone who has dealt with any type of sociopathy, psychopathy, narcissistic personality disorder, borderline personality disorder, or many other mental and personality disorders and illnesses will completely understand what we were dealing with. People with these disorders have a way of getting in your head. Many specialists on TV reviewing Jodi's behaviors have suggested that she may, or may not, have had one or a combination of the issues listed above. I am not a professional, but I do know that what we experienced (and what Travis continued to experience) was not normal.

The majority of the people who have come to know Jodi have met her as a lying murderer. So, it's easy to see through the lies and manipulation. On the other hand, Chris and I met her as the "nicest person" Travis had ever met. When something was bothering us about her, and we brought it up with Travis, he reminded us of how sweet and near perfect she was. At this point in the relationship, we liked Jodi, though less with each passing day. She kept complaining and crying about him, having a complete emotional breakdown, and we just kept repeating, "If you don't like it, move on."

Rereading the emails, I find it interesting that she had a breakdown with us, crying and complaining about Travis and his mistreatment of her. Then she went to Travis and broke down about how mean and cruel we were to her, and how she hated every second of it. She put on the same show for us about how awful Travis was, and then she turned around and put on a show about how awful we were. It's understandable that Travis was so upset with us, just as we were so upset with him for whatever he did to make Jodi so upset. Jodi was playing the victim, and still is to this day. This isn't new to Jodi. She claims to be the "victim" in every relationship she has had. While this is consistent with real abuse victims, there is a plethora of evidence that Jodi was the aggressor on many occasions, Jodi was the manipulator, Jodi was confrontational, Jodi was invading people's privacy and feelings of security, etc. Victims don't do these things. The true victims are the men she lied to, stalked, used, violated, manipulated, and controlled. (While she never claimed in court that Darryl mistreated her, she told us Darryl had taken four years of her life without being willing to give her the ultimate commitment of marriage and a family. She was again the victim by her claim that he wasted her time, and that he was unmotivated and not going anywhere in life. Darryl seems like a really nice guy who still cares a great deal about her. Unfortunately, he, too, got caught up in her mind games.)

In the emails included below, you will read how much I defended her, and this was *after* I had been having feelings for over a month that something was just not right with her. I ignored those feelings for far too long, because what I saw in front of me didn't match the feelings I was having. It was confusing. (I've since learned to immediately trust my intuition.) In the following emails, you will see how kind and good Travis was. As I mentioned earlier, I was pretty hard on Travis. You'll see that in the emails, and even still, Travis quickly forgave.

One day, during a break in the trial, I was in the hall outside the courtroom when a man I didn't know approached me. He introduced himself as Michael Keifer, a reporter for the *Arizona Republic* (one of the people to whom a portion of these emails were leaked to). He showed me the emails, pointing to one particular part, and asked for my response. He turned briefly to speak to someone else, so I read as much and as fast as I could. I read more than he asked me to. The emails he had are not included below. We don't have them and don't have access to them. I will, however, share the notes I made after rushing back into the courtroom and writing down as much as I could remember from them.

In one email, I was apologizing to Travis and complimenting him on his patience, kindness, and forgiveness. I told him that if roles were reversed, I would not have been so understanding. The other email was from Travis; he told us that he loved us and forgave us. Of course, they didn't release those emails. They would show the world the kind of person Travis really was, which was far from what the defense wanted the world to believe.

Though never abusive, Travis struggled with relationships. He knew it, and he would talk openly about it. Travis, like any of us, liked to be liked, but he also had a really hard time committing in relationships. Even if he cared about someone deeply and wanted things to work out, he just couldn't seem to commit completely. He always seemed to leave one foot outside the door. This was less about Travis being mean, a "player," or a jerk, and more about his fear about being loved, being vulnerable, and being abandoned.

The email exchange Chris and I had with Travis occurred not long after Travis and Jodi had met, but it became a focal point of the trial. The defense team could not find anyone to take the stand to say anything bad about Travis. In a feat of legal gymnastics, they desperately tried to make these emails more than what they were, and say things they did not say to try to prove their point. In short, the defense team used these emails to "prove" that Travis was a violent person who ultimately provoked Jodi's wrath. It was all they had, and, frankly, they got a lot of mileage out of it. They strategically presented mere snippets of the emails to tarnish Travis's image. Chris was called to testify at a hearing without the jury present. The defense tried to get Chris to answer a question about the incomplete emails. Chris wrestled with the defense in an effort to see the complete email exchange, so that he could comment in context, but to no avail.

Social media was a buzz about these emails. Since they were never shown in their entirety, everyone wanted to know more about them. The defense ran with the loosely used word "abuse," while in the very same emails, it was acknowledged that it was not the correct word to use. It's very obvious that we were not talking about what they wanted the jury to believe we were talking about. As expected, the defense team did not include the part of our emails where we apologize to Travis.

Were these emails released in full and in context, the core of the defense's story would have been decimated. The email thread, when understood in complete context, would do nothing more than further illustrate what a kind, loving, and forgiving guy Travis was. Did he have a difficult time committing? Yes. Did he beat women and abuse children? No. Was he in love with another woman and trying to re-cover from a very difficult break-up and dating a new woman? Yes. But, that wouldn't serve Jodi's case, so they took a small percentage of the emails, contorted the context, and ran with it.

During the guilt phase of the trial, the defense team hired expert witnesses Alice LaViolette and Robert Geffner, to chime in on these emails. During the guilt-phase retrial, they brought back Geffner and hired L.C. Miccio-Fonseca to testify about our emails. Not one of these experts ever asked us why we wrote these emails, what provoked them, what they were about, or if we thought Travis was abusive. With no more than stories told by Jodi Arias, a proven liar and ruthless killer, one email correspondence in a seven-year span, void of context, details, backstory, and other related factors, they arrived at the same "expert" opinion that Travis Alexander was abusive and Jodi was the victim.

Several times while LaViolette was on the stand, she defended her many conclusions based upon patterns she observed. "I look for pat-terns," she often said. This was not a pattern. This conclusion of hers was derived from one small sampling from one email feed from one incident over a seven-year span. There was no pattern here. They did not bring up the fact that in those same emails, we apologized for the things that were said, and that Travis remained kind and calm in a situation where, if I were in his position, thinking it happened the way Jodi told him it happened, I would have blown a gasket!

Below are the emails that we have. Like I said, I think these are the "worst" of them. I have inserted comments to provide clarity. Knowing that my words have been used to make Travis look bad is heartbreaking. I wish we had access to all the emails, so we could show a fuller context to the story. Even with those emails, there is more to the whole story and situation. It's important to keep in mind that these emails were very early in Travis and Jodi's relationship, yet "experts" applied the content to the entire relationship. Looking back, it seems a bit ridiculous that these emails were even an issue considering Jodi had been living with Darryl Brewer, her ex-boyfriend, the first four months of her dating Travis.

[Note to readers: We have not edited this email feed. We did not correct typos and other errors. I put my responses to Travis in italics to make it easier to follow.

Will indicate the beginning and end of my comments to the reader.]

To: Chris and Sky
From: Travis January 29, 2007
2:27pm

Chris and Sky,

I just got off the phone with a very reluctant to talk to me Jodi. In fact, so reluctant that she doesn't want me to write you guys because of her great fear that you will not have any respect for her if you find out. She mentioned that you instructed her to not e-mail or call me, and to erase me from her MySpace and act if I do not exist. She also mentioned that the last three days have been a discourse on how I am a jerk, I am a abusive to women and that she is blind to the type of person I really am. I didn't pry for a lot of details because it was obvious that Jodi wasn't comfortable telling me much, in fear of upsetting the two of you, as she already feels she has. She mentioned that a comment was made that if she continued to associate with me that you both would lose all respect for her. She also mentioned that you were continually calling her Deanna. To some it up, the past three days you were beating in her head that I am a broken person that is F'd up in the head, who needs counseling. That I am extremely abusive to women and that, the fact that she is interested in me proves that she has her own head problems and needs counseling too. What I find ironic is that your whole basis for all this I am assuming is so that I don't hurt her. What is also ironic, is that Jodi and I have never had an argument, not one. We have always got along and enjoy each others company. Have I ever been rude to her. Well I am sure I have simply because I am rough around the edges and make a joke that isn't funny but sounded funny at the time. Never have I said anything in anger and if you ask Jodi, I would bet that she could easily count on one hand with fingers to spare, how many times I have offended her. Now if that makes me the devil I would ask you the same question that Sky asked Jodi. Has he ever once been a jerk to you? Jodi's answer was yes. Now if you don't have the same answer to the question, then congrats you are better than me and everyone else for that matter. I think that it is a very manipulative question to ask and to try to base a point on a positive answer to the question has Travis ever in his life acted like a jerk. In fact the whole three day experience sounds like a grand brainwashing. What I seriously don't get is if you are so concerned about Jodi's feelings, did you ever consider what it might do to her feelings when she was a number of times referred to as Deanna, told that your respect for her is contingent on her disowning one of her best friends and the person that introduced her to the church, calling her blind and that she needs counseling. How do you think that affects her feelings. I have never ever heard Jodi cry, not once until I talked to her a few moments ago and all I heard was tears and fear. Next time you want to throw me under the bus and there is no denying that that happened quite a bit remember the advice of the secret to not focus on a anti- Travis campaign but more of pro someone else campaign. It would save Jodi and my own feelings a great deal of hurt. That may have been the Doctor Laura approach but it is not the Jesus Christ approach.

Which brings me to my next thought, my feelings. The very little that Jodi would tell me was plenty for me to be reminded of it insight you had about Jason [last name removed]. I will paraphrase the best I can. "If you are so against the type of people we are, don't act like we are friends." If you really think that I am such a horrible person to women why would you want to associate with me and consider me a friend. If I am a bad person to women, then I am simply a bad person. Feeling like you can be my friend and tell Jodi to drop me like a dirty diaper, is not consistent. If I am not good enough to be her friend why am I good enough to be yours. You have always been the epitome of kind to me and excellent friends, in fact, unconditional friends, thats why this approach is so confusing to me. I guess what I am getting at is that I am very hurt by the comments made about me. I think they were unfair, dramatically exaggerated and most importantly, not your place to say. I realize everything was said with a righteous motive. However it was over zealous and inappropriate. I feel you shot beyond the mark. Now in most cases I would first ask from some clarity, but I think we can all agree that they don't get more honest than Jodi. Now if you meant things to come off that way or not it doesn't matter, what I have written is a very mild version of how it did come off. In my opinion you overstepped your bounds and caused more problems than you solved. I know you were trying to help but you went overboard.

Which brings me to my next thought. Regardless of what you may think, I am not mean to Jodi. I adore Jodi. In fact I don't know if it has ever been easier to be nice to someone as it is with Jodi. Has a little of the imperfect Travis come out around Jodi? The answer is you better believe it, but the keyword is a little and I don't think that by any realistic standard can you deem my behavior with Jodi anywhere in the neighborhood of mean. So much so that I can't believe I feel the need to defend myself on the matter. The next issue is her waiting around for me forever, Hence the name of Deanna being used in vain. Let me point out that I have known Jodi four months. I went from intrigued by her to interested in her too caring about her deeply to realizing how lucky I would be to have her as part of my life forever. That has all happened in four months. I would say that is pretty normal. I don't feel that our courtship has been one of her waiting around and wasting her life. Let me reemphasize four months ago we didn't know the other existed. I am scrambling and worrying and receiving extremely intense outside pressure from so many sources to fix myself that I am about to have a nervous breakdown. I realize what I will lose and more accurately have lost a great person in Jodi. I realize how amazing Jodi is. I am aware of my fear of commitment. I think as Jim Rohn would say I have made measurable progress in a reasonable amount of time. At least as far as my relationship with Jodi is concerned. Does that mean I expect Jodi to wait around for four more months or four more years so I can figure it all out? No. My selfish side wants her to wait around but I know it's not fair to her and believe it or not I do care enough to put someone including a girl above my own selfish desires. My point is this I am trying and it hasn't been a very long time and it certainly hasn't been so long that you feel you should be justified to intervene and tell her to never speak to me again. How long did you know each other before you made the big decision. I realize that every situation is different but that is my point. Regardless of the situation four months is not a long time. It makes me wonder who you think I should marry. We have had so many conversations about me needing to get married, but then you tell Jodi that I am mean and abusive and a jerk. I suppose you told her that because you like her and you care for her. So who should I marry then? Someone not as good as her. Someone you don't like or would not have the potential to care about, someone that sucks so bad that she deserves to be abused and wait around indefinitely. If I am as bad as you have depicted me to be then you really believe that I shouldn't be marrying anybody. So my question to you is, am I that bad of a person or just not good enough for the likes of Jodi? What you have accomplished is irreparable damage to mine and Jodi's relationship. She is paranoid that this evil person you have depicted will someday surface. No matter what I say or do she will always have in the back of her mind of this person that lurks in the shadows. She told me "I haven't seen any of what they said about you, but they know you well enough to know that is who you really are. Why would they say that if it wasn't true?" So in other words I am atoning for sins that I have not committed. She respects your opinion so much that you did about as much damage to our relationship with your comments as if I would have backhanded her across the face myself. Three days ago she thought I was a great guy. Tonight she said that I was "someone with major character flaws" she just hasn't experienced the majority of them yet. How do you think that made me feel about my good friends Chris and Sky Hughes. Guys I am sorry but while I am trying desperately to overcome my problems so that I don't lose something great like I have done before. You are kicking me while I am down and ruining any chance that I had. It is one thing if she decides I am not the one based on who I am or what I have done but this is ridiculous. Your remarks have become part of the problem and not the solution. How with such a endorsement am I ever supposed to get married. Before I forget why on earth would you recommend her to date a Non-member who has already asked her to throw the church aside so they could have a relationship. That has got to be the most ridiculous thing of all. Am I so bad that a border line anti-Mormon is better. Against my own desires I have recommended that she go date other good members so that she could at least see a contrast from me but a Non member. I just don't get it.

Guys, I hope I am making an ass of myself and am missing some key factor that makes everything you said appropriate but I am not finding it. What is for certain is you have done your own fair share of hurting Jodi. She loves and respects you so much that she doesn't want to mention anything to you but on the other hand she is not interested in having a Travis Alexander Roast ever again. I would like to think that I have enough redeeming qualities that you wouldn't have to spend three days inflating my imperfections. The only thing I ask of you is that you would both take the time to apologize to Jodi and do what you can to make her feel comfortable that this incident won't cause any weird moments between you guys and her. She is terrified of losing your friendship or even diminishing it in anyway. She loves you as much as you love her and probably even more. As for me you probably don't feel you owe me an apology so I won't ask for one. If you feel inclined to reply back on all of this I would ask that you address every part of this e-mail so that nothing is left unresolved. Your friendship is also very important to me. I love you both so much. Which is probably why your poor opinion of me hurt me. I usually can give a crap. I am fully aware that some people don't like me, but I don't care what most people think. I do however care what the two of you think. I know everything that went on was meant with good intentions, but that is not what occurred. You will have to forgive my sternness. I am just very upset. I don't know who said what and I only know very little of what was said. What I do know is most of it shouldn't have been said. My name apparently is not safe in your home. I know you are aware of my problems but I didn't think they were so big to be violently opposed against me. I realize that how you meant things is way different than how they were perceived. I know you are loving people who want the best for Jodi and I. I think sometimes we just get carried away and desensitized when something is the topic of conversation for a long period of time. I know being chided by someone of the likes of me is probably not easy to take because I am the one usually being chided but I ask you to respect what is written not the writer. Jodi has so much respect and admiration for your entire family. She has told me that she wants to format her family after yours. She thinks that you are going to think she is stupid either vocally or silently and it will never be the same. That can't happen. It would crush her. So please do your best to make her feel comfortable around you is my only request. I don't even ask for an apology just don't send me a rebuttal putting me in my place because I already know my faults clearly and honestly. It would only upset me.

Travis

P.S. After I wrote this I slept on it reread it and edited it and describe how I felt when I wasn't angry. So please take this in the spirit it was sent. I love you both very much.

First of all, this was who Travis really was. So nice, so kind, even when he had every right to fly off the handle and write us off because of what he "thought" had happened. Jodi lied about it being a three-day attack on Travis. Clearly, she lied about that and told him things that never happened and things that were never said. It was one conversation between the three of us: Chris, Jodi and I. Previous to that conversation, Jodi brought up things here and there, and I would tell her how I would respond to Travis. It wasn't us cornering Jodi and turning her against Travis. It was her telling us things about Travis and us giving her our response. Of course, she didn't tell him that we were responding to her complaints. In fact, she told him, "I haven't seen anything of what they said." Jodi brought up everything we talked about, not the other way around. Jodi brought up not being number one on his Myspace account, him not calling her, and his still loving Deanna. Jodi is ever playing the victim. She told us how awful Travis treated her, and then she turned around and told Travis how awful we were to her. She told him that we *threatened* that we would lose respect for her if she continued dating Travis. We never said that. While she was the one who instigated and orchestrated the entire conversation, she told Travis she wanted nothing to do with that sort of thing ever again. She told him it was a bash on Travis session. In reality, she was the one doing the bashing.

Travis was so concerned for her in his email, and he worried about her more than he worried about himself. Like he said, he liked Jodi, he had only known her for four months, and they lived in two different states. It was completely unfair of us to put any pressure on him to commit to her, but as you will see, that was not what this was about. We were watching Jodi's emotions and "heartbreak," as she was ready to marry him, and he just wasn't at that stage in the relationship. At the same time, Travis did things that just weren't cool—not "abusive" in the way the defense and their "experts" would want the world to believe. When the word "abusive," was used in our emails, it was in an

"I wouldn't want my daughter to put up with that" kind of way. He had just gotten out of a relationship with another woman and was still in love with her. He didn't want a bunch of pictures of him and a new girl he was dating posted all over the internet. What he was doing wasn't out of the ordinary in many relationships, but it just wasn't optimal. Once this and other things were brought to his attention, he began to work on them immediately.

To fill in a blank, Travis and Deanna had recently broken up prior to Travis meeting Jodi, but they were still very much in love. They talked all the time and continued to express their love each time they spoke. They were no longer intimate, or at least, trying not to be (they kissed once). They both agreed that the relationship was over and they would be friends. Travis was trying to move on, but his feelings for Deanna made it difficult. Travis really liked Jodi, as you read in his email to us, but because of his feelings for Deanna, he wasn't as available as Jodi wanted him to be.

As a point of interest, before Jodi complained that Travis wasn't ready to commit to her, she was still living in Palm Desert with her "ex-boyfriend" Darryl. It's almost comical. She told us and Travis that she and Darryl broke up and were sleeping in different rooms, but this was a lie. She never broke up with Darryl, and according to Darryl's sworn testimony, he was under the impression that he and Jodi were still together. When he moved out of their house in December 2007, he thought Jodi would be joining him after she sold their house. While on the stand, he was asked by the defense, "How did your relationship ultimately end?"

His response was, "At that point, I found employment in Monterey, and I moved in late December, and we parted at that point. I didn't feel that the relationship had ended, but it definitely had changed." (She never broke up with him! She was cheating on him and lying to them both!)

Then he was asked, "Was there a breakup conversation?"

Had Jodi in fact already broken up with Darryl, this would have been the time for Darryl to talk about that breakup conversation, but that conversation never happened. He thought they were still together the entire time. He said, "There wasn't a formal breakup conversation, as much as we both saw our paths going the other way. I was hoping that Jodi would be back with me after resolving the house issue, but it was an unsure time."

By this time, late December, Jodi had already been baptized. She and Travis exchanged Christmas gifts and had already been physically intimate on several occasions (though not in the ways she indicated in her courtroom testimony).

Now, let's put the string of facts together. Jodi was living with her boyfriend, Darryl, whom she was still formally together with. Darryl said they were not having sex, since she joined the Mormon Church. They were probably still intimate, otherwise Darryl would have said something about that, but he only mentioned the fact they were no longer having sex. (At this same time, Jodi claims she was having sex with Travis and didn't know it was wrong.) She was crying to Travis, Chris, and I because Travis wouldn't commit to her? Incredible. It's sensible to assume that Jodi was living a lie, cheating on Darryl with Travis, and on Travis with Darryl. (While she and Travis were not in a committed relationship, she claimed he was the only guy for her.) She had a life with Darryl, but life with Travis seemed like it was more promising. She was willing to give up everything with Darryl if Travis would commit to her, but if not, she didn't want to lose the life she had with Darryl. I imagine that the pressure of the situation was getting to her, and she was starting to break. Darryl was moving to Monterey in December. She was trying to figure out where she was going to live— Monterey with Darryl, or Mesa with Travis. She was playing them both.

This provides some additional insight as to what may have provoked her rage that ultimately led her to kill Travis. She made a massive gamble on Travis, and it didn't pay off. She lost everything by being rejected by him. She'd already lost Darryl. Now it was totally clear that she'd lost Travis. Was she worried that Travis was going to let the world know about the monster he'd discovered in her, which would close all the doors of possibility she saw in her life? With Travis dead, and the truth with him, maybe she thought the threat of everyone in Pre-Paid Legal learning the true nature of Jodi Arias would be gone with him. She naively assumed she might be able to pursue some of those opportunities she saw for herself. Her premeditated plans to maliciously murder Travis would ruin even those hopes of a bright future.

From Sky to Travis
Monday, January 29, 2007
3:35 PM
Subject: Re: You've crossed the line.

*Travis,*

*I know this is a conversation that needs to happen over the phone, and Chris wants to call you, but will have to later because we have a doctor's appointment and he doesn't want to rush (he may be writing you now). I do much better writing. So I am going to respond via email. I only have 15 minutes, so I won't be able to address everything now, but I wanted to say some things promptly, and if you want me to address the rest, let me know, as I would be more than happy to. First and foremost, you are a wonderful person and we love you (even if it seems that we don't), we are excited for you to get married, and want you to be happy. I knew you would be upset and hurt, and you have every right to be—you should be. I was going to write you an e-mail Saturday night, but it was too late, and then I was going to yesterday, but assumed you would be writing, and wanted you to be able to say everything you wanted to say without any distractions from me. I am so sorry for all of this, I would have rather not been put in this situation, but that's what happens when you care about two people that are involved and I am okay with that. I don't know if this make sense, but with the information she gave me, the advice I gave Jodi, was not the friend thing to do in regards to our friendship (mine and yours), but I felt that it was the right thing to do.*

*I can only imagine all of the pain you are in/have been in over your situation with Deanna, and I know this situation with Jodi doesn't help. Know that I would love to see you marry Jodi, but just because you have never heard her cry, doesn't mean she hasn't been crying. She LOVES you, so much that she is afraid that bringing up anything that is bothering her or letting you know that she doesn't think you are perfect would ruin all chances to be with you. When she explains her CURRENT situation with you to her friends, we are not the only ones that have told her to "move on." Everyone she has explained it to, has given her the same advice. Since it was, it enabled her to tell you how she truly feels with out it coming directly from her, but from people who care about you. Let me sum up the situation:*

*Your sister is in love with a guy that loves someone else. He can't be honest with those he cares most about, about his feelings for her. In fact, he won't even allow her to put pictures up of the two of them in places where "people" may see them. He doesn't call her during the day, he waits until after 1 AM (giving her what is left of him at the end of every day). He jokingly calls her a skank. He tells her to go out with other guys, but makes her feel guilty when she does. Thus keeping control, without having to give any commitment. He kisses her in the dark, when noone is around, and messes around with her, but won't commit to her. People that know both of them, have no idea that they are even an "item." She loves him more than anything, and will do anything for him, and just wants that mirrored, but it is nowhere in sight because he is not available. She feels insecure about where she stands with him most of the time, too afraid to be honest with him because she doesn't want to lose what she does have. She is sad and confused unless she is talking to him. And again, he is not available.*

*WHAT DO YOU TELL YOUR SISTER TO DO? Move on, right?*
*Are we so wrong for advising her to do the same?*

*I have to go, but look forward to talking to you about this later, and*
*Jodi should know I wouldn't "lose" respect for her. I thought I made it*
*clear that even if she changes nothing, we love her just the same.*

*I will send her a copy of this.*

*Love ya! (even though you hate me)*

*Sky*

I don't know where Jodi got all of the stuff she told Travis, nor do I know why she told him we threatened to lose all respect for her. I guess that made her "victim" story, damsel-in-distress so much better, but it just never happened. The whole point in our conversation with Jodi was that Travis was obviously not emotionally available because he was still in love with Deanna. Since Jodi and Travis were not in a committed relationship, we encouraged her to date other people and not wait around. We didn't tell her to banish him from her life, but if she did choose not to date him, that she wouldn't be able to "just be friends" because of how much she liked him. I think Jodi and the defense got their idea for the "secret relationship" story from these emails. After these emails, the things Jodi complained about were addressed by Travis. The relationship was no longer a "secret." Everyone knew they were dating, and that didn't stop when they broke up and continued the physical relationship. People always thought they were dating because they were *always* together.

Travis addressed the "one a.m. calls." He told us he didn't know that it bothered her, but that was the only time they could talk. She was a waitress and mostly worked nights. They talked as soon as she got off work until late, and then she would sleep until late the next morning and go back to work. I brought this up to her, because this was one of the things she was so upset about. She told me that was all true, but she wanted him to call her while she was at work. Confused, I asked her why she wanted Travis to call her while she was working. She explained that she just wanted to know that he was thinking about her. *What? Was she serious?* After talking to Travis, and again to her, there were many things like this where it wasn't Travis being a "jerk," but her being high maintenance and having somewhat ridiculous expectations. For example, she wanted to be his number-one friend on Myspace, but, as in life, Deanna was his number one.

From Sky to Travis
Wednesday, January 31, 2007
3:48 PM
Subject: My Response

*Trav,*

*I will respond in all caps, not cuz I am mad, but cuz it will be easier to differentiate where I responded.*

[Excerpt from Travis's email to us]

Chris and Sky,

I just got off the phone with a very reluctant to talk to me Jodi. In fact, so reluctant that she doesn't want me to write you guys because of her great fear that you will not have any respect for her if you find out. She mentioned that you instructed her to not e-mail or call me, and to erase me from her MySpace and act if I do not exist. She also mentioned that the last three days have been a discourse on how I am a jerk, I am a abusive to women and that she is blind to the type of person I really am. I didn't pry for a lot of details because it was obvious that Jodi wasn't comfortable telling me much, in fear of upsetting the two of you, as she already feels she has. She mentioned that a comment was made that if she continued to associate with me that you both would lose all respect for her.

[Sky's email reply to this excerpt]

*I KNEW JODI WOULD GO TO YOU WITH EVERYTHING I SAID (I DON'T SAY THAT IN A BAD WAY), OR I WOULD NOT HAVE SAID IT. IN FACT, I HAD HOPED SHE WOULD BECAUSE THAT WOULD OPEN THE GATE TO DISCUSS WHY I SAID WHAT I DID, WHICH WOULD ALLOW IT TO COME FROM ME, AND NOT HER, AND SHE COULD TELL YOU HOW SHE FEELS. I'VE BEEN IN THIS SITUATION. IT IS A SELF ESTEEM THING. IT IS EASIER TO SAY THEY SAID THIS, CUZ IT DOESN'T "ROCK THE BOAT" BETWEEN YOU TWO, BUT HER CONCERNS ARE ADDRESSED WIHOUT HER BEING "DEMANDING" OR A "JERK." KNOWING THIS, I HOPE YOU CAN SEE THIS WAS NOT ABOUT RIPPING YOU UP, IT WAS ABOUT HER BEING UPSET WITH WHERE SHE IS IN THIS RELATIONSHIP. IN LOVE WITH YOU, SEEING A FUTURE, BUT BEING A BOOTY CALL (AGAIN, WE WERE LOOKING AT ACTIONS, NOT WORDS). THE CAPITALIZATION REALLY COMES ACROSS AS FIRM/YELLING...MAKE SURE YOU DON'T READ IT THIS WAY.*

[Excerpt from Travis's email to us]

She also mentioned that you were continually calling her Deanna.

[Sky's email reply to this excerpt]
*I will start my responses with these stars.*

[They were asterisks, and we took them out, and used brackets [ ] to make it easier to follow the email back and forth]

*Continually-no. Chris used it as an example that she needs to get change, or she would be in the same boat. I know with the emotions you are feeling, and trying to do what you need to do with Deanna, this was like a slap in the face, but to me it is a way of describing Jodi's undying love for you, in hopes of change, with no change in sight.*

[Excerpt from Travis's email to us]

To some it up, the past three days you were beating in her head that I am a broken person that is F'd up in the head, who needs counciling. That I am extremely abusive to women and that, the fact that she is interested in me proves that she has her own head problems and needs counciling too.

[Sky's email reply to this excerpt]

*I would not have gotten this from it. It was not like that. If it had been where we kept bringing up what a jerk you were and trying to force her to feeling this, I would recommend NEVER speaking to us again. The reality is, she would saddly and torn up, tell us things and I would tell her what I wished I had done in the same situation. It wasn't about you. It was that she should not allow you to hurt her anymore. It was advice from one girl to another about thing you were doing. When she told me what you were saying, I did say, "That isn't right. It's abusive. He is not nice to girls. He is mean, and if he is talking to you like this now, it would be worse when you get married, and you have kids to think about. You wouldn't want your daughter to be with someone that talks to her like this, nor makes her feel like this." And I still think this is true. Had you joked about Josh calling me a skank, fine. Probably not right, but I would laugh. BUT, I am not in love with you. That would hurt her a lot more than me. You said you wanted to be refined. This is how that works. It means giving up parts of you, that are ok to give up. You may feel, "That's me, if she doesn't like me- I'm not gonna be someone else." That's not you, that's the T-DOGG. Travis said he wants to get married and be refined. So I hope this doesn't offend you. When I write this out, it sounds worse than when it came out of my mouth. When spoken, it was spoken with concern, not anger (I did get upset towards the end [not with Jodi], but I will explain that at the end of this letter).*

[Excerpt from Travis's email to us]

What I find ironic is that your whole basis for all this I am assuming is so that I don't hurt her. What is also ironic, is that Jodi and I have never had an argument, not one. We have always got along and enjoy each others company. Have I ever been rude to her. Well I am sure I have simply because I am rough around the edges and make a joke that isn't funny but sounded funny at the time. Never have I said anything in anger and if you ask Jodi, I would bet that she could easily count on one hand with fingers to spare, how many times I have offended her. Now if that makes me the devil I would ask you the same question that Sky asked Jodi. Has he ever once been a jerk to you? Jodi's answer was yes. Now if you don't have the same answer to the question, then congrats you are better than me and everyone else for that matter. I think that it is a very manipulative question to ask and to try to base a point on a positive answer to the question has Travis ever in his life acted like a jerk. In fact the whole three day experience sounds like a grand brainwashing.

[Sky's email reply to this excerpt]

*I am really sorry this happened the way it did, but if you want me to respond to this point by point, I have to take you to that night, so my responses are not going to sound apologetic. I will respond with the logic in my head that night. I've been trying to be nice because I feel bad, but it doesn't give you an explanation to what happened. The whole "basis" was so you didn't KEEP hurting her, so she wouldn't let you keep hurting her and be ok with it. Trav, she was in pain. I think the pain with Jodi you experienced wasn't what we caused, but it was the same pain we saw that night. We caused her to go to you with the pain, but we didn't cause the pain. I simply validated her pain. She was being treated horribly, you weren't beating her physically, but you were emotionally. Granted you may not have recognized it, but it is about time you do. When you are in love with someone, and they supposedly care about you, but you aren't acknowledged as an important part of their life unless the door is closed and you are making out...Or on the phone when no one else can hear...That does something to your self-worth. She has been making excuses for you "we aren't officially together" etc., "so I can't expect certain things." She was very hurt. Especially when people you both know, when trying to figure out if there were anything between you, after watching you, told her, "After watching the two of you, we have decided by the body language nothing was going on." She mentioned this SEVERAL times, so it was obviously upsetting her. The days of of making out with girls, having little meaning ended when you hit about 25, Travis. Especially when coupled with talk of wanting to get married. Jodi is not in love with me, therefore, I do not have the ability to cause the pain you saw. I saw the same pain, and knew, just as you did, this is screwed up! (There is a lot I am leaving out, but it would take days.)*

There are so many things that stand out to me now that I was completely oblivious to when we wrote these emails. Jodi had told us that people said, "After watching the two of you, it looks like nothing was going on by the body language." I'm pretty sure, in addition to so many other things, she made this up.

[Excerpt from Travis's email to us]

What I seriously don't get is if you are so concerned about Jodi's feelings, did you ever consider what it might do to her feelings when she was a number of times referred to as Deanna, told that your respect for her is contingent on her disowning one of her best friends and the person that introduced her to the church, calling her blind and that she needs counciling. How do you think that affects her feelings. I have never ever heard Jodi cry, not once until I talked to her a few moments ago and all I heard was tears and fear. Next time you want to throw me under the bus and there is no denying that that happened quite a bit remember the advice of the secret to not focus on a anti-Travis campaign but more of pro someone else campaign. It would save Jodi and my own feelings a great deal of hurt. That may have been the Doctor Laura approach but it is not the Jesus Christ approach.

[Sky's email reply to this excerpt]

*Again Travis, WE didn't cause the pain you saw. She felt like an idiot. She said, "You guys aren't going to respect me." That was her own fear. I reassured her throughout the conversation that I loved her, and that wouldn't change. But it wasn't right for you to do what you were doing—making out with her, but not giving her the commitment that she deserved.* [Side note: That last sentence sums up the whole point of the emails. He was in love with Deanna and unable to give Jodi what she wanted. He was making out with her, and she wanted a commitment . . . now.] *You have her total commitment, and that is why you are ok with the situation. Or, were ok with it. I never said she should disown you. My whole thing that I kept reiterating, was, "We love Travis, and we love you. But, he is not available, and who knows how long it is going to take for him to get over Deanna. He is not giving you what you deserve, but he is taking a lot. Move on, and he will either realize what he has, fix himself, and come for you when he is ready, or he won't. But either way you will be better off. He will either be there, and available* [I think that's what it says—our copy is blurry], *for you down the road, or he won't. But don't destroy your self-worth in the process." She didn't feel like she could make demands on you, so instead of staying in the relationship the way it was and getting hurt, building up animosity, and causing permanent long term damage, I advised her to move on. Not necessarily with her feelings for you, those aren't going to disappear, but physically go out and have fun- without the guilt.*

[Excerpt from Travis's email to us]

Which brings me to my next thought, my feelings. The very little that Jodi would tell me was plenty for me to be reminded of it insight you had about Jason [last name removed]. I will paraphrase the best I can. "If you are so against the type of people we are, don't act like we are friends." If you really think that I am such a horrible person to women why would you want to associate with me and consider me a friend. If I am a bad person to women, then I am simply a bad person. Feeling like you can be my friend and tell Jodi to drop me like a dirty diaper, is not consistent. If I am not good enough to be her friend why am I good enough to be yours. You have always been the epitome to kind to me and excellent friends, in fact, unconditional friends, thats why this approach is so confusing to me. I guess what I am getting at is that I am very hurt by the comments made about me. I think they were unfair, dramatically exaggerated and most importantly, not your place to say. I realize everything was said with a righteous motive. However it was over zealous and inappropriate. I feel you shot beyond the mark. Now in most cases I would first ask from some clarity, but I think we can all agree that they don't get more honest than Jodi. Now if you meant things to come off that way or not it doesn't matter, what I have written is a very mild version of how it did come off. In my opinion you overstepped your bounds and caused more problems than you solved. I know you were trying to help but you went over board.

[Sky's email reply to this excerpt]

*I know Jodi told you more than a little, and I'm glad she did. Travis, with love, you are a heart predator. You take great joy in making women fall for the T-Dogg. You laugh about what you can get away with. It would scare me to death if my little sister liked you, in fact, I wouldn't allow it. I am a bad person in a lot of ways, doesn't mean you aren't gonna be my friend (well maybe not, after this incident). Women are fragile, and you have shattered a lot of them. Is it possible that the reason it came off so badly is because it was charged with so much pain that Jodi has been going through? Let me try to clarify. What was going on in her head, and what was going on in our house were totally different. For example, she tells us that you call after one, and she thinks to call you all the time. You are often so tired and seem like you are forcing yourself to stay awake. She wished you would just call her to say hi, or because you were thinking about her. Her excitement about you is not mirrored. I tell her she deserves more than that. In a new relationship one is excited, you MAKE time to call that person just to say hi. You*

*make out with her everytime you see her. You keep her up late at night.*
*You owe her more than what you are giving her. She has given you*
*everything, all control, and you give her 1 am calls and make-out-fests.*
*I told her this, and it is what she has been feeling. She asked why? I*
*told her that she is filling the physical spot that Deanna doesn't. But*
*Deanna fulfills everything else for you. That is not to say you don't*
*enjoy talking to Jodi. But with Deanna fulfilling all but physical needs,*
*and with Jodi fulfilling the physical, you feel fulfilled. This is not ter-*
*rible to say, it is true. I told her if she wanted more from you, she needed*
*to make you earn what she is offering so freely, otherwise she is going to*
*stay very confused and hurt. When he is willing to love you the way you*
*need and deserve to be loved, than you won't feel the pain and confu-*
*sion you do now. He has no right to make out with you, make you feel*
*guilty about hanging out with guys (by teasing her you do this), call*
*you so you can check it off his list (that's how she feels), and not commit*
*to you (Not at 29, and always talking about being ready to get married.*
*Making out with someone now means different things than it used to,*
*or at least it should). Now, to me that is not horrible to say, it's simply*
*true, I would think you would give someone the same advice. And you*
*may feel like you give her a lot more than that, BUT SHE DOESN'T,*
*and SHE needs to. It's not to say you are a horrible person, just taking*
*a lot from her without giving much (I am not saying you FORCE her*
*to love you, but she does.) And I told her you aren't available to give*
*her what she wants right now. In her head, her whole reality has just*
*changed and not because I put it there. She had been feeling a lot of*
*what we said and expressed that to us, but didn't want it to be true.*
*We didn't create anything/" brainwash her" we just let her know she is*
*feeling exactly how she should be. She had been making excuses for why*
*it was ok that you were doing the things you were, and making her so*
*sad. I didn't filet you, but what she had hoped "was" with you, wasn't*
*and her excuses were filleted. I wish you could have been a fly on the*
*wall, you still would have been upset, but probably more- so because you*
*would have agreed with us.*

[Excerpt from Travis's email to us]

Which brings me to my next thought. Regardless of what you may think, I am not mean to Jodi. I adore Jodi. In fact I don't know if it has ever been easier to be nice to someone as it is with Jodi. Has a little of the imperfect Travis come out around Jodi? The answer is you better believe it, but the keyword is a little and I don't think that by any realistic standard can you deem my behavior with Jodi anywhere in the neighborhood of mean. So much so that I can't believe I feel the need to defend myself on the matter.

[Sky's email reply to this excerpt]

*Have you treated her better than girls in the past? Yes. And I said that. But that doesn't mean you haven't been mean. She has been hurt...A lot. And you have made her cry, and I really feel it was not what we did that upset her so much. It was the reality that she loved a person whose actions were not in accordance with how she had hoped he felt. I do feel it is mean to talk about wanting to get married, making out with a person every time you see her, but when she walks into a room full of people, you don't stop everything to run give her a hug and a warm hello. I saw this at my house. It took too much time for you to even acknowledge her arrival... It was mean, but I don't think you were try-ing to be mean. NO ONE even knows there is anything going on with you guys! Unless they have stayed at our house and seen you go in the same room. This is sad for her. She can't even say to guys that ask her out, or in conversation that she is seeing Travis Alexander (unless it is John [last name removed]). Call it what you want, but this secrecy says more to her in the way it makes her feel than anything. You don't want people to know, and whatever your reasons for that are, it is what it is, and that is mean. I know who Sean [last name removed] is making out with at night because I see him and how he acts with her during the day, same with Jesse [last name removed], and I don't even know these guys that well I know who you are making out with at night, but I have no idea what is going on with you during the day. Jodi is an awesome girl, and whoever she ids making out with should be proud to let EVERYONE know. It should show in his relationship with her in public. If you care about her, don't keep it a secret- for her sake. This causes her a lot of pain, and I told her she doesn't deserve it. You are being a jerk. This is what I said, and this is how I feel. I know you have crap you are dealing with, and I feel for you Trav, I really do, But don't put Jodi through emotional turmoil so she can relate better to you. It is unnecessary damage that can be prevented.*

This is all we have of the emails. I would guess that the rest will be made available at the conclusion of the sentencing phase, and, hopefully, with the information above (and without it) you will be able to see that they were not at all what the defense and their experts would like everyone to believe. It's evident that what we were talking about in the emails was in no way related to what LaViolette and others indicated. We weren't talking about Travis beating Jodi up and being verbally abusive. We were talking about Travis not being a perfect gentleman in every way, shape, and form, but he was still better than many people. These two concepts are on opposite sides of the spectrum, and the way *they* represented it was not even in the same galaxy! These emails had nothing whatsoever to do with what the defense said we were talking about. They wanted people to believe Travis was abusive and mean. Speak to any of Travis's ex-girlfriends, and you will get a completely different picture. These emails were about Travis being in love with another girl. He wasn't emotionally available to be in another relationship. Travis was easy to fall for, but he had a difficult time committing. That is not abusive, nor was he *intentionally* being a jerk.

In these very same emails, Chris said Travis was "abusive," then said that wasn't the right word. Chris told Travis to stop "gutting" women and that he himself had done his share of "gutting" women. The defense used our words against Travis, and that was brutal! During Nurmi's closing statement during the retrial of the penalty phase, he was reading directly from my email on the screen. It was talking about Travis's rough upbringing. Nurmi stopped reading about three lines from the end of the paragraph, as I sat there thinking, *Please jury, keep reading! Read the entire email exchange!* The last three lines were something like: It's amazing that with all you have been through, you turned out the way you did. You are a miracle. You are a wonderful person.

Jodi continued to confide in me after the emails and never once said Travis was abusing or mistreating her. She wanted him to ask her to move to Arizona, commit to her, and marry her, but those complaints were not complaints of abuse. The way she kept bringing up Deanna, and then told Travis that we kept bringing up Deanna, makes me wonder if she wasn't setting a foundation for driving a wedge between he and Deanna, and eventually all of his friends. So many things became clear to us as time went on. Eventually, we saw Jodi for who she was.

CHAPTER 8

# Evil at the Door

*We mentioned that Travis loved Christmas because he loved*
*to give, but he also loved it for other reasons. Since Travis*
*was young, he loved Christmas because it meant he got to*
*see two of his favorite people in the world: his uncle, Mike*
*Alexander, and his cousin, Mike Alexander. He loved them*
*so much and always looked forward to their visits.*

NOTE TO READERS: OVER THE years, we have told the following story several times. We realize some minor and inconsequential details may differ from one telling to the other. Chris or I may have chosen to add more or less details in some of the many retellings of this story. We have done our best to recount these incidents in the way we remember them. Regardless, the major details of the story have never changed and remain intact in this telling.

It was early 2007, and I could not shake the feeling I had about Jodi. I felt bad because she had just been baptized and was now a member of the Church of Jesus Christ of Latter-day Saints. I felt that it was my duty to befriend and support her. According to her, she had no family and wasn't close to anyone. I felt like I needed to be there for her. I finally said something to Chris. "I know this may sound weird . . ." and I went on to tell him how I had an uneasy feeling about her. Chris encouraged me not to ignore my feelings, but to pay attention to them. He suggested that I watch her more closely to see if I noticed anything. So I did.

The feelings I was having about Jodi persisted. I even asked myself if I was acting out of jealousy or being territorial. But it wasn't like that at all. This feeling would not go away and, in fact, it intensified. It wasn't a "I don't like having her around" feeling; it was a "something is not right, protect your family" feeling—loud and clear! I was confused. What I had observed in her before I really started watching her was not congruent with this warning I was getting. We had observed some "issues" with her, but I chalked it up to her immaturity. She was extremely immature and emotionally underdeveloped. Looking back, it's odd to consider that a woman could still be so immature while being in a four-year relationship with a man twenty years older and essentially being the stepmother to his child.

The confusion didn't stay with me long. The more I watched her, the more disturbed I became. Jodi was conniving, manipulative, and calculated all rolled up into a dangerous, little ball. It's difficult to put a proper description to what I observed in her, but I can share what I saw.

One night, at a training meeting at the San Bernardino Hilton, my friend Hollie and I were sitting at the registration table positioned at the very end of a long hallway. There was another event being held in the banquet room at the opposite end of the hall. We would later learn that the event was hosted by a research company that paid random people $20 to rate commercials for a few hours. The majority of this group was male, most of whom were unkempt and shabbily dressed. The banquet rooms were on the right side of the hallway. The double doors into their banquet room were propped open. Just beyond the open doors was a wall of mirrors. Jodi would start at our end of the hall and walk to the very end of the hallway, look into the banquet room, flip her hair around, glance into the mirror, look into the room again, flip her hair again, and walk back, only to turn around and do it again! She made this walk several times, as if she was on a catwalk! Hollie and I couldn't figure out what she was doing. It was so bizarre! Finally, we figured it out. As she walked back the final time, she walked a little faster. We then saw a guy come out of the room and follow her. When she reached our table, she said, "I think this guy is gonna try to talk to me. Tell him I'm Travis Alexander's girlfriend."

The man stood next to her and started talking. She immediately began to flirt with him, so I said, "She has a boyfriend." He quickly apologized and walked away.

Jodi turned to me and asked, "Why didn't you say I was *Travis Alexander's girlfriend*?"

Why did that matter? He didn't know Travis! It was just Hollie, her, and me. Who cares? She did! She was obsessed with Travis! Perhaps she was trying to impress Hollie and I? Who knows? She and Travis weren't even "together." I felt like I was in sixth grade all over again. Finally, she went into our training. Hollie looked at me and said, "There is something very wrong with her."

But this was just the beginning. Jodi would talk to, flirt with, and text married men at all hours of the night, but it wasn't to make people laugh or make them feel good, like when Travis would flirt. It was her attempt to make Travis jealous. She tried to show him she was wanted by other men. One night, around two or three a.m., Jodi, Travis, Chris, and I were hanging out in our living room. Jodi had been texting with a married guy we worked with in Pre-Paid Legal. He was one of the top-earning associates in the company, and one of the many men Jodi had her picture taken with. I asked her to hand me her phone, and I typed out and sent a text that read something like, *Stop texting Jodi, and go get in bed with your wife. Sky.*

Jodi freaked out. "What if he tries to ruin my business?" she asked.

She didn't have a business, but I asked her, "How would he do that?" For which she had no intelligent reply.

This wasn't the only married guy she pursued a relationship with. She flirted with one of our colleagues—we'll call him "Jack"—all the time. Jack was married with a great wife and kids. In December, there was a big Pre-Paid Legal training in Mesa, Arizona. A large group of Pre-Paid Legal associates were driving in from Southern California and Utah and were going to stay at Travis's house in Mesa. Chris had a car full of eight guys, including himself. Jodi called Travis and said that she wanted to come to the event as well. Travis told her that his house was packed and there wasn't any room for anyone else. (Travis's house was indeed packed, but it also had to do with the fact that Deanna Reid would be there. Travis still cared about Deanna. He was having a hard time letting her go, and he wanted to spend time with her). Jodi called Travis back a little later and told him that one of her friends, who happened to live in Mesa, called to see if she wanted to come spend the weekend with her. What a coincidence! Jodi was like Lady Luck. She experienced inexplicable coincidences and chance, never-in-a-million-years occurrences, on a regular basis. She told Travis she would be staying at her friend's house, and began making plans to get to Mesa. She called Chris to see if she could ride with him, but his car was full, so she asked if she could follow him. They agreed to meet up near Palm Desert, where Jodi was still living, which was also along the route from Southern California to Mesa.

Jodi pulled up in her Infiniti G35, an expensive car for a waitress who rarely worked. She rolled down her window and asked if anyone would like to ride with her because she didn't want to ride alone. Jamie, the only single guy in Chris's car, volunteered. But, Jack immediately jumped out of Chris's car and into Jodi's.

Jack and Jodi drove to Mesa together. Needless to say, Travis wasn't pleased to see Jodi, but everyone played nice. Later that night, Jack took Chris aside and told him that Jodi was his soul mate, and that upon his arrival home on Sunday, he would announce to his wife that he was leaving her. Chris did everything he could to talk sense into him. Eventually, thank goodness, he did.

Jodi never went to her "friend's house," the one who invited her to Mesa in the first place. Travis asked her about it, but she said she would just stay at his house, as if she was doing *him* a favor. He informed her that there was no room, and there really wasn't. There were people everywhere. In true Jodi fashion, she ended up staying the night at Travis's house with everyone else. The house was packed, so Jodi ended up sleeping on the floor.

When Chris returned home, he told me what happened with Jack. I was not surprised. Jodi had been working on him for weeks. I'd previously noticed Jodi frequently and inappropriately flirting with and hanging on Jack. I decided to talk to her about it. I explained to her that he had a family, and she didn't want to be "that girl." She said she felt terrible and acted like she had no idea what I was talking about. But, she swore she would stay away from him.

Upon returning to California, Jack was making every effort to avoid Jodi, but she did not make it easy! At the next several Pre-Paid Legal meetings, she was all over him. We went to Mimi's Cafe after a meeting one night, and Jack sat at the end of the table near Chris and me. Several people pulled chairs over, and our end of the table was packed, but there were several available seats in the middle of the table and at the opposite end. Rather than sit in a chair that was available, Jodi had the nerve to ask the man next to Jack to move over. It wasn't that simple. The man had to move his chair back, because there was no room to slide over, then Jodi plopped down next to Jack. I whispered to Chris, "She has no shame!"

Jack was trying to talk to Chris, and Jodi kept trying to talk to Jack. When he made it clear that he wasn't going to give her any attention, she did something unbelievable. She stared down at the table as if thinking. Then she wrapped her arms around Jack's arm, pulled it into her, and laid her head on his shoulder! Who does that? Especially after her show about how "sorry" she was, and how she was going to steer clear of him. She had told me she was going to be on her "best behavior."

Going back to the event at Travis's house in December, it was there that Jodi and Deanna met for the first time. In court, Jodi testified that when Deanna saw her, Deanna became upset and ran upstairs. That was a lie. Jodi and Deanna shook hands, and Deanna stayed downstairs and hung out with everyone. All of Travis's friends were Deanna's friends, so everyone was excited to see her . . . everyone except Jodi. Jodi also testified that she and Travis slept on side-by-side couches, and she kept trying to hold his hand, but anytime someone came around he would drop her hand, not wanting anyone to know about them, or something like that. Another lie. Travis gave his bed to two of our friends. Travis slept on the floor of his office, and Jodi found a spot on the floor in the living room.

There were three guys Jodi used to make Travis jealous: Abe, Jon, and Mark (not Marc McGee, the individual who inserted himself into this case with false claims about us, Deanna, and Travis). Jodi used these three men in hopes of encouraging Travis to commit. She also used them in hopes of convincing Travis what a "prize" she was to be fought for. On more than one occasion, Jodi told me how Abe called her frequently. She asked me if she should tell Travis or keep it from him. More than once, I reminded her that they were not in a committed relationship, and that it was fine for her to talk to and date other people, so I didn't see the point of telling Travis. If I didn't give her the answer she wanted, she would escalate it to, "Well, he keeps asking me out," or, "He tried to kiss me" (and, of course, she always expressed her devotion to Travis). All of this was manipulation on her part. She wanted me to tell Travis that she had all these guys pursuing her, and he'd better commit to her before he lost her! I never told him anything about it until later when we talked about their relationship and our concerns in April 2007.

We later found out from Abe that he did not "try" to kiss her. He *did* kiss her! In fact, they had a pretty heated make-out session in a parking garage. He even put his hand down her pants. In reference to the undergarments that some Mormons wear, Abe said, while tugging on her thong, "Those aren't magic underwear!" to which she responded, "But there is magic in them!" Classic. This is the girl who tried to make Travis look bad for talking to other women while he was getting to know her, and who continued to talk to and date women after he and Jodi "broke up." The defense team didn't want Abe to testify about this experience in court during the penalty-phase retrial for fear it would "prejudice the jury," but they were allowed to trash Travis all trial long with conjured stories of abuse, pedophilia, and philandering.

Jodi claimed under oath that she and Travis were in a committed relationship beginning February 2, 2007. It's unclear if there was ever an official "commitment" between Jodi and Travis. I can say there was a change in the relationship around February 2007, because of our January emails, Travis was made aware of certain things that were bothering Jodi and fixed them. But, as far as a "committed relationship," Jodi said that she and Travis were not girlfriend/boyfriend in an email she'd sent to Travis in mid-February. The email she sent to Travis was one that she had claimed she sent to Abe. Abe never received the email. This is just one more piece of evidence that shows how Jodi would manipulate Travis.

I want to take a step back and look at Travis's intimate life. Travis would certainly not be proud of his not adhering to all of his values all of the time. Travis made mistakes. But, let's cut him some slack. His "sex life" that was put on display for the world—dissected, and blown out of proportion—paled in comparison to many high school boys, and certainly paled in comparison to Jodi's. The guy was thirty! While the defense team argued that it was deviant behavior for Travis to talk to other women while being a single guy, testimony about Jodi and another guy sexting was not permitted. This is the same girl who was flirting with a guy on the way home from a memorial for the man she "loved" and slaughtered. The same girl who, within hours of nearly decapitating Travis Alexander, was rolling around with another love interest. But back to the disturbing things I noticed.

Jodi would "accidentally" send Travis emails that were "meant" for other guys. She would bring stuff up to Travis under the guise of "being completely honest," or because his name "came up" in a conversation so he had a right to know what was being said about him. She would do this to try to get a rise out of him. She told Travis things Abe said about him and vice versa in an effort to create a rivalry over her. Travis and Abe knew *of* each other, but didn't know one another. All they knew about each other was what Jodi told them. I have been able to get to know Abe through this trial, and he and Travis really would have liked one another had they not met in Jodi's web.

Similar to the negative dynamics she concocted between Travis and Abe, Jodi turned Travis against her own family by the things she told him about them. Travis had never met them, but he would later compare Jodi to her mother in a negative way. Everything Travis knew about her family was from what Jodi told him, and what we all believed about Jodi's family was a far cry from reality. It was all so juvenile and annoying. It was almost as if Jodi lived in her own world with its own set of ethics and rules. She worked hard to orchestrate the outcomes that she wanted, like a puppet master. It was all so disturbing, especially as we look back on those days. Jodi was the master manipulator. Sometimes, her maneuvers were shrewd, cunning, and undetectable, but at other times, she was like a child with her hand inside a cookie jar, trying desperately to convince an adult that she had never even seen a cookie jar. Sadly, Travis couldn't see it until the end.

After that terrible weekend when Jodi lied to us about how Travis was treating her, and then lied to Travis about what we said about him, we came to the conclusion that she liked Travis way more than he liked her. We simply saw this as her amateur effort to get Travis to commit. In a maneuver of self-interest, Jodi apologized to us profusely, admitting that she exaggerated, and that she should have let me talk to him first, as she agreed. Armed with all the facts and the perspective of time, there is no question that she choreographed the entire blowup, grotesquely manipulating all of us in an effort to get Travis to commit to her and drive a wedge between us and Travis. Unbelievably, it worked. According to mental health experts, this is classic sociopathic and psychopathic behavior. She had already begun her effort to isolate Travis in an attempt to have more power over him.

She had successfully driven a wedge between us and Travis, bringing herself and Travis closer together. Our friendship recovered quickly, but all three of us had been completely duped by her. While most girls would become more comfortable and secure with this situation, it seemed to have the opposite effect on Jodi. She became more clingy and more possessive. She bemoaned nonstop about the fact that Travis would not ask her to move to Arizona. I did not think it was possible for her to complain any more about this than she already had. I was wrong. She did. It became incessant. She was desperate to know if she was totally "in" with Travis, and if she should make her new home in Arizona, or if she should call the whole thing off and go north to reconnect with Darryl. She was in too deep. She couldn't call it off. She had to figure out how to get to Arizona. During this time, she was at our house more and more. We didn't understand how she was making money. Servers make most of their money on the weekends, and it seemed like she was at our house almost every weekend.

It became a rare thing that we ever had time alone with Travis. It was almost as if anyone who spent time with Travis without her posed a threat to the fantasy life she'd created in her mind.

One weekend, in February (I think it was February) 2007, Travis came to stay with us, and for some odd reason, Jodi wasn't able to join him at our home for a couple of days. We had a great time reconnecting with Travis. Not long after he arrived, I was washing dishes when Travis said he wanted to read something to me. He held a piece of paper in his hand. Pensively, he expressed concern about the email; he explained that it was an email Jodi had received from an "anonymous" stalker. He read it to me.

The anonymous man began by showering his precious with praise. Paraphrasing from memory, it included the following: *Jodi, you are so amazing, you are so incredible and beautiful.* Then he said, *You are such an amazing artist,* and something about her hand being an asset, and complimented her photography skills. Praises galore! Then the man started in on Travis. *He doesn't deserve you, he's not good enough for you, he doesn't appreciate you!* Then, the man got ultra creepy when he said something like *I know where you live. I've been watching you. I will have you.* Finally, the climax came—the whole point of the email was revealed in Jodiesque splendor. It was something like, *You're in California. Travis is in Arizona. Travis can't protect you because he lives too far away! I will have you.*

It was all I could do to hold back the belly-shaking laughter this ridiculousness deserved! She might as well have signed her own name at the bottom of the email. As elementary and moronic as this terribly embarrassing attempt to manipulate Travis was, he couldn't see it! He continued reading, but I couldn't hold it in anymore! I erupted! Travis looked so confused. This was a life-threatening email, and he was baffled by the fact that I was laughing hysterically.

"Sky! How can you possibly laugh about this email? This is scary stuff!"

I turned off the water, dried my hands, grasped the counter with both of my hands, and leaned closer to him. I stared into his eyes and said, "Travis, Jodi wrote that email! She wants nothing more in the world than for you to ask her to move to Arizona. This is her attempt to get you to do that. I promise you—she wrote it." He looked both bothered and shocked that I would think something so terrible about the "nicest girl" he had ever met. He tried to convince me that she was frightened by this email and didn't feel safe. I told him again that she'd written it and nothing he could say would convince me otherwise.

On another occasion when Travis and Jodi were at our house, Jodi said she needed to talk to me alone, so we took a walk. She told me that she was concerned about her and Travis's relationship. Of course, she complained about not being invited to move to Arizona, as usual. She told me that Travis left his email open and she happened to see it. She noticed some emails from others and read them. She said Travis was being very flirtatious, so she forwarded every email to or from a female to herself. I remember thinking, *This is scary!* I don't recall what I said to her, other than she needed to tell Travis about what she had done. We continued walking and talking for a while before going back to the house.

We are uncertain if it was this visit with Travis and Jodi, or the one following, where we saw something in Jodi that we would not wish upon our worst enemy. I do, however, remember telling Chris around this time, "You gotta tell Travis he can't marry her. Something is not right." Chris completely agreed.

I believe it was April 2007. Jodi and Travis were staying with us again. In the months leading up to this day, Chris and I had observed Jodi being even more clingy, manipulative, and obsessive. We had more than one discussion where we had determined it was time to talk to Travis about our concerns and the red flags we'd observed. We were really hoping that the relationship would deteriorate and be short-lived, but we also knew Travis was happy. All signs pointed toward a more serious relationship. We'd more than lost that loving feeling for Jodi and definitely wanted to talk to Travis. Her behavior was disturbing, but we weren't afraid of her at this point. That was about to change.

From the moment they got to our house, it was crazy—crazy uncomfortable, crazy disturbing, crazy bizarre, and soon, crazy terrifying! They were there for several days. Jodi wouldn't leave Travis's side. It was like she was tethered to him! If he got up from the couch to get a drink, she would follow him and stay right next to him. She didn't just sit next to him; she was halfway on top of him. It was obvious that it was bothering Travis, too. She was literally smothering him! He had to keep asking her to get off him.

Somehow, Travis succeeded in escaping to the bathroom without her noticing. In a panic, Jodi came in the kitchen asking if I had seen Travis. I told her he was in the restroom and motioned to the back bathroom, which was in the laundry room. She headed back there, but didn't come back, so I just thought she went outside. Nope! I went to the laundry room to throw a dish towel in the laundry and there she was, standing with her back to me, leaning against the bathroom door. Not wanting her to know I had seen her and to avoid an awkward moment, I went back into the kitchen with the dirty rag still in hand. I heard the toilet flush, as she rushed back into the kitchen. Travis had no idea she was out there.

Later, the four of us got in the Jacuzzi. It was so awkward! She was all over him! If they were just kissing and being cute that would be one thing, but it was far beyond that. She was straddling him, crawling on him, sucking and kissing his neck, while giggling in a forced, high-pitched baby voice. Without changing a thing, it could have been a *Saturday Night Live* skit. I turned to Chris and asked, "Does she not know we are right here?" Travis was noticeably embarrassed. He was pushing her off and asking her to stop, but she was relentless! She would stop for a moment, and then go back at it.

In a firm voice, Travis finally said, "Jodi! Stop! Please!" I wish it ended there, but it didn't.

We went back into our home after getting out of the Jacuzzi. Our kids were in bed, Chris and I were downstairs, and Jodi was in her room . . . or so we thought. We heard a loud thud upstairs and thought one of our kids had fallen out of bed. We bolted up the stairs, only to startle Jodi, who was standing outside Travis's bedroom. She threw her hand up making a fist and said, "Oh! I was just about to knock!" Travis had been on the phone with Deanna for quite a while. No one knows how long Jodi was standing there listening to his conversation.

The next day, we took a drive around our neighborhood in Murrieta, California, to look at some houses that were being built. I was driving, Chris was in the passenger seat, our two boys and Jodi were in the middle seats, and Travis was in the backseat. When I looked in the rearview mirror, I saw Jodi had turned around to face Travis in the back of our SUV. He looked out the left window and then the right, but he wouldn't make eye contact with her. He had a silly smile on his face and was clearly just playing around, but Jodi didn't think it was funny. She was noticeably bothered. I nudged Chris and told him to look. He took his visor down and watched in the mirror, as Travis was being Travis. She got mad and turned around, folded her arms, and pouted for the rest of the drive. We would later discover why she was so upset; Travis would not "stare into her eyes!"

At some point during this weekend, I said to Chris that he needed to tell Travis that she was obsessed with him and it seemed to be getting worse . . . quickly! Chris assured me that he was thinking the same thing. Chris and Travis went into Chris's office to talk shop, and I went into the kitchen to do some computer work. Jodi joined me and immediately started complaining and whining about Travis not asking her to move to Arizona. She felt he should be asking her to move and that they needed to take the next step in their relationship. While Travis was enjoying getting to know Jodi, she had one thing on her mind, and that was marrying Travis Alexander! She was hyper-focused on it now. She was obsessed, and it was starting to show in everything she did. She wouldn't let up. I had hit my limit. I got my phone and sent Chris a text. I didn't know that his phone was face up on the desk, within reading distance from Travis. The alert caused both Travis and Chris to look down at the phone. Chris saw the text was from me and read it. He immediately grabbed the phone so Travis didn't see it, but it was too late. It said something like, *she is driving me CRAZY! Get her away from me!*

Looking confused, Travis asked, "What was that?"

Chris was so uncomfortable and just started laughing. "Nothin', bro. It's all good."

"Chris, I read the text," Travis said sternly. "What's going on?"

"We need to talk," Chris said.

"Start talkin' then!" Travis barked.

Chris suggested that the three of us—Travis, Chris, and I—chat later in private. Jodi was still upset about Travis not staring into her eyes, so she went to bed in her room downstairs, and the three of us went upstairs to talk in our bedroom.

With the bedroom doors closed, we told Travis that we were concerned about him, and shared with him all that we had observed in Jodi that caused us to worry.

"She is absolutely obsessed with you, Travis," I said. "I'm afraid we're gonna find you chopped up in her freezer!"

Travis was shocked. This came out of left field and knocked his feet out from under him. He was disoriented and in disbelief. Then he became very sad, realizing all the effects this conversation was going to have on his life. We were Travis's good friends, and Chris was also a mentor to him. He didn't want to disappoint us, but he liked Jodi a lot and realized that we didn't. It hurt. He began a sales pitch about her, highlighting her positive qualities, how nice and kind she was, and that she would never hurt a soul. We countered. We told him about the emails she'd forwarded to herself from his account, about the married men, and about the guys she was using to make Travis jealous. We pointed out all the bizarre things we'd witnessed that weekend and previously, the crazy clinginess, following him around the house, eavesdropping on him while he was in the bathroom and on his private phone call with Deanna.

He refused to see it! He kept making excuses for her. He said he had noticed that she had been really clingy, but he intended to talk to her about it. He was trying to put out a forest fire with a squirt gun. Our minds were made up. She was bad news! There were so many signs yelling, "Danger! Not safe!" But he didn't want to see any of them.

Suddenly, a terrible cold chill ran through my body. I have never experienced that feeling before, or since, and I hope I never have it again. It was awful! I didn't feel safe, and to make matters worse, I somehow knew that Jodi was standing outside our bedroom door. Pointing to the door, I quietly mouthed the words, "She is out there." Just in case she *was* "out there," Chris and Travis successfully changed the topic of conversation. A moment later, there was a knock at the door. All of us were freaked out. Travis got up and opened the door.

"Is everything okay?" Jodi asked.

"Yes, it's great!" he replied.

"Are you going to bed any time soon?" she asked.

"Ya, in a little while," he assured her. "I'll come say goodnight before I go to bed."

She went back downstairs. We heard her door close, and then Travis checked to be sure. We figured she'd gone back to bed, and we continued talking. I couldn't shake the creepy feeling I had. It was maybe thirty to forty-five minutes later when I got that same cold feeling, but stronger.

While frantically pointing at the door, I mouthed to Chris and Travis, "She's out there!"

Travis mouthed back, "No way!"

I nodded my head "yes."

Travis crept over to the door and ripped it open. A possessed-looking Jodi was standing there with an expression on her face that cannot be adequately described. A horrible feeling came over my body. Pure evil is the only thing that comes to mind. She just got caught eavesdropping in someone else's house, but she didn't seemed phased or even embarrassed. She plowed forward.

"Is this a private conversation?" she asked in an accusatory tone of voice, spewing with anger.

"Actually, it is," Travis said calmly. "I'll be down to talk to you in a few minutes."

We were all on edge. She could have done anything in that moment, and Chris and I would not have been surprised. Angrily, she turned and walked away. There was a palpable discomfort experienced by all of us after she left.

Travis looked at us, obviously torn up, and asked, "So you don't think she can change?"

We both shook our heads. "I'm so sorry, Travis," I said.

Upset and confused, Travis said goodnight and went downstairs to chat with Jodi before going to bed.

As soon as the door shut, Chris turned to me, "Did you feel that?"

"Yes! What was that?" I asked. "Are the kids safe? Are we safe? What are we going to do?"

Laying in our bed, more scared than we had ever been, I asked, "How did we get to a place in our lives where someone we are very afraid of is staying in our home? Is she going to set our house on fire?"

"Should we bring the kids in our room?" Chris asked. "Do you think she will hurt them?"

"I don't want her here ever again. She can never come back!" I said firmly.

"I agree," Chris said.

"First thing in the morning, tell Travis that she can't come back. He's gonna hate us . . ." I said.

"He will have to understand that we don't have a choice. He had to have felt that. He saw her face," Chris said.

I got up and checked on our kids every fifteen minutes the entire night. Each time I went to check on the kids, I noticed that Travis was not in his room. Jodi's light was on downstairs and I could hear talking. As the sun was coming up, I was up again to check on my children, and I noticed that Travis had gone to bed and Jodi's light was out.

No one got much sleep that night. That morning, I dreaded seeing her. *What would I say? How is Travis going to tell her that she isn't welcome here? What will she do?* Travis woke up later that morning. I saw him in the hallway, and he looked awful.

"I want you to tell her everything you told me," he said. "She needs to hear it from you."

"I'm not gonna do that, Travis!" I contended. "That is so awkward!"

He insisted and wasn't going to back down.

I assumed Chris had already told him that Jodi was no longer welcome in our home, and that was why Travis looked so busted up, but Chris hadn't told him yet. Travis didn't know Jodi was about to be kicked out of our house and our life.

Reluctantly, I honored Travis's request. Jodi and I went into her room to talk. I told her everything and how disturbing it all was. I told her we knew she was obsessed with Travis. I talked to her about her flirting with married men, and how I thought it would get better after our last talk, but it had only gotten worse. She protested, suggesting that she had been on her "best behavior."

"If that's your 'best behavior,'" I said, "then I would hate to see you acting poorly."

She was completely emotionless for the several long, insane hours we talked. She kept talking in circles. I finally told her I needed to get back to my kids. She had shown no emotion the entire time we spoke, even when I told her I wasn't comfortable with her in my home or around my family. I had been very bold with her.

As I was getting up to leave, she asked, "Are you going to tell Travis not to date me?"

"I already did."

She lost it! Finally, she showed emotion. She was sobbing, repeating, "I can't lose him! I can't lose him!"

I felt bad, but not bad enough to ignore the feeling I had the night before. She was evil. I knew it and I couldn't deny it. I was done with her, or so I thought.

While she and I were in her room talking, I heard our friends, Hollie and Jacob, come into our home. Thank goodness they did, because my kids were so hungry! It was between one thirty and two in the afternoon, and they hadn't eaten lunch. Chris and Travis were taking some work-related calls, and Hollie was making lunch when I came out of Jodi's room.

Chris had brought Jacob and Hollie up to speed about our unbelievable night. Hollie, and anyone else in or near the kitchen, must have been able to hear the intensity of mine and Jodi's conversation. When I finally walked out of Jodi's room, Hollie gave me an "Are you okay?" look.

Jodi just got kicked out. I told her I wasn't comfortable with her in my home, and that she wasn't welcome anymore. Any normal person would have packed their things and been miles down the road by now, but Jodi continued to show that she was anything but normal.

I didn't tell her that I thought she was evil, or that we were scared she was going to kill us all. I told her that I wasn't comfortable with her in my home nor around my family. To my complete shock, she walked out of her bedroom and into the kitchen, and sat at the table. It was bizarre and so incredibly uncomfortable! She sat there for an hour until Travis came in the room. They both headed out back and stood by the parked cars, talking until after five p.m.

I don't remember apologizing to Travis, but I'm sure I did over and over. He was so upset. He just didn't get it. He couldn't see that it was a real-life *Fatal Attraction*, and *The Hand that Rocks the Cradle* movie was playing out in his life. From that day forward, I started referring to Jodi as "Rabbit Boiler" from the movie *Fatal Attraction*, and "Peyton" from the movie *The Hand that Rocks the Cradle*. Sadly, this wasn't name-calling. It was prophecy.

Over the next few days, I had several conversations with Travis, each of them more difficult than the next. Our relationship was strained for the next couple months. He was really mad at us, but more so, he was hurt. He just couldn't understand why we were so set against her and wanted nothing to do with her. Every time she came up, we argued, so we avoided talking about her all together for several months. He wasn't the only one who was upset with us. There were others in our business network who felt that we were judgmental, overreacting, and too harsh. All I could tell them was that they didn't experience what we experienced.

The defense team and the few people who support Jodi want to blame Travis, or have accused him of pushing Jodi to the brink and "making" her a murderer. This evil had nothing to do with Travis. We saw it seven months after meeting her, not to mention the warnings I got from whatever you want to call it: God, the Holy Spirit, gut, the

Universe, intuition, inner voice, etc. Oprah calls it the sixth sense. It warned me right away. I didn't listen.

The way Jodi interacted with detectives when under arrest for murder, how she lied to the media and then lied about her lies, and her control and manipulation in the courtroom and of the law was a testament to what we had observed. She lied, used, manipulated, and controlled people throughout her life. Imagine dating her! Imagine being so manipulated by her that she is controlling you, and you have no idea that she is! Many people don't realize that this pattern of obsessive, stalking, and invading other's privacy that we saw Jodi doing to Travis was not new to Jodi. It plagued her other relationships as well.

Bobby Juarez was an ex-boyfriend of hers that we learned about during the trial. Jodi met him when she was very young. She also got into his emails, wouldn't let the relationship go, and stalked him. I was told that Bobby Juarez moved to Hawaii to get away from Jodi. I was also told that she cut his phone lines. When he was no longer interested in her, she moved on to his roommate, Matt. She also got into Matt's emails, then claimed that some random people came into the restaurant where she was working at the time to inform her that Matt was cheating on her. At some point she slept in Matt's bed waiting to confront him, after driving hours to confront the girl he was cheating on her with. When being interviewed by the defense, Matt indicated he'd tried to break up with Jodi, but she kept crying and wouldn't let him.

People who worked with Jodi and Darryl have indicated that the two of them began their relationship while Darryl was still married. I don't know the validity of this. It was also reported that Jodi tried to become like Darryl's ex-wife. She got breast enhancements, colored her hair to match his ex-wife's, and purchased the same kind of car his ex had. According to an interview with Darryl, he tried to create space between him and Jodi to focus more on his son. Jodi wasn't having it, and continued to try to force the relationship.

Jodi broke into Travis's email account and his Myspace account on multiple occasions. Rather than confronting Travis with what she had learned, thus having to reveal that she had violated his trust, she made up a story, like she did for Matt, saying people came into her place of work and told her that Travis was talking to other women. She read Travis's text messages and listened to his conversations. Travis told a friend that he had no privacy for a year because of Jodi's intrusive behaviors. The list can go on, and on, and on, and on, and on.

During the trial, I made a list of "things that only happen to you if you are Jodi Arias." When you see the list, it's overwhelmingly clear that Jodi just makes stuff up. She has a script that she sticks to when it comes to relationships. Either Jodi is the most unlucky girl in the world, or she is just a pathological liar. I'm going with the latter, for obvious reasons. She was "spun around" by both Travis and Bobby when they were "assaulting" her. Her family has been threatened and insulted so many times it's hard to keep track of it all. People seem to come into restaurants to tell Jodi any time a guy is cheating on her. Her boyfriends are great about leaving their email accounts open with evidence of their infidelities. She has been attacked by family members, boyfriends, and intruders (she gets attacked a lot). "Falling to her knees" is a common occurrence when Jodi is "attacked," so is being "caught/grabbed by the wrist" when fleeing. She has a playbook, and it seems she's been running those plays since she was a little girl.

Fortunately, I didn't have to see Jodi until our Pre-Paid Legal team training event at Daniel's Summit, Utah, in June of 2007 (between two and three months after we kicked her out of our home). We stayed at a beautiful mountain lodge where we swam, boated, water-skied, four-wheeled, rode horses, hiked, hung out, and attended trainings. I was not looking forward to seeing her. As I was getting gift bags ready for our executives and top-money earners, two women volunteered to help. This was when I met Julie and Clancy, Travis's good friends, and good friends to many people in our business. They were talking about Travis and Jodi, and how they did not like them together. Neither of them liked nor trusted Jodi, and both felt something was not right with her. I didn't say anything until they were done talking. I asked them if they had told Travis how they felt. Both said they hadn't . . . yet. I asked that they make sure they did, but to also make sure to tell Travis that I didn't say anything about Jodi. I was really worried about Travis, and it was clear that Julie and Clancy were as well. They were not fooled by Jodi for a second.

They eventually spoke to Travis later that day, and he came straight to me. He was mad and accused me of being on a "witch hunt." He was convinced that I was on a mission to turn everyone against Jodi. I told him I didn't have anything to do with what Clancy and Julie thought, that they had come to their conclusions independent of me. He wouldn't believe me. This was only the beginning.

Later into the weekend, Travis came down the hall toward me as I was leaving my room. He was coming right for me. *Oh great!* I thought.

"I hope you're happy!" he said, very upset.

"About what?" I asked.

"Jodi is crying in my room, so I hope you are happy!" he snapped.

"Why would I be happy about that?"

"She's crying 'cause she's afraid that if she goes to the pool in a bikini, you're gonna call her a slut!"

"Annnnd . . . why would I do that?"

"Because she only has a two-piece bathing suit, and she's afraid you're gonna tell everyone she's a slut," he explained.

"Are you being serious, Travis?" I was trying not to laugh. This was unbelievable. I could not believe he was buying into her sixth-grade nonsense! How could he not see how she was manipulating him?

"Um, Travis . . . why would I care?"

The look on his face said it all. He looked so confused. "Good point," he said, "Sorry." And he walked away. I stood there in a stupor, wondering what the heck that was about.

I felt sick to my stomach. It was obvious that Jodi was doing every-thing she could to turn Travis against us. It was sad and terrifying, all at the same time. Not long after this bizarre interaction, everyone, but Travis, went to a nearby lake for team-building activities. Travis borrowed our car to go to visit the home of one of his relatives. Jodi was beside herself. She was going from person to person at the lake, asking if they had seen Travis, or if they knew where Travis was. She was in a complete panic. I thought she was going to tear her hair out and scream at the top of her lungs. She was pacing and was clearly about to lose it! Any description of her meltdown will fall short. She was pacing back and forth, going from person to person, looking all over, from the parking lot to the beach, checking her phone over and over, like an overwound wind-up toy, or, more accurately, like a woman possessed. I finally asked someone to tell her that Travis wouldn't be back for several hours.

Not long after our business event in Utah, things were obviously not right in their relationship. They had been having issues for a while. Jodi was way too controlling and obsessive. Travis cared about her a lot, but he knew it wasn't going to work. They broke things off at the end of July 2007. We were thrilled! So was Travis. He still cared about her, but he wanted to get his life back on track, and he was looking forward to dating other women.

There's a misconception that Travis was "using" Jodi. Even some of Travis's friends have said that he was just using her to "keep his bed warm until he found a 'good' Mormon girl." This is absurd and couldn't be farther from the truth. Others have indicated that Travis was looking for a virgin to marry, and since Jodi wasn't one, she was automatically disqualified. These people clearly do not know Travis.

First of all, Travis wasn't a virgin, and to mark people off the list because they had partaken of the "forbidden fruit," as it were, is just stupid. He just wasn't like that. Travis loved people and he loved Jesus. He believed in repentance. He knew everyone makes "mistakes," and he certainly wasn't going to hold that against anyone! He had his fair share of making mistakes himself. Many people outside of Mormon culture feel that Travis and Jodi weren't doing anything wrong, but because of his religious beliefs, Travis knew he was out of bounds. He wanted to be true to what he believed. It wasn't Jodi's sexual past that made Travis decide not to pursue a relationship with her! It was her obsessive, immature, and intrusive behaviors and her lies that made him realize it just wasn't going to work. He couldn't trust her. He knew she wasn't a virgin when he met her. He couldn't have cared less, and he was hoping the relationship would lead somewhere. Travis always cared about Jodi. We see that he still cared about her even toward the end of his life, but deep down, he was afraid of her. He told several friends, including the Hiatts, whom he considered family, that he was afraid of her. I think everyone assumed he was kidding, because he laughed while talking about her killing him. On May 18, 2008, just weeks before he was murdered, Travis wrote the following on his blog:

*This type of dating, to me, is like a very long job interview and can be exponentially more mentally taxing; desperately trying to find out if my date has an axe murderer penned up inside of her and knowing she is wondering the same thing about me.*
http://travisalexander.blogspot.com

CHAPTER 9

# The Beginning of the End

*Travis loved to be creative. He enjoyed inventing things. He wanted*
*to get a patent on a pair of flip-flops he'd created by lining the flip-*
*flops with shag carpet. He called them, "Shaggs." He loved them and*
*wore them everywhere. The only problem was they shed like crazy!*

AUGUST THIRTEENTH THROUGH THE FIFTEENTH, after Travis and Jodi called
it quits, a bunch of us from our Pre-Paid Legal team went on a four-
wheeling trip to Marysvale, Utah. Among those on the trip were Clancy,
Julie, Mike Bertot, C.A. Murff, Chris, and I—all good friends of Travis.
Travis was always the life of any trip or gathering, but sadly, that wasn't
the case for this one. Travis was not himself. We would discover later in
the day that Travis and Jodi fought on the phone most of the drive.

Travis Alexander being "Superman" on the four-wheeler.

Travis rode down with Mike Bertot, and he heard them arguing. Mike wrote:

In August 2007, Travis drove from his home in Mesa up to Utah to join me and a group of our friends on our annual four-wheeling trip. There were several people in other vehicles, and Travis rode with me in my truck for the three-hour drive to our destination. Travis did not seem himself at all that day, and it didn't take long to learn why. Once on the road, Travis's phone rang, and it was Jodi. I did my best to not eavesdrop on their conversation, but the longer it went on, the harder it was to ignore. Eventually, one of them hung up on the other—I'm not sure who, but I now had a chance to inquire as to what was happening.

"Hey, bro, what's going on?" I asked.

"Just crap with Jodi," he replied.

"Like what? I've never seen you get mad before." I said it jokingly, but I couldn't remember ever seeing Travis get mad at anyone or anything before.

"I just don't know what to do about her anymore. She doesn't want to accept the fact that we're not together anymore," he said.

"Don't worry about it. She'll get over it. Besides, she lives hundreds of miles away" was my advice.

"I wish that were true. She just moved to Mesa . . . after we broke up. She lives less than a mile from me now."

I was shocked. "What the . . ."

"Yeah, crazy, huh?"

"That's one way to put it."

Travis proceeded to tell me everything that had happened over the past few weeks since she had moved to Mesa, and even before that. He expressed how he constantly felt like she was around even though he didn't see her, like she was following him . . . everywhere, but he couldn't see her. He even thought she had been sneaking into his home and worried that she would sneak in again while he was out of town.

"That's some crazy, stalker s***, bro," I said. "You need to be careful."

Travis didn't think it was that serious. "I think she'll get over it. I just wish she wasn't that close to me."

"I hope you're right."

During the rest of the drive, their conversation continued, at least until we lost phone service in the mountains of southern Utah. They would speak again until one hung up on the other, then switch to texting until one or the other stopped responding. The conversation was clearly becoming more and more heated as it went on.

When they were actually talking, I heard Travis say many things that made it clear that he wanted no part of a relationship or anything else to do with her. Things like:

"Why did you move to Mesa? You've got no reason to be there besides me!"

"A normal person wouldn't do that."

"Leave me alone. We're not going to be together."

"Stop lying, Jodi."

For the rest of the trip, Travis was not himself. Instead of being social and happy with his friends, he was withdrawn and preferred to be alone much of the time. He was ultra-sensitive the entire weekend. Normally, he could take a joke, but that weekend he got angry if any of us teased him. He was not the person we were accustomed to being around. I felt even more uneasy about Jodi, and for the first time, I was really worried about my friend. Travis was right—a normal person wouldn't do the things she had done.

When Mike and Travis arrived at the cabins, we were all excited for the party to begin. But it never did. Travis was the party, but something was wrong. He was miserable . . . really upset and sulky. When everyone was having fun, telling jokes, and being silly, Travis was in the background, by himself, staring blankly at the ground. The following day, the group was riding on a trail when Travis suddenly stopped his four-wheeler, turned around, and went back to his cabin. This was where he spent much of the weekend, on the phone quarreling with Jodi. Cell signal was in and out, so he often drove to find service.

Everyone in the group was feeling bummed. None of us had ever seen Travis like this, and it was affecting all of us. When Travis was around, there were several offshoot conversations happening about him. When he wasn't around, he was the focal point of many of the main conversations. We were all worried about him and tried to figure out what was wrong. We knew he had been fighting with Jodi, but didn't know what could cause him to be so upset.

Finally, Mike shared with us what had happened with Travis on the drive to the cabins. Mystery solved. I snapped. I saw him leaving his cabin, where he had been talking to Jodi on the phone. I intercepted him before he made it to the group sitting around a campfire. I couldn't keep it inside any longer.

In the many years of our friendship, this was the only time Travis got really mad at me, and I deserved it. He had been mad, or bugged, by me many times. He was mad when we kicked Jodi out of our house, but this was different. I got in his face about Jodi like I never had before. I was mad and frustrated. I saw what this relationship was doing to him, and at this point, I was totally convinced she was nothing but evil. I knew she was manipulative because I had witnessed it! I had been manipulated by her, as well as watched her manipulate him and others. They had broken things off, and Travis was in a really good place. He was getting his spiritual life back on track, and he was excited about dating other people.

Holding nothing back, I told Travis exactly how I felt about Jodi Arias. It was an impassioned tirade, one I have lived to regret. What Travis needed was a hug. He needed someone to simply comfort and support him. I was at a breaking point. I loved him so much, and I could not stand what she was doing to him. The infection had been lanced, and what happened next could not be stopped.

"How can you not see what she is doing to you? You were doing so well. You were so happy after you guys broke it off. She's evil! She's manipulative! She's ruining your life! How can you not see it? How can you not see it, Travis? She's absolutely obsessed with you! She's possessed! She is not normal! She is dangerous! She is a stalker! She has hacked your life! Think about it—if you even mention another girl or talk to someone new, she immediately becomes their best friend. Look at her Myspace page, Travis. She is you! Everything you like, she likes! She has patterned her life after yours. Can you not see this? At Daniel's Summit, she had a freaking meltdown 'cause she couldn't find you. She was about to have a nervous breakdown! She follows you around! She follows you to the bathroom and stands outside the door! She wrote that crazy email to herself, acting like an anonymous stalker! She wrote that email, Travis! That is so crazy! How can you not see it? Almost since the day you met her, she's been manipulating you to commit to her and to invite her to move to Mesa. She's been playing you against other guys, and other guys against you! She's manipulated you! She's manipulated us and a long list of other people! She's lied to you! She's lied to us! She's a real-life fatal attraction! She's crazy, Travis! She's evil! She eavesdrops on your conversations! She eavesdropped on *our* conversations, in my own home, outside my bedroom door! And you caught her! Didn't that scare you, Travis? Could you not feel that evil feeling? Did you not feel like you were in danger? Why do you keep talking to her, Travis? You've been doing so well! You're getting your spiritual life back on track! You've been so happy since you broke up with her. Why are you allowing her back in? I don't understand it! You need to be done with her, and you need her out of your life! I don't get why you even talk to her! Be done with her for good! Tell her you want *nothing* to do with her!"

I let it all out, and though I would feel badly about it later, it felt good in the moment. I finally told Travis everything I had ever wanted to tell him, the way I wanted to tell him. I had summed up Jodi Arias.

"You don't understand!" he said intensely.

"You're right!" I said loudly. "I don't understand! She's ruining your life and you keep talking to her!"

"Sky," he said sternly. "I'm all she has. She has no family. She has no friends. And every time I try to break things off completely with her and move on with my life, she threatens to kill herself!"

"How can you not see what she's doing, Trav? She's manipulating you! She's not gonna kill herself, and if she does, it's not your fault! People break up every day! People move on, every day! If she kills herself, that's on her, not you," I said.

"I couldn't live with myself if she killed herself because of me," he said, more calmly now. "You can't guarantee that she won't hurt herself, and I couldn't live with that."

I leaned forward, and firmly said, "She's not gonna kill herself, Travis, and if she does, so be it! You'd get your life back!"

The look on his face broke my heart. It wasn't one of anger. It was one of pure sadness. He stood there completely defeated. Soberly, he said, "You're being a b****."

He headed back toward his cabin, and I headed back to the campfire. As I rejoined the group, I couldn't get the hurt look on his face out of my mind, and the guilt began to set in. I'd known him for six years, and I'd never seen him so sad, and I'd never heard him cuss until that moment. I still remember the look on his face. He wasn't mad; he was hurt and almost looked helpless. I wouldn't drop it, and at the time, I had no idea just how badly she had manipulated and controlled him. I knew he was struggling, but I didn't realize how pained he was. Obviously trying to hold back tears, he told me how I just didn't understand. My disdain and disgust for her grew exponentially that day. I hated what she was doing to him. I feel terrible about that whole experience, and looking back, knowing what I know now, I wish I would have just hugged him instead of getting so angry. We were really look-ing forward to this four- wheeling weekend, but it was awful. The fun we had with our friends and business associates was overshadowed by Travis's sadness.

Travis cared about Jodi a lot, but he knew they weren't good for each other. He enjoyed talking to her and enjoyed her company. Travis spent a lot of his childhood feeling unloved and alone. She would con-stantly remind him that he was all she had. She would beg him not to abandon her and made him feel so guilty. It put him right back to his childhood, and he could not be responsible for someone feeling alone and abandoned. She would throw it in his face that he baptized her, and he couldn't just walk away. Travis had begged and pleaded with Jodi that she not move to Mesa, but she did anyway. Not only did she move there, but she moved only a few minutes from his house. Under oath, Jodi said Travis asked her to move there and even paid for it! Everyone on that four-wheeling trip knew he didn't want her to move there. Jodi lies. It's just what she does. He wanted to move on. He wanted to be done, but she wouldn't let him go. It wasn't long after she moved there that Travis just wasn't his usual self. Though he wanted to move on, he felt an incredible sense of responsibility for Jodi's psy-chological wellbeing. He was in a quandary, one that would prove to be terribly tragic, and, ultimately, lead to his demise.

CHAPTER 10

# Unraveling

Travis loved Broadway musicals. He knew all
the lyrics to the songs in *Les Miserables.*

ALL OF TRAVIS'S FRIENDS WERE taken aback to learn that Jodi had moved
to Mesa . . . after they broke things off. It was one of many warning
signals that something bad was about to happen. Her moving to Mesa
didn't happen without a fight.

On the one hand, he had this ex-girlfriend hanging around whom
he still liked, cared for, talked to often, and felt responsible for. On
the other hand, he was enjoying the single life again, and was excited
about the prospects of finding Mrs. Alexander. He thought he'd found
her. Her name was Lisa Andrews.

Travis and Lisa went to church together. Travis was older than Lisa,
and it might not have seemed like a fit, but eventually it was. Lisa decided to give him a chance, and they began hanging out. In October
2007, Travis won a trip for two to Newport Beach. He and Jodi enjoyed
traveling together, and even though they had broken things off three
months before, he invited her to join him. While there, Travis was taking a shower in his hotel room. He left his phone in the bedroom, and
Jodi, never one to let an opportunity escape her, read through his text
messages and most likely his emails. While going through his phone,
she saw a text from Lisa saying that she missed him. Jodi, acting like

Travis, sent a reply text that said something like, *Cuddle time with Jodi. I freaking love this girl!*

It was on this trip that Jodi went missing for over an hour with the same married guy she had been texting in the middle of the night at our house. Hollie and Jacob were on this trip and tried to convince Travis that Jodi was bad news. Especially Hollie. While Jodi was off doing who knows what with the married guy, Hollie talked with Travis about his relationship with Jodi. She told him of her concerns and fears. She had never trusted Jodi and always knew that something was wrong with her.

When Travis and I talked on the phone, I would avoid asking him about Jodi. I knew they were still spending a lot of time together, and I assumed they were messing around. When Jodi did come up in our conversations, I never pressed him for the details of their "non-relationship" relationship. However, after learning how much he liked Lisa, and realizing how serious they had become, I felt the need to defend Lisa by putting pressure on Travis to end *everything* with Jodi. Everything. Travis told me he wanted us to meet Lisa and asked if they could stay with us for a few days because he wanted to take her to Disneyland. I told him absolutely, because it would give me a chance to tell Lisa that he was still hanging out with Jodi. Travis defended his relationship with Jodi, saying they were nothing more than friends. I knew he was full of it and kept badgering him about it. Finally, he admitted they had "messed around a few times," but had both agreed that it couldn't continue. I told him they would continue to mess around as long as they hung out, and the only way to prevent it would be to sever all ties. He had either fooled himself, or thought he was fooling me when he said they could still hang out and be friends, but not be intimate in any way. My threat to tell Lisa might have scared him a little too much. Unfortunately, the Disneyland trip with Lisa never happened.

As Travis and Lisa got more serious, she got cold feet. She knew Travis was looking for a wife, and she wasn't ready for marriage yet, so she put on the brakes. It didn't take long before she realized how much she loved Travis, and they were back together. Travis adored Lisa. He was so happy when he was with her. I can't remember if there was a certain occasion, but he took a piece of poster board and filled the whole thing with a message written with candy bars and candy, and left it by Lisa's door.

This was a very difficult time for Travis, because Jodi would not go away. One of the detectives, who worked on Travis's murder case, described the relationship between Travis and Jodi as a cycle of Travis trying to abstain and Jodi seducing him. Travis would be regretful and tell Jodi to stop coming over in the middle of the night. She would apologize, and then they would not be intimate . . . only for her to seduce him again. I remember one conversation where the detective told me that "no guy could have refused the things she was doing." He said she would just show up in the middle of the night.

I asked, "Like trench-coat style?"

He responded with, "Exactly."

The detective told me that he felt bad for Travis, because it was obvious he was really trying to live the way he felt he should, and she was making it near impossible. The detective and the prosecutor on the case both said it's apparent that Travis was a really, really good person after reading through all the evidence.

In December 2007, Travis called and told me someone had slashed the tires of his car. He conveniently left out the fact that his car was parked outside Lisa's house when it happened, but I didn't need to know where his car was when it happened to know who did it. Something inside me screamed, *Jodi slashed his tires!*

"Jodi slashed your tires, Travis." I said matter-of-fact.

"No, she didn't, Sky," Travis passionately defended her. "She would never do anything like that! I know you think she's an evil witch out to destroy my life, and granted, she's got her issues, but she's not the type of person who would do something like this."

He defended her, but I could tell that he knew deep down. He just didn't want me to know, and he certainly didn't want me to know that he knew. He got his tires replaced. The following night, his brand-new tires were slashed again, only this time he didn't tell me about it. Interestingly, at some point Travis called his sister, Samantha. She can't remember if it was the first or second tire-slashing, but Travis told her that Jodi had slashed his tires in the night while he was at Lisa's house. Samantha, who is a police officer, encouraged Travis to call the police and make a report, so there was a record. He called the police, but it took too long for them to arrive at Lisa's home, and neither Travis nor Lisa could wait around.

Travis confronted Jodi. Of course, she lied and said that she could never do something like that. When Travis told her he had called Samantha and told her he thought Jodi did it, Jodi freaked out. Apparently, she guilted Travis into calling Samantha back to retract his story. Either with Jodi in his presence, or with Jodi on a three-way call, Travis called Samantha back. He told her that Jodi couldn't stop crying. He explained that she was terribly upset that the Alexander family thought she had anything to do with slashing his tires, and he assured Samantha that he was wrong. "Jodi didn't do it."

Travis's relationship with Lisa was progressing quickly and Jodi was unraveling. Her measures became more intrusive and desperate. In February, Lisa's tires were slashed while her car was parked in Travis's driveway. (In the eBook version of this book, I was recounting all of the tire slashing incidences from memory- eight years prior. I had distinct memories of mine and Travis's conversation after his tires were slashed the first time. He was NOT happy that I thought it was Jodi. I didn't remember a conversation about a second tire slashing, so I didn't think he had told me. After the eBook version was published, text messages between Travis and I became available. He *did* tell me about the second tire slashing, but he never told me about Lisa's tires getting slashed. It was Lisa who told me about *her* tires being slashed after Travis was killed.)

As Travis spent more time at Lisa's house, all hell broke loose. Some of the following things happened the night Travis's tires were slashed, and some happened on other nights. Someone opened the front door to Lisa's house. When Travis went to check it out, no one was there. Someone knocked on the front door or tapped on windows, but when Travis and Lisa looked, there was no one there. Understandably, Lisa was afraid and asked Travis to stay. Lisa woke up to an email from an "anonymous" person telling her how awful she was for having Travis spend the night. The email told Lisa she needed to repent, that she was a whore and that God loved her, among many other things. This is an excerpt from the email Lisa received:

> *You are a shameful whore. Your Heavenly Father must be deeply ashamed of the whoredoms you've committed with that insidious man. If you let him stay in your bed one more time or even sleep under the same roof as him, you will be giving the appearance of evil. You are driving away the Holy Ghost, and you are wasting your time. You are also compromising your salvation and breaking your baptismal covenants. Of all the commandments to break, committing acts of whoredom is one of the most displeasing in the eyes of the Lord. You cannot be ashamed enough of yourself. You are filthy, and you need to repent and become clean in the eyes of God. Think about your future husband, and how you disrespect not only yourself, but him, as well as the Lord and Savior Jesus Christ. Is that what you want for yourself? Your future, your celebration, and your posterity is resting on your choices and actions. You are a daughter of God, and you have been a shameful example. Be thou clean, sin no more. Heavenly Father loves you and wants you to make the right choices. I know you are strong enough to choose the right. Your Father in Heaven is pulling for you. Don't ignore the promptings you receive, because they are vital to your spiritual well-being.*

Travis later told people that Jodi sent that email to Lisa. While Lisa and Travis were hanging out at Travis's house, Jodi snuck in and Lisa saw her. She told Travis, and he ran out the door after her. During Jodi's testimony, Juan Martinez, the prosecutor, questioned her about sneaking into Travis's backyard and spying on him while he was making out with a girl on the couch in the house. She said that he took the girl's bra off. The girl was Lisa, and her bra did not come off. Travis told some of his friends that Jodi was following him on dates. Both Deanna and Lisa said that on more than one occasion, they would come downstairs and lights were on that they knew they had turned off, or a door would be unlocked that they were sure they had locked. None of Travis's roommates had been home. Travis later told Lisa that it was Jodi.

In Jodi's interview with Detective Flores, the lead detective working Travis's murder, she told him that she was surprised to find out Travis was dating Lisa, because that made Jodi the "other woman." She claimed she did not know about Lisa. This was, of course, another lie. Jodi had plenty of experiences with Lisa. She had texted Lisa from Travis's phone, and it was believed by many that Jodi sent the crazy anonymous email to Lisa. Then there were the weird occurrences at Lisa's house that many attribute to Jodi. Travis's tires were slashed at Lisa's house—twice. Lisa's tires were slashed at Travis's house. She had followed Lisa and Travis, and had tried to break them up. How do you do all of that without knowing you were the "other woman"? Travis accused Jodi of the December and February tire-slashings again shortly before she killed him.

While Deanna was still living in Arizona, Travis would ask her to feed and take care of Napoleon while he was out of town. On one occasion, she entered the house, only to find Jodi in the kitchen on Travis's computer while waiting for cookies to bake. Deanna said it was extremely awkward. She described it as being "very eerie." She called Travis to let him know. Travis told us that he was not happy about Jodi being there.

Jodi's invasion of Travis's privacy by hacking accounts and following him on dates mixed with her using other men against Travis, lying about chance encounters with information-providing strangers, and relentless advances to keep Travis "hers" by seducing him, she was making Travis's life unlivable. Any time he would meet a new girl, Jodi would immediately "friend" that girl on Myspace, or do whatever she could to get close to that girl. He was miserable and still so conflicted. He would be so past his limit and ready to be done when she would reel him back in again by saying he couldn't abandon her, threatening suicide, or with sex. During the trial, defense expert, Alyce LaViolette, presented something called the Abuse Cycle. If we were to follow the Abuse Cycle presented by LaViolette, including the issues with control and use of guilt, Jodi was clearly the abuser, and Travis the abused.

CHRIS:

One of the most colorful personalities in the Jodi Arias murder trial was a man named Gus Searcy. Gus has been referred to by some as the "Forest Gump" of Pre-Paid Legal, because of his long list of incredibly obscure accomplishments and life experiences. He owned a world-championship Frisbee dog who "made more money than some people make in a lifetime," he was the "youngest person ever to own a 7-11 franchise," and he has been among the "highest-paid magicians in the world." As a witness for the defense, he went head to head with the prosecutor on many occasions. In one instance, he defended Pre-Paid Legal as more of a "circle," rather than the pyramid shape the prosecutor erroneously suggested. When pressed for information he was not willing to discuss, he pled the Fifth. After having done so, the judge asked if he had an attorney. While looking at his wristwatch, he said, "At this time of day? No." This was a black eye to him and to all of us as Pre-Paid Legal Associates. Pre-Paid Legal members can call their law firm about *any* legal issue during business hours and can call twenty-four-hours a day with emergency issues. Additionally, he misspoke when he stated that Jodi was on my Pre-Paid Legal team. She wasn't. He also suggested I had never helped anyone on his team. This also was not true. Over the years, I've done several Pre-Paid Legal seminars for Gus and his team. Needless to say, he was a real stand-out in this case.

Gus took an interest in Jodi after meeting her in 2007. He volunteered to "mentor" her, even though she was not on his team and would not benefit him financially. Gus even gave her a cell phone, the same phone Jodi used to record her and Travis's sexually charged phone conversation, which was referenced many times during the trial. Some believed Gus had a romantic interest in Jodi, even though he was old enough to be her father, and perhaps even her grandfather. Regardless, he denied any romantic interest in Jodi and sided with her during the trial as a friendly witness for the defense.

In his testimony, Gus tells the story of Jodi staying with him in his motor home in Las Vegas when she received a phone call from Travis. He testified that he could hear Travis shouting at her before she stepped outside to finish the call in private. He further testified how emotionally distraught she was at the conclusion of that phone call, literally "shaking" when she re-entered his home. This occurred around February 25, 2008, the same time that Lisa and Travis discovered Lisa's tires had been slashed while her car was in Travis's driveway. We have no way of knowing for sure, but could it be that Travis called Jodi accusing her and confronting her for slashing Lisa's tires? He had every right to be irate. Why did Jodi run off to Gus's place in Las Vegas? Perhaps because she had just slashed Lisa's tires and needed an alibi? The conversation might have gone something like this, "I'm in Las Vegas, Travis! Not only would I never do something like this, I couldn't have done it! I'm in Vegas with Gus Searcy!"

This was the third set of tires that Travis had to buy in three months. His tires were slashed twice, and then Lisa's tires were slashed. With all the traveling he had done and neglecting his business in the process, this was a major financial hardship on him. Jodi texted Travis incessantly while she was with Gus, and Travis was clearly ignoring her. In her testimony on February 17, 2013, when asked why there were so many text messages from her without a reply from Travis, she said,

"All of his must have been deleted because they aren't here." They had a record of all text messages between Travis and Jodi from the phone company, and she claimed they were deleted. Clearly, Travis was very upset with her and didn't want to talk to her.

SKY:

Up until January 2008, Travis had asked Jodi to move out of Arizona several times, but by January, he was *begging* her. Her obsession and stalking were worsening, and his life was deteriorating. Travis continued seeing Jodi, even while in a committed relationship with Lisa. Lisa broke up with Travis again. His spirits went from bad to worse. He called me to tell me that he and Lisa had broken up, and that she wouldn't talk to him. I told him that she probably knew about Jodi. Travis was bothered I'd said that, but it was true. He was suffering terribly. I was very worried about him.

Fortunately, Chris and Travis would each earn an all-expenses paid vacation for two from Pre-Paid Legal to Cancun, Mexico. The trip was still several months away. We were really looking forward to the trip until Travis informed us that Jodi was going with him. We were really bummed out, because that meant we wouldn't be spending time with Travis.

A couple of months before the trip, Travis asked his friend and fellow Pre-Paid Legal associate, Brenda, if it were possible to take Jodi's name off his reservation and take someone else. She told him to call corporate, as it would depend on whether or not they had bought the ticket. Travis called. Fortunately, they told him that the ticket hadn't been purchased, and he just needed to let them know who he wanted to bring. We were ecstatic! We counted down the days, knowing that we were going to have the time of our lives, enjoying Mexico with Travis and our other friends, with no Jodi in sight.

The same "voice" that told me to protect my family from Jodi in December 2006 was now telling me to help Travis. Toward the end of

March 2008, I invited him to stay with us for an extended period of time. I told him I was very worried about him. We'd previously had several conversations about his financial difficulties, so I knew he was in a bad place. He reassured me that everything would be fine because Jodi was moving back to Yreka, California, in a few weeks, at which point he could focus on rebuilding his business. He would have his life back, and he was really excited.

He had messed things up really badly with Lisa, and he knew it. It caused him a lot of grief. There was a huge change in Travis around this time. The once-happy-almost-all-the-time Travis was now morbidly sad much of the time. He had completely ruined his chances with Lisa. Travis hoped she'd give him another chance, even though he knew he didn't deserve it. He was trying to figure out how he could get her to talk to him. He would try to be at the places he thought she might be, so they would run into each other and she would have to talk to him. All of his attempts failed.

During this time, a woman named Mimi gave a talk in Travis's church. They both attended the same singles' ward, but Travis had never really noticed her before that day. He was impressed with the talk she gave at church. Though heartbroken from losing Lisa, he'd hope to take his mind off it by trying to get a date with Mimi.

Mimi came from an amazingly talented family. After meeting them, Travis called me one night terribly discouraged. She and her siblings were well educated, spoke multiple languages, were extremely successful, and all were incredible musicians. He felt that there was no way Mimi would want to give him the time of day considering where he came from, and his lack of a college education. He knew that he really had to impress her!

For their first date, Travis would be taking Mimi to a rock-climbing gym. Mimi was very athletic, so Travis knew he needed to bring his A-game. The day before their date, he spent time on YouTube learning the ins and outs of rock climbing. Then he went to the rock climbing gym to familiarize himself with rock climbing and the wall, so he could show her what a "man" he was. He climbed up and down those walls for hours, and left feeling confident that she would be impressed by his abilities the following night. He could hardly wait.

He called me the following morning in an absolute panic! He was so sore from the night before, he couldn't move any part of his body. He said it was the worst pain he'd ever experienced in his life. I suggested he do something else or postpone the date. Neither option would work. He wanted to see her that night, and she was looking forward to rock climbing.

Later that night, Travis called us to give us a report about his date. Chris and I laughed so hard we cried. He relayed this experience where she would scale up the rocks like it was nothing, while he was struggling to lift his arm from his side while still standing on the ground. Every time he tried to lift his legs or arms, he winced in pain. He said it was horribly embarrassing! He walked us through all the thoughts going through his head, and it was a riot! We couldn't stop laughing! He was too embarrassed to tell her that he had been there the night before practicing so he could impress her, so he just gimped around all night looking silly and feeling mortified!

Travis wanted so badly to impress Mimi, but at the same time, he needed to do something he feared would certainly ruin his chances with her. Guilt was bearing down on him about how he'd been living his life. He needed to come clean about his sexcapades with Jodi.

The Church of Jesus Christ of Latter-day Saints has a system in place to help its members who have fallen into sin repent and get back on the path. Like most other Christian denominations, premarital sex is discouraged for a long list of reasons. In the Mormon Church, it's looked upon as very serious sin and requires confession (similar to "confession" in Catholicism without the anonymity). Travis wanted to confess all that had been happening between him and Jodi.

Because of the nature of Travis's actions with Jodi, he knew the church would hold what's called a disciplinary council for him. He had previously confessed to his bishop, but because of the repetitive nature of what Travis was doing, it was taken to the next level. It's important to keep in mind that Travis going to his bishop was completely voluntary. The main purpose of a disciplinary council is to lovingly determine an appropriate path of repentance and recovery. These councils are not meant to be a punishment, but are a way to work together to help someone overcome transgression. Unfortunately for Travis, in a stroke of unbelievably bad luck, he learned that one of the men who would participate in his disciplinary council was Mimi Hall's father.

During the council, Travis spoke about the nature of his relationship with Jodi, including the transgressions the two of them committed. Mimi's father, along with others, compassionately listened while Travis cleared his conscience. Though what happens in these councils is strictly confidential and not to be discussed by the church leaders who participate, Travis felt that after Mimi's father heard what he had to say, he would never let his daughter date Travis. Travis told me that Mimi's father was incredibly kind to him before and after the council. Travis's privileges to attend the Mormon Temple were revoked until he completed the repentance process.

After his disciplinary council, Travis was working hard to get his spiritual life back on track. He was doing his best to keep his distance from Jodi, knowing that she represented a threat to his healing. She was making plans to move out of Arizona. Travis could finally see some light at the end of the dark tunnel he'd been traveling in. Thankfully, now that he had befriended Mimi, he decided he wanted to invite *her* to Mexico. Initially, Mimi declined the invitation, but after some convincing by Travis, and the fact that she would not be rooming with him, she decided it sounded fun and that it was a great opportunity. She was in!

Completely unrelated to the council, Mimi wasn't that into Travis romantically. She liked him as a friend, and they had fun together, but there was no love connection for her. She made it clear that she was going to Mexico as his friend, nothing more. Travis was fine with that, and we couldn't have been happier about it. We had heard so many great things about her and looked forward to meeting her and spending time with her. We were taking our kids and a babysitter, so we arranged to have Mimi and our female babysitter share a room. Travis would be staying with my little brother, Zion, who had also earned the trip.

I can only imagine being uninvited to this trip was quite the blow for Jodi. It was a big opportunity for her on many fronts. First of all, it was free. She wouldn't have to pay for anything, nor would Travis. Pre-Paid Legal would be picking up the tab for everything—airfare, lodging, transportation, food, drinks, gratuity . . . everything! She'd get to spend time with Travis and his friends, not to mention all the top money earners in Pre-Paid Legal. Additionally, she could check Cancun off her list! She and Travis both had the book, *1,000 Places to See before You Die*. The two of them had traveled together, often checking off some of the most desired travel locations in the world. This trip would allow her to check off a couple more, including Chichén Itzá and Tulum. I can't imagine how irate she must have been to learn she wouldn't be going. To make matters worse, not only had she been uninvited, she had been replaced. This was more than she could handle.

As the trip got closer, I continued to worry more and more about Travis. Obviously, I know now what that feeling was about, but at the time, I just felt like I needed to get him out of Arizona. I asked him again and again to come stay with us in Murrieta, California, but each time he reassured me that he was fine. Things were looking up. Jodi was gone, and Travis was thrilled! But, he was still incredibly sad about ruining things with Lisa. I believe this was around the time when his friends, Taylor, Regan, and I all got a similar text from Travis talking about how he had messed up his life so bad that he wanted to "blow his head off." It's so heartbreaking.

On April 30, 2008, our third son, Taj, was born. In the Mormon Church, babies are typically blessed in front of the congregation by their fathers and others the family invites to participate. We decided that Chris would bless Taj at the beginning of June. I invited Travis to join Chris in blessing Taj, but he didn't immediately commit. He said he had to check on some things and would get back to me. He was checking with his bishop to see if he was able to participate. (In the Mormon Church, you must be living the tenets of the faith to participate in many of the ordinances.) At this time in Travis's life, he was back on the right path spiritually, but he was still in the midst of a repentance and healing process, which would disqualify him from participating in the baby's blessing. Finally, he texted me back saying he wouldn't be able to make it to the blessing. I told him not to worry about actually participating in the blessing but to come and hang out with us. I also suggested that he bring Mimi. They could stay at our house, go to Disneyland, and then fly out of the Los Angeles International Airport to meet us in Mexico. He took a while to get back to me, but said that Mimi was unable to get the time off work. I tried, but I just couldn't get him away from Arizona. Still, I was terribly uneasy.

Sometime during May, I had left Travis a couple of messages and hadn't heard back from him, which was rare. I texted a final message warning him that if he didn't call me back in thirty minutes he would force me to load my new baby in the car and drive to Mesa. He called me right back. He said he didn't understand why I was acting crazy; he assured me again that everything was fine and that he was doing really well. Oh, how I wish I would have somehow made him come to California.

On Tuesday, June 3, 2008, I was busily packing for Mexico. My family and I were going to Mexico for five days before Travis and Mimi were scheduled to arrive. This would have been the last time I ever spoke to Travis had I answered my phone or called him back that night. I was doing laundry and worried about getting everyone packed for our trip. I saw his call coming in, but I needed to get everything done while my kids were sleeping. I think I called him back and left a message on Wednesday, June 4. I didn't hear from him, but knew I would see him in Mexico the following week.

# CHAPTER 11

# Her Name Is Jodi

*Travis loved the ocean. One of his favorite things*
*was to have a bonfire. He would often sneak away to*
*pray and meditate down by the water's edge.*

EVERY WEDNESDAY EVENING, CHRIS HOSTS a training call for his marketing team. Sometimes he would train, and other times he invited other leaders to train. This particular Wednesday, June 4, it just so happened that Chris had invited Travis to train. Chris sent a text to Travis about noon on Wednesday to make sure that he was prepared for the call. Travis texted Chris back a little later to confirm. This was the last known contact Travis had with anyone.

We left for Cancun on Friday, June 6, 2008. Once there, we began planning all the things we would do when Mimi and Travis arrived. We planned guided trips to see the ruins in Chichén Itzá and Tulum. We planned an outing to swim with whale sharks in the open sea. Our friends, Jacob and Hollie, would be joining us, and we sent several texts to them, as well as to Travis to make sure they wanted to do all the activities we were considering. Each trip required a deposit to guarantee our spots. We needed to make sure that everyone was on board, so we wouldn't lose our deposits. Hollie and Jacob confirmed, but we never heard from Travis.

By the evening of June 9, Chris was really worried. He'd reached out to Travis several times, starting on June 4, after Travis was a no-show on his conference call. Chris assumed he just spaced the call, but having not heard from him in five days, Chris knew something was wrong. The next evening, Chris called Travis again. This time, he didn't leave a message. He couldn't. Travis's voicemail was full.

"Something's wrong with Travis!" Chris said in a panic. "He missed our call on Wednesday, he hasn't responded to any of our calls or texts, and now his voicemail is full. We need to call the cops!"

I explained a that a police "wellness check" might take some time and the cops wouldn't go inside his house if no one answered. I suggested that Chris call one of Travis's friends to check on him. Chris didn't have any of the phone numbers we needed of the guys in Arizona, but we had Dave Halls. Many of the guys who had lived with Travis over the years were a part of Dave Halls's Pre-Paid Legal team, and we knew that Dave would know how to reach them. Chris called Dave to explain that we were worried about Travis, and asked if Dave could hunt down someone in Mesa to go check on Travis.

At approximately ten p.m. Cancun time, we went to sleep, still awaiting Dave's call. Around that same time, Mimi had become worried because she hadn't heard from Travis either, and they were supposed to leave for Mexico the following day. Mimi called Michelle, a mutual friend, to ask if she would meet her at Travis's house. Michelle brought her boyfriend, Dallin. Together on Travis's front porch, they knocked on the door. They could hear Napoleon barking on the other side of the door, but no one answered. They called Taylor, Travis's good friend, to get the garage code from him, so they could enter the house through the garage.

Taylor stayed on the phone with them as they walked into the house. Once inside, they noticed a foul smell. They assumed Napoleon had an accident and it hadn't been cleaned up. Passing Travis's office, they noticed his cell phone and wallet sitting on his desk. Travis's room was on the left, at the top of the stairs. They turned right to follow the music they heard coming from Zach's room, one of Travis's roommates.

They asked Zach if he knew where Travis was. He told them Travis was in Mexico. Mimi countered, saying that she was going with him, and they weren't supposed to leave until the morning. Together, the group walked over to Travis's room. His double doors were locked. After going downstairs to retrieve a key, Zach returned to the group standing outside Travis's bedroom. When he unlocked and opened the door, he was assaulted by a horrendously foul odor. He immediately saw a pool of blood on Travis's carpet near the entrance into Travis's large bathroom. Zach yelled at the girls to stay back, as he proceeded further into the bathroom. I think Dallin may have followed. There was blood everywhere in the hallway leading up to the shower. With the shower in view, Zach saw Travis's lifeless, decaying body, crumpled up on the shower floor. Horrified, he ran out of Travis's room, telling the others that Travis was dead.

Immediately, Michelle called 911. After establishing that Travis was dead, the 911 operator asked Michelle if Travis had been threatened by anyone recently. Before she could even finish the sentence, Michelle said, "Yes, he has. He has an ex-girlfriend that has been bothering him, and following him, and slashing tires and things like that."

"And do you know the ex-girlfriend's name?" asked the operator.

"Her name is Jodi."

Taylor arrived just as the police arrived. He grabbed his computer from his car, took it to an officer, and pulled up a Myspace page. "This is the girl you are looking for. You need to find Jodi Arias."

Travis's good friend, Brint Hiatt, who Dave Hall called to go check on Travis, arrived shortly after Taylor. Once briefed, he called Dave and told him what happened, and Dave called us. Chris and I were asleep when the phone rang. I answered.

"Hello," I said, quietly, trying not to wake Chris.

"I need to talk to Chris," Dave said.

"He's asleep," I replied.

"Wake him up," he said sternly.

"It's Dave Hall," I said, to Chris, while handing him the phone.

"Hello?"

"Chris, I have terrible news. Travis is dead."

"No! No! No!" Chris whimpered, as he began to cry.

I knew Travis was gone.

While Chris was still on the phone, I heard Travis's voice behind me so clearly and distinctly that I turned around expecting to see him standing there. I heard him say, "Take care of Deanna."

I don't remember crying. I might have, but I just remember not being able to feel anything. I don't know if I was in shock, or what was going on. Chris hung up with Dave and said, "Jodi did this. Jodi killed Travis." I didn't want to believe it. I knew she did, but I didn't want it to be her. The following day, a new group of Pre-Paid Legal associates were coming into Cancun. This was the day Travis and Mimi were supposed to arrive. There was a solemnness throughout the resort. Everyone was talking about it in hushed voices, wondering how could this have happened.

It was this day or the next that we talked to Detective Esteban Flores from the Mesa Police Department. He was the detective assigned to this case, and the one who processed the horrendous scene left in Travis's house. We spoke with him several times, and each time, passionately imploring him to find Jodi Arias. Initially, all we had was a long list of intrusive, dangerous stalking behavior and a hunch. But throughout the day, we would piece together a story that would implicate Jodi even further.

A Pre-Paid Legal associate from Utah told us that Jodi had just been to Utah to spend time with Ryan Burns. Our friend, Mark, a former cop, went to dinner with Ryan and Jodi and several other associates. Mark recalled Jodi having bandages on her fingers. I called Ryan to get the story first-hand.

He proceeded to recount this fantastically ridiculous story Jodi had told him, one only Jodi could make up. She told him she was going to drive from her grandparents' home in Yreka, California, down to Los

Angeles to take pictures for a friend. Then she was going to drive from Los Angeles to Utah so she could hang out with Ryan, whom she had a romantic interest in. But her plan and what actually happened were very different.

First of all, she was forty hours or so late showing up to Ryan's house. Where was she? Well, even though it's a straight shot from Southern California to Utah on the 15 freeway the entire way, she claimed to have gotten lost. She said she went the wrong direction for hours. But she couldn't call him because she lost her phone charger (never mind the fact that every truck stop from California to Utah would have a charger she could purchase). Tired, she pulled over to take a nap. Then, miraculously, while "cleaning out" her car after her nap, she found her charger. This was a rental car; how messy could it have been that she "lost her charger" in it? Finally, she showed up in Utah, and, likely with Travis's blood under her nails, she rolled around with Ryan into the wee hours of the night.

If we wouldn't have felt so strongly that Jodi had done it, we would have known it after hearing this wild tale. The story she told Ryan about why she was delayed was so incredibly ridiculous. While still reeling from the shock of it all, we called Flores again and told him everything. We gave him names and phone numbers of people to call about Jodi's story. We knew Jodi did this, and we told everyone. Most of our trip to Cancun was just a blur, a sad memory. We spent our time making phone calls and putting together a case against Jodi. We asked Flores if anyone had told Travis's family. He said they didn't know how to get in touch with them. We told him we would find someone to go to his grandmother's house to tell Travis's family. We called Mike and Sherree Chapman. Mike was one of Travis's best friends, and Sherree had grown up with Travis and his family. Her dad, Les, was a good friend of Travis's family and was their former bishop. I can't remember if we called Les, or if Mike and Sherree did. Les was given Detective Flores's phone number, so he could call him before going over to the Alexanders. The most difficult call we had to make was to Deanna.

We loudly implicated Jodi for Travis's murder, but not everyone agreed. Some people even got mad at us. Jodi had a lot of people fooled. Some of her biggest defenders were Travis's closest friends . . . our friends. Many people we'd been friends with for years began to judge us and talk about us behind our backs. We hung out in a pretty tight circle, so virtually everything that was said about us came back to us from someone else in the group. Some said we were out of control, or on a witch-hunt, or too quick to judge. Others, though not many, defended Jodi, saying, "There's no way she could have done this." There was a definite divide between the two camps. We knew that Jodi killed Travis, and we beat that drum tirelessly until she was behind bars.

# CHAPTER 12

# A Visit From Travis

*Travis really wanted to get into biking. He bought all the fancy gear, a nice bike, and a killer spandex outfit. Deanna said, "He would do like two laps around the neighborhood and then be done." He put more effort into squeezing into his spandex than he did riding his bike. Taylor Searle was his bike-riding buddy.*

Travis and Taylor

At the risk of sounding completely crazy, Travis's story would not be complete without sharing our last experience with him. Some might find this hard to believe, but anyone who really knows Travis, will know that Travis stopped by our room in Cancun, Mexico, on his way from this life to the next.

Not long after we called Dave Hall to have someone go check on Travis, we laid down to go to bed, but initially, we didn't sleep. I don't remember the exact order of all of these events, but they did occur.

In our room, within feet from the bottom of our bed, there was a huge Jacuzzi. As we were lying in bed trying to go to sleep, all of a sudden, the Jacuzzi came on, shot a burst of water all over the ceiling, and then turned off! Chris jumped, and I laughed. Chris was freaking out as to why it would do that. Our boys were in the Jacuzzi earlier that night, so I assured him that it was nothing. Chris doesn't do well with the "paranormal."

Moments later, a large section of the chiffon drapes flew several feet in the air like a burst of wind had caught them. Chris continued freaking out, and I assured him it was just the wind. I went over to close the door, but it wasn't open, and there were no vents by the drapes. Chris was losing it now.

"I'm not sleeping in here!" he yelled. "Start packing, we are changing rooms!"

I told him that the kids and babysitter were asleep next door, and we were not going to wake everyone up and move. "Besides," I said, "if this person wants to bother you, they will just follow you to the next room!"

All the lights in our room were off, but before we could even begin to relax, a bulb in one of the canned lights next to the bed flashed on and popped (like it does when a bulb burns out). Chris couldn't take it anymore, and he put the blankets over his head. I was laughing, but I like paranormal stuff. It reminds me that our loved ones who have passed on are not far away. I kept teasing Chris, saying things like, "They are after you!" Then, inexplicably, the radio turned on for a few seconds, and then back off. Chris was ready to fly home. Fortunately for him, the weird stuff stopped happening. Eventually, we fell asleep, only to be awakened with the tragic news.

I really wish I would have noted what time all these strange things occurred, so I could compare it with the time Travis's body was found. We know it was around the same time, but I don't know exact times. Chris read somewhere many years ago (not in a "Mormon" book), that if a person dies in a situation where their body is not immediately discovered, their spirit can attend the body until it is discovered. Who knows if they have that option or not. We found it interesting that once things were set in motion to check on Travis, and Mimi, Michelle, Dallin, and Zach had discovered him, all of a sudden, we started having these unbelievably bizarre experiences. Any one of these four things that we experienced would not be cause for alarm. But when all four of these inexplicable events occur back to back, it must be more than a coincidence. When was the last time you had your lights off and one bulb flashed on and popped? Or one jet in a Jacuzzi tub turned on and shot water at the ceiling? Or your curtains flew up in the air? Or the radio turned on and then turned off with no one near it? Now, when was the last time all four of these things happened together within just a few minutes?

Travis in Hawaii with Chris

I know it was Travis. I can only imagine him letting out a huge "hyena laugh" every time something happened and Chris freaked out! Was this his way of asking us, "What the heck took so long, you fetchers"? ("Fetchers" is a nerdy Mormon cuss word.) Or maybe he just came to pester us with love, as he often did, or perhaps he just came to say good-bye and to let us know he was okay. Either way, we are glad he came. In the middle of the night, when we put two and two together and realized Travis had come to see us, it gave us incredible peace in the midst of this tragedy.

# CHAPTER 13

# "She Killed My Brother"

*Travis loved fashion. He was quite the dresser. He had some
really loud custom-made suits that he would match with an even
louder custom shirt and tie. He pulled it off. He was always well
dressed. He loved the book* Queer Eye for the Straight Guy. *It
deals with matters of fashion, style, personal grooming, interior
design, and culture. He used it as a guide for those things.*

UPON OUR RETURN FROM MEXICO, we learned about all the gruesome and
tragic details of Travis's murder. He had been stabbed twenty-nine
times, shot in the face with a .25 caliber pistol, and his throat was slit
from ear to ear. He had several defensive wounds on his hands. He
had been stabbed several times in his back and the back of his head.
My heart broke again! Our poor, poor Travis! We wept at the news. It
was gut wrenching to imagine Travis having to go through that.

After getting settled in, we heard through the grapevine that Ryan
Burns had continued talking to Jodi, even though she was murder
suspect number one. He didn't believe that she could have done it.
When we learned they were still talking, Chris called him and spent
hours telling him all about our experiences with Jodi and the scary
things she had done to Travis. He explained that she was not who
Ryan thought she was. Chris finally said, "Ryan, please, for your own
good, don't return her calls. Don't text her. Completely ignore her.

Act like she doesn't exist, and mark my words, when you do, watch out, because she's gonna turn on the sex!" That was her method of operation. If the boys didn't like Jodi for who she thought they wanted her to be, she reverted to sex.

Ryan didn't talk to her for a few days, and she did exactly what Chris said she would. She put it on him. She started sending him provocative messages, telling him what she wanted to do to him, and with him, when she saw him next. Sadly, Ryan still wouldn't believe us. He said there was just no way she was capable of such a thing; after all, he reminded us, he was a psychology major. He felt that if she had brutally killed Travis, or anyone for that matter, just before coming to his house to hookup, he would have known something was off. But he said she acted totally normal. Ryan later said he had wanted to stay away from Jodi, simply because he respected Chris, but he really liked her and could not fathom the possibility that she was the culprit. Staying away from her didn't last long.

As a side note, after killing Travis, Jodi headed to hook up with Ryan Burns. After leaving Ryan's house, Jodi reached out to my little brother, Zion, who set Ryan and Jodi up (against my warnings). She told him, via text or a phone call, that she didn't feel things between her and Ryan were going to work out because Ryan, according to her, wasn't a very "devout Mormon." She told Zion that Ryan didn't have a "strong enough testimony of the gospel of Jesus Christ." He wasn't spiritual enough for her. This is coming from the "Mormon" chick who just had sex with Travis, slaughtered him, and tried to have sex with Ryan. Hollywood could not have come up with anything more absurd.

I believe it was Michelle who took Travis's dog, Napoleon, home. It wasn't long after Jodi "heard the news" of Travis's death that she began trying to get Napoleon. She was calling people trying to get in touch with Michelle, stating, "Travis wanted me to have Napoleon in the case anything happened to him." We caught wind of this and immediately called Taylor and told him that Napoleon goes to Deanna, and to please tell Michelle to not give him to Jodi. Michelle suspected that Jodi killed Travis, but we didn't know that. When she couldn't get his beloved Napoleon, she went after his car.

Mike Chapman was the original executor of Travis's will. He had been called as a Mormon bishop and just didn't have the time to do all that came along with being executor, so he asked Chris, who was listed as the backup, if he could do it. Before he had turned things over to Chris, he had received a call or two from Jodi. We had previously told him that we were convinced that Jodi had killed Travis, so he called us in a panic! He told us that she had left him a message to call her back. He asked what he should do. Chris told him to call her back and see what she wanted. He called her back, and she told him that Travis had given her the BMW, and she needed the title. He told her he would get back to her and immediately called us. We told him she was lying, and that she was making payments on it (more on this later). We recommended that he ask her for proof that Travis had *given* it to her. He was nervous about making her mad for obvious reasons, but he went ahead and made the call to ask for some sort of proof. He said it caught Jodi off guard as she stumbled around with her words; she said she didn't have anything like that and said good-bye. She called him back shortly after and said she just remembered that Travis sent her an email stating he'd given her the car and no money was owed. Mike asked if she could send him that email. She did. After looking at it closely and comparing it to other forwarded emails, it was clear that she fabricated the email. It wasn't even a good fake. Mike was freaking out. This was his first interaction with her.

Two weeks after Travis's murder, there was a memorial in Arizona, and, no surprise, Jodi showed up! Not only did she show up, but she asked Aaron, a friend of hers and Travis's, to drive her by Travis's house just to see it. Sickening. Once at the memorial, she played the part of a grieving widow. She thanked people for coming and told them how much it would have meant to Travis that they came. One of our friends, Larry, reported that she gave him a hug and thanked him for coming. He said every hair on his body stood up, and a cold feeling came over him. He thought, *Oh my gosh, she killed him.* As Deanna gave the eulogy, Jodi stared at her with an eerie smirk on her face.

Elisha Schabel, a friend of Travis's, shared the following experience about the Arizona memorial:

*There are so many memories with Travis in that building. My first Sunday back as I sat there, flooding memories came back of Jodi Arias approaching me at Travis's memorial service, now almost seven years ago. That's why I was so devastated when he wasn't picking up his phone that early June day in 2008, as I was sobbing in my car, driving home to my now ex-husband, knowing my marriage was going down the drain. I was struggling to cope with that. I JUST knew that if I called Travis he KNEW what would make me smile and laugh and then I would be able to go on my merry way, feeling better about my situation. I felt particularly drawn to calling him, because I had missed him for SO long. He was dating Jodi during the time of my marriage. My then-fiancé forbade me to carry on a friendship with Travis after we were married. I was sick about that, and thought my ex would eventually come around and soften up to the idea of us remaining friends, and even double date with Travis and whatever girl he was dating at the time, even Jodi. I respected my fiancé's wishes and never contacted Travis after I was married. It about killed me, but I needed to focus on my marriage and my family. I had to turn away the single life and live as a married person. However, I did watch him on Myspace and saw who he was dating at different times, and I would just watch from afar, wishing I could be a part of it and know all the details. That's how I knew about Jodi and apparently how she knew about me.*

*When I showed up to Travis's memorial service at the building just off of Hawes and Guadalupe in Mesa, Arizona, in June 2008, Jodi Arias approached me immediately upon my arrival into the chapel. At this particular time, a feeling washed over me that I hope to never feel in my lifetime ever again. It was clear as day and said, "That is the girl who killed Travis." "Um, what?" As you could imagine, I was startled and taken back, way back. I mean, it's not every day, you "hear" those words come to you so clearly and concisely, yet no words were ever spoken audibly. It came from my right side and washed over me, like truth I had recognized in the past. The way the message came was not foreign to me. The message, of course, was foreign to me. I wasn't even sure at that time that it was a murder. I had only heard bits of information from the news and friends, but I didn't know what was truly going on. I was so wrapped up and distraught in my failing marriage that I couldn't keep anything straight. It was such a devastating time for me. To have what I think was a witness come to me still haunts me. But I knew the truth, no matter what anyone ever said to the contrary. So, as Jodi approached me, this is what I was feeling. I was just about to have my very first encounter with his murderess. I was shocked and heartbroken and yet was somehow able to keep my cool, maybe because I felt that if I didn't she would turn on me too. Jodi was "pleasant," and even hugged me, forcefully. It was not a welcomed hugged, but I reciprocated to "play nice" and show that I was a respectful person. She rattled off all these facts she said she knew about me, starting with, "You're a professional photographer too!" and, "Travis talked about you all the time!" and, "I would LOVE to learn from you more about photography and even have you shoot my wedding someday." Looking back, I feel she must have done her homework on me and ALL of the women in his life. It is scary to me now. Travis never talked to me about her because of our disconnection as friends.*

*One of the last text messages I ever exchanged with him, I asked if he and Jodi were still together. He said no and quickly changed the subject. All it took was literally one second for me to know what she was all about. I can easily tell the difference between truth and lies. She was full of lies that night. She was putting on one heck of a charade. Knowing what she did made me sick, yet it allowed me to watch her very intently and be acutely aware of her whereabouts and just observe her. And that's what I did the entire night. I observed her and others. I was repulsed by what I observed.*

*Jodi had made a picture book for all of us to sign at the memorial service of all the pictures she had taken of Travis. There was a small group of us left after the service was over. I remember the tears in everyone's eyes and the horror on the faces of those who found Travis's body. I won't speak for them, but I know their lives are forever altered. My life is forever altered just by seeing their faces and experiencing these moments with them and Jodi at that service. As we all sat there trying to find comfort in each other, asking the tough questions as to whom could do this to our friend, she was nodding along and pretending to be distraught too. Jodi was playing a role and was an actress that day. I saw right through her.*

*Jodi was also looking over our shoulders as we wrote our final good-byes in this book she had made. She looked over my shoulder as I was writing the words, "This isn't good-bye, Travis, this is, 'See you later, my friend. I love you forever.'" Jodi commented on my writings and said, "That's neat what you wrote there, that this isn't good-bye," and she flashed her fake smile. I looked up and gave a respectful yet annoyed look, hoping she would get the hint to step away from me as I took this moment to pay my final respects to my best friend. As you can imagine, it was awkward, painful, and uncomfortable with her there knowing that she was his killer. I shall never forget this day and the feelings I felt. It was pure evil coming from her, but pure and genuine love and sadness from his friends and family. There was no sadness coming from her, whatsoever.*

It took a while for the coroner to release Travis's body, so Travis's funeral was planned for June 21, 2008, in Riverside, California. We were at our house with a bunch of people when we started talking about Travis's funeral. Our friend Mario said something about picking up Jodi from the airport. Chris thought he misunderstood.

"What'd you say?" Chris asked.

"I'm gonna be picking Jodi up from the airport," said Mario.

"Bro, do you not know?" Chris asked.

"Know what?" asked Mario.

"Mario, Jodi killed Travis. We know for a fact she's the one who did it. They're building their case against her."

Mario was shocked.

"She's not welcome at the funeral, Mario. She did it," I said, "We know she did it. If she shows up, I'm going to jail, so it would be best if you call her and tell her you can't pick her up." He was quietly resistant, but he agreed to call her and come up with some story about why he couldn't pick her up from the airport.

Later in the day, Mario said that Jodi called Maria, another one of our friends, for a ride. At one point, Travis had taken an interest in Maria, so in true Jodi fashion, she became friends with her. Maria was planning on picking her up until I called her and explained that Jodi killed Travis. I told her that Jodi wasn't welcome at the funeral. I asked her if she would please call Jodi and let her know she wasn't welcome. Maria was resistant. She's such a nice girl, and she felt bad about canceling. Finally, I said, "Just call and tell her that I told you she was the one who killed Travis. And that she's not welcome at the funeral." Reluctantly, she called Jodi. I can't remember what she ended up telling her, but Jodi never showed up.

Either the day before or the day of the funeral, Jodi called Abe, one of the men she had used in an attempt to make Travis jealous. She explained to him how upset she was that she was not going to make it to the funeral. The story she told him was that she was driving (not flying), and that she got a flat tire. It took the tow truck hours to get to her, and she was devastated that she wasn't going to be able to make it. She wasn't driving, because she had asked people to pick her up from the airport, and I really question whether she ever got a flat tire. She was trying to arrange a ride from the airport only days before.

Travis's funeral was held at a Mormon church in Riverside, California, Travis's hometown. The funeral was a wonderful celebration of Travis's life. Long before the funeral started, the chapel had been completely filled. There was a collapsible wall at the back of the chapel that separated the chapel from the gymnasium. The wall had to be collapsed, as the gym filled all the way to the back. There were about one thousand people in attendance, in addition to the several hundred at the memorial in Arizona! He had touched the lives of so many people. Everyone was either laughing or crying, or both, almost the whole time, which was how Travis would have wanted it. Deanna gave the eulogy, Chad Perkins and Chris gave great talks, and members of Travis's family shared wonderful memories of him. Chad had met Travis in high school, and they remained very close over the years. He absolutely adored Chad and his wife, Heather. Brint and Brea Hiatt, and Dave and Pam Robinson provided beautiful musical numbers. The Hiatts were a second family to Travis. He would often go to their home for Sunday dinners. Dave was Travis's youth leader who had a huge impact on Travis's life.

Travis with the Hiatt Family

After the funeral, we drove to the cemetery. It was over one hundred degrees, and even still, hundreds of people came to the graveside. Mike Chapman, Travis's longtime, close friend, gave a talk and prayed at the grave. My brother, Zion, played his guitar and sang a song he had written.

Travis Alexander, Zion Lovingier, Chris Hughes, and Mike Chapman

After the graveside ceremony, the funeral director apologized as he stepped in and said something like, "I don't speak at the funerals I direct, but I just had to say something to all of you. You make me wish I had known this young man. I have never experienced anything like this. From the service, to what happened here, there is obviously something very special about this man. I am amazed that there are so many people out in this heat. Travis must have been quite the person to elicit such a response. Thank you."

You can see Travis's funeral program at: www.ourfriendtravis.com/program

It was obvious that the funeral was overwhelming for Norma, Travis's grandmother, or Mum-mum, as she was called. Travis was very special to her, and his death broke her heart. It might have just been too much to handle, as her health quickly deteriorated after his death. I do feel it was a blessing that she passed away shortly before the trial started. His death nearly killed her. I can only imagine her having to sit through all of Jodi's lies as she continued to butcher him again and again, long after his death. It would have been unbearable for her. What his family had to go through as they sat in that courtroom, day after day, month after month, was torture to watch. I was so sorry to hear of Mum-mum's passing just weeks before the start of the 2013 trial, but I felt comforted that she would not have to endure the trial. As a disturbing side note, after Travis's body was discovered, Jodi sent Mum-mum lilies. Upon seeing whom they were from, Mum-mum threw them in the trash.

Detective Flores called me one day and told me they were no longer looking at Jodi, because it looked like she didn't have anything to do with Travis's murder. I almost dropped the phone. I panicked and tried to convince him otherwise. He held his ground, saying they had a new lead. He gave me two names and asked if I knew them. I told him I didn't know them, but I knew they were friends of Travis.

After hanging up, I immediately told Chris what Flores had said. Chris was stunned. He couldn't believe it! We needed to do something! We needed to find evidence that proved that Jodi did this. We needed to find out what was going on between them in the days and weeks leading up to the murder. Travis and Chris shared a web developer. Chris called him and asked if he, by chance, had Travis's password to his blog. He did and he gave it to us. We used that password in an attempt to get into Travis's Gmail account, and to our great surprise, it worked!

We spent the entire night scouring every email and Google Chat between Travis and Jodi, from the time they met to the day she killed him, and oddly, even after. We also read many other email exchanges between him and other people. It was all there! Jodi's motive and her attempts to cover up her crime were all in his Gmail account. We knew we had the evidence Flores needed to arrest her! We were both overcome with relief.

I told Chris we should print all of Travis and Jodi's email and chat exchanges. I guess I had watched too many crime shows and was afraid this evidence would somehow be lost. Some of it was risqué, and Chris said he didn't want any of it in our house. I wish we would have printed it though; if not all of it, at least our emails back and forth with Travis. It would be so nice to have those.

I called Flores first thing in the morning. He probably thought I was on drugs. I started screaming, "She did it! She did it! Jodi killed Travis and we have proof!" I told him about a big fight they had via email and Google Chat. The fight occurred on May 26, 2008, just a week before his murder. I also informed him of the fact that Jodi wrote emails to Travis after he was dead in an effort to cover her tracks. She had already killed him, and she wrote an email talking about how since he was in Mexico, she was going to come to his house, eat his oatmeal, and sleep in his comfy bed "like she always does." The next email she wrote to him explained that she was worried because she hadn't heard from him and was wondering if everything was okay. She said she had wanted to call their friends, but didn't, suggesting that it would be weird. I told Flores, "These emails are written to you, the cops! Not Travis! She was not allowed in his house when he wasn't there, and she knew that!" Travis had accused her of stealing his journals and an engagement ring he purchased for Linda years earlier that he was going to trade in when he was ready to get married. Jodi was banned from his house when he wasn't there. Flores asked for Travis's Gmail login name and password. Within minutes of giving it to him, the password had changed, and we were locked out.

Even with this new information, no arrest was made and we were really on edge. We knew Jodi hated us, and we didn't feel safe. At the time, we were living on a sixty-acre horse ranch in Murrieta, California. Chris refused to feed the horses alone in the dark for fear that Jodi would jump out with a gun or a knife, or both! I was afraid to let my little boys play in the yard without us there for fear that Jodi would grab them and take them out of the country and raise them, or worse. I finally called Flores. I told him my concerns and that I needed to know my family was safe. He assured me they were, and that they knew Jodi's every move.

Later, we would discover Detective Flores had intentionally thrown us and others off in an attempt to preserve the case. Jodi had been the prime suspect the entire time. Some of Travis's friends, those who were also close to Jodi, were getting information about the investigation and feeding it to Jodi. I didn't know at the time, but Flores was trying to prevent information from getting to Jodi, and, possibly attempting to put her at ease so she didn't flee. He wanted her to think they were looking at someone else. Little did we know, Flores already knew, for certain, that Jodi Arias killed Travis Alexander on June 4, 2008.

Chris and I were later subpoenaed by the defense for going into Travis's email accounts. We were questioned by the defense at a hearing long before the actual trial started. Kirk Nurmi, the lead on the defense, kept trying to get us to commit to a specific number of emails and chat conversations we read. Neither of us took the bait. We believed Nurmi wanted us to commit to a number of emails we read, so that he could accuse us of destroying evidence. So ridiculous. First of all, I would be way too scared to do that, because it's wrong. Secondly, were we to have deleted something, computer experts can see what was deleted and when. And finally, there was so much in there that was so damning to Jodi, I wanted to scream it from the rooftops, not delete it!

On July 15, 2008, I was rocking my baby, Taj, who was two and a half months old at the time, when my phone rang. It was Travis's little sister, Hillary.

"They got her! She killed my brother! Jodi killed my brother!" she said sobbing, "They arrested her for murdering my brother!"

I cried for hours, and then on and off for days. We knew it was she, but I wanted so badly to be wrong because of what that meant for Travis. We knew he suffered physically, but to be tortured and stabbed repeatedly by someone he loved? The emotional torture of being stabbed over and over and over again had to be so much worse than the physical pain. I can only imagine him asking her with every stab, *Why are you doing this to me?* while begging her to stop. What kind of a monster could do what she did to him? She never cared about him. I think she is incapable of caring about anyone other than herself. When she was finally arrested for his murder at her grandparents' home in Yreka, California, she didn't cry, she didn't show emotion. She only asked if she could get her makeup.

## INTERROGATION

When being booked, Jodi smiled in her mugshot. Classic Jodi. When asked about it during a TV interview, Jodi gave three reasons for her seemingly happy demeanor just shortly after being arrested for one of the most gruesome murders in Arizona history. First, she stated that were Travis in the same situation, "He would be smiling. He would be like, 'Hey!' and flash his grin that he always does." Next, she said she knew her mugshot "would be all over the Internet, so why not?" And finally, she claimed, "I'm innocent."

Just as she gave multiple reasons for her smiling mugshot, she would eventually give multiple stories about what happened to Travis that day. The first story she offered the day she was arrested was, "I wasn't there." That story wasn't going to fly. While interrogating her, Detective Flores did a masterful job of hanging her up. He let her go on and on about how she had not seen Travis since April 2008. She was feeling pretty smug, I'm sure, until he informed her he had photos of her and Travis together in Travis's bedroom the day of the murder.

In her haste to get out of Travis's house before his roommates came home from work, Jodi wrapped up Travis's camera in his sheets and threw it all in the washing machine. They had used this camera to take pictures earlier in the day. In addition to pictures taken of Travis and Jodi, it appeared that the camera had been knocked off the counter and on it's way down it snapped a picture of Jodi standing over a bleeding Travis. Detective Flores also informed her that he found her bloody palm print on Travis's bathroom wall. Incredibly, she continued to deny that she was at his home the day of the murder. Flores even *showed* her a nude photograph of her at Travis's house, time and date stamped June 4, 2008, the day of the murder. Leaning across the table, as if to take a better look, she said, almost in a questioning tone, "That looks like me?"

Apparently, she reevaluated her tale overnight, and realizing she was caught, she had to change her story. If she was to have a remote chance at a defense, "I wasn't there" was not going to work. The new story was, yes, she was there, but the real culprit, or culprits, were two masked intruders, a man and a woman. They attacked her and Travis, but luckily, she was able to escape. She told Detective Flores that Travis was alive when she escaped.

There was a third story the media never covered in great detail. It never grew legs because it was, perhaps, her most ridiculous story to date. In short, the story was that Travis was a pedophile. The accusations revolved around alleged letters from Travis to Jodi where he admitted to having "sex with boys" and to beating her. The letters were fabricated, forged, and concocted by Team Jodi. The entire story from start to finish was a cesspool of desperation and lies. More on this in chapter seventeen.

CHAPTER 14

# Motive for Murder

*Travis enjoyed having serious conversations with*
*people. He loved getting to know people, and finding*
*out what they were passionate about.*

O<small>N</small> M<small>AY</small> 26, 2008, J<small>ODI</small> and Travis got into a big fight. This fight began in texts, and moved to email and Google Chat. During their fight, they also reference phone calls that took place. It is this May 26 fight that gave us the "proof" we were looking for when we thought Detective Flores needed to be convinced that Jodi had killed Travis. It's important to understand where Travis was mentally before this fight. Travis had been begging Jodi to move back to California since she moved to Arizona in the summer of 2007 after he had broken things off with her. His begging increased in January 2008, and continued to increase until she left in April 2008. On April 7, he texted her that if she didn't tell him the truth, he was going to tell us, the Udys, the Freemans, and her parents all the crazy things she had done. He was in complete turmoil, because he was living outside of integrity. He had no privacy for a year and a half, and she had been lying to him since the day she met him. He kept trying to get away from Jodi, but he kept finding himself back in her arms. He told her that he was addicted to her. Keep in mind, this fight was everything coming to a head. He was so sick of this destructive cycle, her constant lies, her intrusive behaviors, the betrayal, manipulations, and he was convinced she slashed his tires twice, slashed Lisa's tires, stole his journals, and she admitted to stealing an engagement ring from his drawer. And that is the shortlist of the things she had put him through. Finally, after all this time, Travis saw Jodi for who she really was.

Below, we only have the fight that took place on Google Chat, and we don't have the times. It will be interesting when all the evidence is released to put their fight together with emails, texts, and gaps where phone calls took place. However, this will give you a good idea of where Travis was mentally and what seemed to put Jodi's plan to slaughter him into action. Nine days after this fight, Travis was dead.

[The argument seems to go back and forth between Jodi's invasion of Travis's privacy, her chronic lying, and their sexual indiscretions. We did not make any corrections to this chat.]

> *Travis: i don't want bull shiz that neither of us believe*
> *Travis: just call me and tell me*
> *Travis: i want to hear it*
> *Travis: because I feel it will be the first pure truth youve ever told me*
> *Jodi: this is difficult. It will only piss you off more.*
> *Travis: why*
> *Jodi: Because sometimes the truth suck!*
> *Jodi: s*
> *Travis: call*
> *Jodi: call you?*
> *Travis: yes*
> *Travis: and tel me*
> *Jodi: right now?*
> *Travis: yes*
> *Jodi: deal*
> *Travis: but say it*
> *Travis: right*
> *Travis: right*

*Travis: right*

*Travis: hello*

*Travis: Jodi?*

*Jodi: I'm here*

*Travis: right*

*Jodi: right*

*Travis: so let's wuit with the bull shiz*

*Jodi: ok*

*Travis: all of that talk has happened many times and it has never changed anything*

*Travis: so lets quit with it*

*Travis: ur not sorry*

*Travis: im ok with that if ypull admit it.*

*Travis: it should be libersting to you*

*Travis: liberating*

*Travis: right*

*Travis: right*

*Travis: right?*

*Travis: am i talking to myself*

*Jodi: No*

*Travis: am I talking to myself?*

*Jodi: no*

*Travis: why cant you respons*

*Jodi: you're not talking to yourself*

*Travis: what is taking you so long*

*Jodi: I reading what you mssaged me on Facebook.*

*Jodi: I didn't know you were chatting w/me there.*

*Travis: oh well*

*Travis: so we are clear*

*Jodi: Yes*

*Travis: so tell me the truth*

*Travis: tell me that you are not sory*

*Jodi: I can't just say it as a blanket statement like that. It's too convoluted. It's not black and white*

*Travis: and be specific*

*Travis: okay well say it with details*

*Travis: okay*

*Travis: so*

*Travis: what your point*

*Jodi: My point is that all of the things you said when you were playing the tough Travis is true.*

*Travis: i know they ae*

*Travis: are*

*Jodi: So there is really no point in me continuing to breathe. And that's not a poor-me cry for sympathy.*

*Travis: listen*

*Travis: weve been over this*

*Travis: Right?*

*Travis: might as well just give ut up*

*Travis:okay?*

*Jodi: ok*

*Travis: so we are done with all the pretenses*

*Travis: no more faking soy no more faking like im throught with you*

*Travis: through*

*Travis: sorry*

*Travis: my r's arent working*

*Jodi: Travis, in the most non-pretentious way, you are like an angel that gets snared by evil influences. But I. too, am like an angel that gets ensnared by evil influences. And along I come, looking like an angel, speaking sweetly, acting nicely, pleasing you in ways you had only fantasized and of course it's easy to get caught up in that. I*

*Travis: well?*

*Travis: it will save us a lot of time and energy*

*Travis: ur not sorry so quit apologizing*

*Travis: and that way I can quit forgiving*

*Travis: deal*

*Jodi: umm...ok?*

*Jodi: I just don't want you to be miserable any more.*

*Travis: u don't care jodi*

*Jodi: I only contribute to the misery factor in your life.*

*Travis: just stop*

*Travis: its ok*

*Travis: I serve a purpose of yours*

*Travis: whateve it is*

*Travis: thats fine*

*Jodi: Then what do you want me to say? Whatever the purpose is, I don't understand it. I've tried to figure it out. It's not marriage. It's not sex.*

*Travis: I thought I might break away this time but you knew I couldn't*

*Jodi: I've proven it's not friendship*

*Jodi: Violated that one plenty of times*

*Travis: you knew one call and youd reel me in*

*Travis: you don't care jodi*

*Travis: just say this im not sorry*

*Jodi: I don't ever dare to hope for that at this point*

*Travis: and Ill be okay with it*

*Jodi: OK, maybe a spark of a dare*

*Travis: im not saying it's friendship*

*Travis: it is what it is*

*Travis: no reason to label it*

*Travis: lets just quit with it all*

*Travis: if you want to sneak around just tell me what you want and ill give it to you*

*Travis: youll get it anyway*

*Travis: then Ill yell*

*Travis: and then forgive*

*Travis: why go through all that*

*Travis: it was*

*Travis: the email and everything as true as it was*

*Travis: was my way of getting you closer*

*Travis: because i am addicted*

*Travis: you are ruining my life but I'm addicted*

*Travis: so thats fine*

*Travis: ruin it*

*Travis: but lets not hide behind the facad*

*Travis: jus tdo what you intend to do*

*Travis: Im am going to quit acting tough*

*Travis: you know it's my own facade*

*Travis: anyway*

*Travis: So Ill quit with mine*

*Travis: now you quit with yours*

*Jodi: Honestly, aside from what I wanted to say, it was me that wanted to hear your voice just once. It's like a little fix. You're not the only one addicted.*

*Travis: well lets just ruin each others life then*

*Travis: I don't care any more*

*Travis: if you want my freaking passwords just ask*

*Jodi: Because I'm horrible*

*Travis: whatever you may have found it wasn't bad enough to deter you from whatever your purpose is so who freaking cares*

*Travis: im just tired of all this*

*Travis: its killing me*

*Travis: seriously I can't stand it*

*Travis: I cant keep up with this cycle*

*Travis: so lets cut out the act*

*Travis: so there*

*Travis: its out*

*Travis: lets just quit with the pretense*

*Travis: I trued to stay away this time*

*Jodi: No. I don't want to hurt you anymore. Bless you for your forgiveness, but you deserve better, and I don't deserve you.*

*Travis: but you called*

*Travis: and you made sure I heard your voice*

*Travis: u knew that would be enough*

*Travis : not how many infractions*

*Travis: It's obvious by anyones reason that I should have never have anything to do with you*

*Travis: you just kill me*

*Travis: every time*

*Travis: and I keep taking you back*

*Travis: I hqve come to terms with it*

*Travis: I am in partial addicted to you*

*Travis: the positives*

*Travis: if all you were is positive*

*Travis: or your good facade that is in fact an act*

*Travis: I'm addicted to it*

*Travis: But it's bull s@#%*

*Jodi: well there aren't any positives left now, so you won't be addicted much longer*

*Travis: yet I'm addicted to it*

*Travis: and you know it*

*Travis: and you know Ii will always take you back*

*Travis: you always know*

*Travis: you know Ill get pissed but ill take you back*

*Travis: you know if you just equal the drama with my anger ill take you back*

*Travis: and thats why you don't hesitate to keep ruining me*

*Jodi: I wish I were better*

*Travis: because you know you can*

*Travis: and youll get away with it*

*Travis: you know it*

*Jodi: I don't want to*

*Travis: okay jodi you win*

*Travis: im addicted*

*Travis: I know how thisis gonna unfold already*

*Travis: im gonna fogive you and you are gonna do it again*

*Travis: i know that*

*Travis: and I am gonna forgive you*

*Travis: and you are gonna do it again*

*Travis: I know it*

*Travis: why can't you reward me for trusting in you over and over again*

*Jodi: Because there is no excuse for me to be alive*

*Travis: i want a real answer*

*Jodi: I don't deserve any rewards*

*Travis: u dont*

*Travis: I want a real answer*

*Jodi: I don't have an answer. I really am awful. Truly. Can't you agree that that's the truest thing I've typed thus far?*

*Travis: please Jodi*

*Travis: why*

*Travis: what was your reasoning*

*Travis: why did you try to cover it up afte I told you I knew*

*Travis: why do you always li*

*Travis: e*

*Travis: thisisn't fair to me*

*Travis: please*

*Travis: dont you see*

*Travis: the pattern*

*Travis: you do something to make any sane person shun you*

*Travis: what do i do I forgive you*

*Travis: I lash you and forgive*

*Travis: then you do it again*

*Travis: I talk tough and forgive*

*Travis: you do it again*

*Travis: I talk tougher and still for give*

*Travis: this has happened about 30 times*

*Travis: thats how many times youve been caught*

*Jodi: Just because I'm not whoring around doesn't mean that I wouldn't act any different. I need to keep myself out of that situation.*

*Jodi: Which of course isn't a problem at this point*

*Travis: so have messed around with anyone else*

*Jodi: you're the last person I've ever been intimate with.*

*Travis: nut you would like to be with someone else wouldn't you*

*Travis: but*

*Jodi: My sex drive is gone.*

*Travis: i doubt that*

*Jodi: I haven[t dittled myself since I moved here except for the times when we were on the phone and we did it together.*

*Travis: well it didnt seem to be a problem on the phone*

*Jodi: Of course not. That's the affect you have. Nobody else can do that. Absolute kryptonite. I don't want to be a whore. I could joke that if being a whore for Travis is wrong then I don't wanna be right. But this isn't the time for jokes. I've been a bad influence*

*Travis: like I said Im not mad about that.*

*Jodi: I know Travis*

*Travis: Why did you get in my facebook*

*Travis: after all thos*

*Travis: these times I have forgiven you*

*Jodi: Because I suck*

*Jodi: The sexual part for me was an unevolved way of trying to be more loved. I knew you weren't in love with me. I knew you cared, but that it wasn't that kind of love. So when we made love, I was able to actually convince myself, yes lie to myself. It really felt for that space of time that it was something bigger and better. But that's the intoxication felt from sex. And you made it so good. You became another person. It's like you nearly worshipped me. I felt sooo so so loved when we did that. It became absolutely addicting.*

*Jodi: But you weren't just a piece of meat.*

*Jodi: Either way, that doesn't speak for the way I've treated you outside of your bedroom.*

*Travis: no ill admit you were noble in the sack*

*Travis: but its because it served you to be*

*Jodi: I know. The better I was, the more you wanted me, and the more you wanted me, the more we got to be together.*

*Jodi: I was a whore for you because I was a whore for that feeling.*

*Jodi: I was a whore in general and I still am.*

*Travis: and you like being a whoe*

*Travis: whore*

*Travis: unless you could get something sexual from me*

*Travis but outside of that nothing else about is worth anything to you*

*Travis: and how do I know*

*Travis: because your actions speak it loud and clear*

*Travis: and you have nothing to say in eply*

*Jodi: Everything I feel moved to say wouldn't hold an ounce of weight with you.*

*Jodi: But what I was going to say is this*

*Jodi: So I guess that means that at the core I'm not sorry.*

*Jodi: but I still struggle with guilt and regret over it.*

*Travis: ur not sorry for invading my privacy either Travis: but atleast I know where my value to youis Travis: and its not much more than that*

*Travis: i was a source of pleasure*

*Travis: thats it*

*Travis: nothing else*

*Travis: at the core I don't think you cae if I live or die*

*Travis: I really dont*

*Travis: the pain u have caused is worse than death*

*Travis: at times*

*Travis: i thought you were something that you were not*

*Travis: you scamed me*

*Travis: and you knew you were scaming me*

*Travis: i think you would choose a dollar bill over my life*

*Travis: its the other stuff that is blatant lies that I have a problem with*

*Travis: ur not sorry*

*Travis: u know ur not*

*Travis: so why say it*

*Travis: u know ur not sorry*

*Travis: If I was there ud prove how not sorry u r*

*Travis: so lets just leave it at that*

*Jodi: If you were here, I don't know. But you're not here and I'm not there, and we're behaving ourselves.*

*Jodi: I get so caught up in wanting to do the right thing*

*Jodi: And then when you come around I want to do a different version of the "right thing" and it may be a two-way*
*Jodi: street, but I*
*Jodi: nevermind. We shouldn't even be discussing this.*
*Jodi: I don't know what else to say.*
*Travis: say ur not sorry for it*
*Jodi: Part of me is glad we did that. Is it wrong to feel that way?*
*Jodi: Don't answer.*
*Travis: i don't know*
*Jodi: It is*
*Travis: but ur not sorry*
*Travis: i know ur not*
*Jodi: It is a struggle inside of me. I want to take the high road, but the selfish part of me wants to take you and if you were here and the opportunity presented itself, then I most likely would.*
*Travis: i think you are just demented and somehow thought taking from me somehow benefit you.*
*Jodi: Speaking of taking*
*Travis: i think I was little more than a dildo with ah eart beat to you*
*Jodi: I would have been content just cuddling, but I wasn't strong enough.*
*Jodi: Again I am sorry for that.*
*Jodi: I was way overcome.*
*Travis: no your not*
*Jodi: It was wrong*
*Travis: i know you're not*
*Travis: I ask that you not lie*
*Travis: you ae not sorry*
*Travis: youre not*
*Travis: i don't ask that you be sorry*
*Travis: i ask that you dont lie Travis: youre not sorry*
*Travis: and I don't care*
*Travis: im ok with you not being sorry about that*

*Travis: its me too*

*Jodi: Yeah, but it was more me.*

*Jodi: I should have been better.*

*Travis: theny why*

*Travis: why did you try to ruin me*

*Travis: why*

*Travis: just tell me why*

*Travis: u arent who you say you ae*

*Travis: so tell me why*

*Travis: even now you only talk but your actions show that you hate me*

*Travis: even right now*

*Jodi: I don't know what you mean by ruin you? I would never deliberately set out to do that. I was bitter, yes, but I tried to be a big girl in other ways: by lending you my few hundred dollars when your re-fi depended on it, by giving you a [Pre-paid Legal] membership [sale] that would have taken me out of charge-backs, by devoting time to pushing you through those last few counters [sales] at the last hours of the month so you would qualify [for your bonuses]. It was an endless struggle. I was resentful for other things, but I've always wanted you to succeed. I haven't deliberately set out to try and ruin you. I am so sorry for what I have done.*

*Jodi: Those nice things listed above don't even begin to add up to*

*Jodi: counter balance the horrible things I've done.*

*Jodi: It should have all been different. It's my fault.*

*Jodi: I am 100% responsible for this.*

*Travis: you did those thing to reel me in*

*Travis: it was about you*

*Travis: why did you manipulate me into loving you*

*Travis: why me*

*Travis: i was a good guy*

*Travis: why did you have to do it to me*

*Travis: why do you hat eme*

*Travis: me*

*Travis: what was your objective*

*Jodi: There have been times when you've screamed into the phone so loud at me that the speaker was distorted and then you hung up. The pain was so sharp and so deep that I just couldn't process it. I could only scream in response to the air. And I would scream at the top of my lungs until my throat was raw, "I HATE YOU! I HATE YOU! I HATE YOU!" Until I had no energy left to say it and it had wittled down to a little whimp,"… i hate you…" And I just sobbed and cried until I couldn't breath.*

*Jodi: But you know what? I deserved all of that. Every angry phone call. Every unpleasant word*

*Travis: what was the point*

*Jodi: doesn't compare to what I've put you through*

*Jodi: It doesn't begin to measure up.*

*Jodi: I've done you more wrong and that is apparent without even keeping score.*

*Travis: you only showed that you hated me*

*Travis: never love*

*Travis: only hate*

*Travis: ur words were lies*

*Jodi: I did try, but I didn't try hard enough.*

*Travis: your actions were truths*

*Travis: no*

*Travis: you didn't ty*

*Travis: What you did to me wasnt trying to love*

*Travis: it was succeeding to hate*

*Travis: cant you just tell the truth*

*Travis: please*

*Jodi: Yes, I just became so resentful. It was all very selfish. An act to try to protect myself from the pain, but it didn't work. I didn't want to hurt you either. I am so sorry.*

*Travis: so many times I have stared you in the eye and said if you ever had any love for me youll tell me truth right now and youd look straight into my eyes and lie*

*Travis: and I knew it*

*Jodi: If it was unconditional love, it would have never hurt you.*

*Jodi: I'm just not worth it. I'm not.*

*Jodi: You have so many bright and wonderful things on your horizon.*

*Travis: i know that*

*Travis: i want you to admit it*

*Travis: your actions prove you hate me*

*Travis: tell me the truth I hate you*

*Travis: say it*

*Travis: I want the truth just once*

*Travis: and then tell me why you hate me and desire to ruin my life*

*Travis: why do you only try to ham me*

*Travis: ive sacrificed so much for you.*

*Travis: I have taken so much heat for you*

*Travis: and dfended you*

*Travis: defended the lies you told others with the lies you told me*

*Jodi: I'm sorry Travis*

*Travis: i gave you anything I could I sacrificed everything I could and you just tried to murder me from the inside out*

*Travis: how could you*

*Jodi: It wasn't really my intention to harm you*

*Jodi: Please understand that*

*Travis: you ae so concerned with how many tears ive cried*

*Travis: you dont know what horror you have caused me Travis: you can not conceive*

*Travis: you have not felt as much pain in all your life than what you have repeatedly caused me with your lies and your invasions and the psycho s@#$ you have subjected me to*

*Travis: you have made me want to die*

*Travis: on countless occasions*

*Travis: you have hurt me so bad over and over again*

*Travis: and how do you repay me forgiving you by doing the same thing again*

*Travis: couldn't you ever try to love me*

*Travis: u never saw me of more value as a piece of s@#$ unless I was serving some purpose*

*Travis: i am less than nothing to you*

*Jodi: I really did love you. But I let it get so distorted.*

*Jodi: I'm so so so sorry*

*Jodi: I have no excuse*

*Jodi: none*

*Travis: say the truth*

*Jodi: I just wish you weren't hurting right now.*

*Travis: i am s@#$ to you*

*Travis: it would be the first true thing you have ever said to me*

*Jodi: I wish that's all you were to me. I try to tell myself that everyday. That you mean NOTHING. And every time a*

*Jodi: feeling started to creep back in I suppress it*

*Jodi: and I tell myself that you are worthless to me*

*Jodi: I"m so sorry,*

*Jodi: I really am.*

*Jodi: You deserve so much more than the crap I've given to you*

*Jodi: You deserve a wealth that is beyond this world.*

*Jodi: And I deserve a pile of s@#$ for what I've done to my friend*

*Travis: if I do why do you only try to harm me*

*Travis: u*

*Jodi: I don't want to care about you*

*Travis: dont*

*Travis: csare*

*Travis: you dont care*

*Jodi: I don't want to care about you at all.*

*Travis: just be honest*

*Jodi: If I didn't care, I would n't hurt and you wouldn't have gotten hur*

*Jodi: t*

*Travis: just quit lying*

*Travis: quit*

*Travis: cant you quit*

*Travis: all u have ever done is lie*

*Travis: you have only told partial truths to cover up lies*

*Travis: don't you see*

*Travis: u are why your life sucks*

*Travis: it ur lies!*

*Travis: just tell the truth*

*Travis: write something you stupid idiot*

*Travis: wow*

*Jodi: I may be a liar, I may be a whore, I may be evil, I may be a coward, I may not be worth the air that I breathe, I am most likely the most horrible person you've ever had the misfortune of knowing, but one thing I am NOT, is violent. I did not and would not and would never slash your tires*

*Travis: wow wow wow*

*Travis: u r something else*

*Travis: u r comical*

*Jodi: Nor did I have anything to do with that. I didn't and I wouldn't.*

*Travis: u r a laughing stock*

*Travis: after all I have done*

*Travis: how could you be the way you've been to me*

*Travis: how*

*Travis: I want an answer*

*Travis: NOW!!!*

*Jodi: I don't have an answer.*

*Jodi: I don't know why*

*Jodi: I hurt too*

*Travis: Let me tell you why*

*Jodi: I guess maybe it was my way of trying to renounce you*

*Travis: because you only care about Jodi*

*Jodi: I acted immature*

*Jodi: I acted stupid*

*Travis: u don't care about me*

*Jodi: I shouldn't have gone about it that way.*

*Travis: thats why*

*Jodi: What can I really say though? Jodi: "I agree" ??*

*Travis: u can tell the truth*

*Travis: tell it*

*Travis: once*

*Travis: u slashed the Fing tires*

*Travis: u did*

*Travis: I know u did*

*Travis: u r a liar*

*Travis: u don't care either*

*Travis: dont you see your lies why youir life is worthless*

*Travis: It will always be intil you tell the truth.*

*Travis: you have got to learn*

*Travis: can u learn*

*Travis: If not*

*Travis: you are taking up people air*

*Travis: ur freaking pathetic*

*Travis: that is what took u so long to write*

*Jodi: Well it would have been done sooner, but I was watching you type*

*Travis: u said u wee almost done and you lied again*

*Travis: u r worthless*

*Travis: u r s@#$!*

*Travis: cant you tell the truth*

*Travis: is it impossible*

*Travis: seriously*

*Travis: is it impossible*

*Travis: i loved someone who never existed*

*Travis: what I thought was real never even existed*

*Travis: finish your utterly worthless email*

*Travis: where is it*

*Travis: u sasid it was almost done*

*Travis: cant you tell the truth*

*Travis: i know you got into my computer and erased a letter I sent to Lisa*

*Travis: I know you did*

*Jodi:What?!*

*Jodi: No*
*Travis: shut up*
*Travis: shut up*
*Travis: i don't want more lies*
*Travis: u stole my journals*
*Travis: you slashed my tires*
*Travis: and I know it*
*Travis: i know it*
*Travis: why continue lying*
*Travis: dont you ever want to tell the truth*
*Travis: ever*
*Travis: u never have*
*Travis: is there any desire*
*Travis: any*
*Jodi: I can't send the email?*
*Travis: at all*
*Travis: why not*
*Travis: b@#$%*
*Travis: i have waited*
*Jodi: It's not letting me put your address in the recipient bar*
*Travis: and now you tell me no*
*Travis: copy it how freaking conveinant*
*Travis: did you ever even write one*
*Jodi: OK, I figured it out*
*Travis: that is ur email*
*Travis: who freaking cares about you*
*Jodi: I'm a full time bartender now a Mexican restaurant*
*Travis: u think I care about ur sob story after what you have done to me*
*Travis: a bartende*
*Travis: r*
*Travis: perfect*
*Jodi: It's not a sobe story*
*Travis: a sluts joc*
*Travis: b*

*Travis: maybe you can get tips for BJ's*

*Travis: oh im sure you can*

*Travis: u r good at that*

*Jodi: Yeah, according to what you've said, I'd have that car [Travis's BMW he sold her] paid off in one shift with vacation money to spare!*

*Jodi: Maybe I can use you as a reference*

*Travis: yeah you are a 3-hole wonder*

*Travis: you are good for something*

*Travis: and always have been*

*Travis: u have never given out the truth for truths sake*

*Travis: u never have*

*Travis: how must it be to be solely be a liar*

*Travis: nothing else*

*Travis: to live a life identical to satan*

*Travis: and you after everything send me some bulls@#$ thing down the pipe as you log into my facebook*

*Travis: you are a rotten lunatic*

*Jodi: What does that mean???*

*Travis: can't you remember when you chose to take away my human rights what I have done for you*

*Travis: cant all the things I have done to help you stop you from taking away what belongs to me*

*Travis: how can you be such an ingrate*

*Travis: how many times can someone pay someone for service by stabbing them in the back*

*Travis: how do you live*

*Travis: how does a heartbeat in such a corrupted carcass*

*Travis: ur email obviously wasnt almost finished another lie*

*Travis: do you know how to tell the truth*

*Travis: r u capable of it*

*Travis: have u ever*

*Travis: ever in ur life*

*Travis: when you have had the temptation to lie have you ever resisted it and told the truth*

*Travis: even once*

*Travis: of course not*

*Travis: ur parents must be proud*

*Jodi: They're not proud of me.*

*Travis: they shouldn't be*

*Jodi: they didn't even come to watch me sing even though the rest of my family did. Not that you care, but that's just to illustrate how much they're not proud.*

*Travis: miss high class server, can't even get a job at a freaking dine*

*Travis: even when you say u are telling the tuth you are lying*

*Travis: even when you come clean it is a partial version of the truth to seerve your purpose*

*Travis: you have been nothing but a liar from the beginning*

*Travis: u r evil*

*Travis: if I was*

*Travis: it is gone because of you*

*Travis: send your piece of s@#$ lie fest so I can mock it*

*Travis: we already know based on all the last emails you send, and then invaded my privacy that it is b@#$*%@#*

*Jodi: look, I don't want to be like this.*

*Travis: You ae like this*

*Jodi: I know*

*Travis: like I said I have never dealt with a more solid form of evil*

*Jodi: I don't know what to do*

*Jodi: I really am sorry for everything.*

*Jodi: I know you don't want apologies.*

*Jodi: I don't know what to say.*

*Travis: you are not sorry*

*Travis: what I want is for you to quit blatantly lying*

*Travis: we both know by your actions that view me as pure s@#$*

*Jodi: Can I just send the email? I'm almost finished…*

*Travis: pure freaking s@#$*

*Jodi: No, Travis*

*Travis: ur email is s@#$ too*

*Jodi: One day, it will be clear.*

*Travis: i hate you*

*Jodi: I've acted so wrong.*

*Travis: do realize that*

*Travis: i hate you*

*Travis: so much*

*Travis: you have been more cause of pain than the death of my father*

*Travis: You are relentless in your torture of people that have loved you and protected you and served you and what do you do*

*Travis: you try to destroy them*

*Travis: you are the lowest of the low*

*Travis: you are sick and evil and knowing you makes me want to kill myself in punishment*

*Travis: im so stupid*

*Travis: i don't even know if u r human*

*Travis: hitler had more of a concious*

*Jodi: I am so, so sorry. If anyone should it is me. You are light unto this world. I can't even compare.*

*Travis: than you*

*Travis: shut up*

*Travis: just shut up*

*Jodi: Only you would say that. Anyone else would see it for what it is: an Anchorman joke. I was just giving him a hard time for showing off and being such a ham. You and I had a conversation about this Facebook pics and their content. I was just razzing him.*

*Travis: no you were flirting with him and you know better*

*Travis: its danny jones.*

*Travis: maybe you are just on to the next d@#$*

*Travis: and he is an easy target*

*Jodi: His temperature is cold when it comes to that.*

*Travis: so you have checked it then*

*Travis: what a freaking whore*

*Travis: u r too much.*

*Travis: maybe kyle kimbrell then*

*Jodi: It's based off a vibe I got at [a business training] many months ago.*

*Jodi: I tried having a conversation with him, and he was cordial, but never flirty or anything like it.*

*Travis: im glad to see you are checking the vibe of danny jones you must feel so classy*

*Travis: yet you flit anyway*

*Jodi: Like you, I flirt because it's "harmless", "means nothing", and there are "no intentions" behing it.*

*Travis: don't freaking ignore me*

*Jodi: I'm emailing you!*

*Travis: and dont send me some worthless email with all your bogus lies*

*Travis: you dont know how to tell the truth*

*Jodi: OK Travis. What do you want me to do?*

*Travis: ur words are worthless*

*Travis: in everything you throw at me its all on agenda to save your own a@#*

*Travis: just like that disgusting call today*

*Travis: have you forgotten what is like to be human*

*Jodi: Perhaps.*

*Travis: have you forgotten you are dealing with humans*

*Jodi: no*

*Travis: by the way your little comment to Danny Jones makes you look like a cheap whore*

(Google Chats compliments of Beth Karas and karasoncrime.com)

It's morbid to realize that when she killed him, she did everything to him that he said she was doing to him in this fight. She stabbed him in the heart. She stabbed him in the back. And, ultimately, she killed him. After reading this, it makes me realize that the tongue-lashing I gave Travis on the four-wheeling trip, and my subsequent talks with him about cutting her completely out of his life were the equivalent of shaking an alcoholic or heroin addict while screaming, "Just stop it! Why won't you just stop?" Many people look at Travis and ask, "Well, if he was scared of her, why did he keep going back to her?" From what this fight tells us, he kept trying to get away. She called him, knowing he just needed to hear her voice and she was in complete control. While addicts know their addiction is killing them and they hate it, they keep going back to it. Travis pretty much surrendered to her. *Whatever you want, just tell me! You know you are going to get it anyway!*

Chris and I both cried while reading this fight, but we became sick when we read, *Why did you manipulate me into loving you? Why me? I was a good guy! Why did you have to do it to me? Why do you hate me?* And, *You are ruining my life, but I'm addicted. So that's fine. Just do what you intend to do.* This is so difficult for us to read because it shows how trapped he was. He was helpless and hopeless. Here is a woman who is slashing his tires, stole his ring, stole his journals, is violating his privacy at every chance she gets, is making his life unlivable, yet he can't get away from her. She has invaded his privacy so many times, he is sick of hearing her say sorry because she just does it again. Travis was always saying he was done with her even though he knew he wasn't strong enough to walk away for ever. He thought he could break away, but she knew he couldn't and she capitalized on it.

He realized that she was not who she pretended to be. He was the one who felt used, not her. He points out that all of her actions, and the chronic lying are evidence that she hates him. He said, "I was little more than a dildo with a heartbeat to you!" He tells her that she has hurt him more than anything in his life. These are hardly the words of a man who is "playing" or using a woman. He cares about her, but she was scamming him, and he told her so.

Like we said, in addition to these Google Chats, this fight continued via email as well. In one of those emails, Jodi said, "Two things you are wrong about: I didn't steal your journals, and I didn't slash your tires." But then we read something even more disturbing. We can't remember how it was brought up or the exact wording, but Jodi had done something very bad and possibly illegal. Travis was really upset about it, and Jodi said she would call an attorney first thing in the morning, or Monday morning. So what happened that Jodi needed legal council? Was this fight about the sexually explicit phone call Jodi had recorded without Travis's permission, or had she done something even more criminal? Had she stolen someone's personal information and sold it, or used a credit card illegally? (She was doing sales for Travis, and would have had to gather personal financial information.) Did she kill Travis because she knew he had found out what she was doing and was going to make sure she was held accountable?

Beth Karas from karasoncrime.com was able to access text messages which provide us with further insight. (You can see these text messages on karasoncrime.com.) On May 22, 2008, Travis knew that Jodi had done something wrong and wanted her to admit it. These are the text messages between the two of them (the texts have not been edited):

Travis: I'm not mad. But I know what you did and until you will admit we won't talk.
Jodi: Alright call me then I'll tell you everything I know.
Travis: Are you going to admit it. If not then we r not talking.
Jodi: You need to hear about what happened and why. Am I guilty? Yes. But it's more than just that. The stuff involving you is just a fraction of what has happened. I'm in a BIG mess. I have a lot of apologizing to do to a lot of people. I didn't even see this one coming, and I can't believe how stupid I was! I really really screwed the pooch on this on[e]. So badly I have to call Parker Stan tomorrow.

("Parker Stan" is Parker Stanbury, a law firm in California. As a part of Jodi's Pre-Paid Legal membership coverage, she could call them and get legal advice.)

Jodi: What's the deal? Call me and we'll talk. This is serious, you need to know.
Travis: In a minute.

I thought this fight may have started because of the call Jodi recorded, but how would Travis "know" what she did if she didn't tell him? He wanted her to fess up to something he knew she did. It doesn't make sense it was the recorded call because why would she need to apologize to a lot of people? The next texts between them are not until May 26, 2008, the day of the big fight. This fight begins with texts from Jodi wanting to talk about what she was involved in, and let Travis know how he was involved. It sounds to me that she has involved him without him knowing. She did not want to incriminate herself, and refused to put anything in writing, and he didn't want to speak to her.

> Travis: Put it in a email.
> Jodi: I can't. It'll literally take less than 5 min. Maybe only 4. It's important because it effects us both.
> Travis: Then leavit on a voicemail. I'm not speaking to you leave me alone about it.
> Jodi: Let's just say it's too incriminating for an email/voicemail whatever. Just let me say it and I'm done.
> Travis: I don't really care. You haven't seem to care about privacy in the past. Just leave the voicemail or nothing.
> Jodi: Well I'm not going to leave you the incriminating part on the voicemail or anywhere. So we can forget that part. I'll tell u the other part but I need a response from you about it. Deal?
> Travis: I sent you a response to your dire conversation, that I hope you read because you need to read it. Maybe it will spark human emotion in you, something that only seems to exist when it comes to your own problems. But everyone else is just part of your sick agenda. By the way, your pic comment to Danny Jones makes you look like a pure whore, even more to the people who know you. You should be embarrased by it. If he knew what I knew about you he'd spit in ur face. So would everyone else. I have never never in my life been hurt so bad by someone. But why do I even say it because you don't care. It

doesn't serve your evilness. You couldn't get off your lazy butt to
to read it could you. That's the sociopath I know so well. It freakin figures. I don't want your apology I want you to understand
how evil I think you are. You are the worst thing that ever happened to me. You are a sociopath. You only cry for yourself. You
have never out me and you have betrayed me worse than any
example I could conjure you are sick and you have scamed me.

We will probably never know what this fight was really all about. Even
if his moving on, going to Mexico with Mimi, and Travis finally seeing Jodi for the monster she is contributed to her wanting to kill him,
whatever this fight was about, whatever Jodi had done, would die with
Travis. Regardless of what the fight was about, we know it triggered
something in Jodi that motivated her to put her vile plan into action.
After this fight, everything went into motion. May 28, 2008, a .25 caliber gun was stolen from Jodi's grandparents' house, where she was
living. Darryl said it was "the end of May" when Jodi called and asked
him for two gas cans for a trip to Mesa. Jodi asked another man to borrow money because she had to "go to Mesa to fix things." Darryl and
this man are the only two people who knew Jodi was planning on going to Mesa. Ryan told me it was the "Thursday or Friday before Travis
was killed" that Jodi told him that she was going to come see him,
making it May 30 or 31. She picked up a rental car on June 2. On June
3, she bought a five-gallon gas can from Walmart, and borrowed two
from Darryl. She went to Pasadena, fueled up her car and the gas cans
(even though she claimed to have the gas cans because fuel in Nevada
and Utah was cheaper than California, she fueled up in California).
She turned off her cell phone, stopped using her credit cards, and
headed to Arizona. Travis didn't know she was coming. There were no
text messages from him asking her if she was staying awake, her estimated time of arrival, why her phone was turned off, a "can't wait to
see you" . . . nothing! There weren't even voicemails! Travis was dead
around 5:00 p.m. Wednesday, June 4, 2008. Ryan was expecting her

at his house in Utah earlier that same day. Jodi's phone was off and he began to worry. Once Jodi was out of Arizona, she powered on her phone, and was laughing and flirting with Ryan like nothing had happened. She told him that she had lost her phone charger, but was able to find it. She said she had gotten lost, taken a nap, and was on her way. Within hours, she was rolling around with Ryan in Utah and telling friends how she looked forward to raising her future family with Travis's future family because they would always be friends.

# CHAPTER 15

# Letter to the Alexanders

*Travis, Chris, and some friends were on a snowmobiling trip. They were all hanging out in one room. Travis had a huge Russian fur hat with strings on each side, with a furry ball on the end of each string. He put it on while in his underwear, and everyone in the room began laughing, because he carried on like everything was normal. Someone dared him to go out in the hall in his underwear and the hat. He asked, "I just have to walk out there and come back?" Joking about how that wasn't even a challenge, he cracked the door to make sure no one was out there. Another guy shoved him out the door and locked it. Everyone in the room erupted, but quickly settled down when they realized there was no effort from Travis to get back in. They opened the door, and there he was in his underwear with his Russian hat on doing jumping jacks in the middle of the hallway!*

Travis snowmobiling with Chris and friends in Daniel's Summit, Utah

On Travis's birthday, July 28, 2008, Jodi wrote Travis's family a letter from the Yreka, California jail. It was an eighteen-page letter she felt duty-bound to write because they "deserved to know the truth." We were given a copy of the letter and have included it below. Brace yourself.

*To Travis' Family,*                          *Monday, July 28, 2008*

*Of all the letters I must write, this is one of the most difficult, second only to the one I must write my own parents. I've thought at length of the things I should tell you all, but after talking with Detective Flores and Blaney, they convinced me of the importance of telling you all that I know, that you deserve to know. Now, I know that they told me this not primarily out of principle, but to build their own case. That is their job, it's what they do. I knew that. Nevertheless, their pleas have stayed with me since I last spoke with them 12 days ago. And the more I have pondered it, the more I have come to agree with them 100%, for if it were my own brother, I'd want every detail that could be had. And if an arrest was made, I'd have a million questions for the person in custody, first and foremost: Why? I don't have all of the answers that you seek, but as I sit here today and put pen to paper, even on Travis' birthday, I'm going to try to answer as many as I can. Because this is not a Q and A forum, I don't know what questions you have precisely, but I do presume that you've gathered enough of everyone else's opinions to form your own notions of the kind of person that I am, and the kind of relationship that Travis and I had. Since things have culminated in this way, and since the detectives have already made it clear that my case is hopeless and theirs is rock-solid, I have no reason to hold anything back at this point, nor do I want to go to my grave having withheld anything that might help you piece some things together. It is no longer about me and the things I don't want you all to know. You deserve to know. Besides that, Detective Flores said anything I might reveal about Travis would never and could never change your opinion of him, and since my fear of such was the only thing holding me back, I feel like I can now shed a little light on what was our situation. I have a tendency to ramble but I will keep most trivialities to a minimum. However, I do feel that starting from the very beginning would be best so that you will have a brief synopsis of our history from beginning until now. This may or may not clear up some of your questions, but to me, it's worth trying.*

*I met Travis at the Rainforest Café at the MGM Grand in September 2006. We later marveled and mused at the irony of meeting in such a place, as we later discovered our mutual passion for a healthy planet and the environment in general. He confidently walked right up to me, stuck out his right hand and said, "Hi, I'm Travis." I cordially responded with the usual niceties and figured that would be it, since in that moment, his was just another of the many new names I was trying not to forget. I continued to meet other people as we walked through the casino, but Travis made it a point to walk by my side and keep a running conversation. There wasn't any kind of magnetic attraction that I could feel, but in that short time we discovered just a few of the things that we had in common: traveling, the UFC, the 49ers, and the drive to create an amazing life. After that weekend, I didn't expect to hear from him again. But surprisingly, he called the very next day. A few days later he invited me to accompany him and some friends to church in Murrieta. That following Wednesday, he gave me a copy of the Book of Mormon. On November 26, 2006, Travis baptized me at the Church in Palm Desert, where I was living at the time. He said he'd never met anyone more prepared to receive the Gospel. Joining the church was one of the best decisions I'd ever made and has been one of the greatest experiences of my life. I know that Travis will be richly rewarded for the role he played in bringing me into the fold.*

*Our relationship during that time was ambiguous and undefined. There was no doubt a mutual attraction but we were in no way officially dating. By Christmas of 2006, Travis had grown to mean a lot to me. He was determined to "Mormonize" me further, so I received a generous lot of gifts that Christmas to serve that very purpose, everything from a CTR ring & scriptures with my name engraved on them, to a copy of a painting of Jesus Christ, the Proclamation of Families, and a biography of Gordon B. Hinckley. His generosity never wavered the entire time that I knew him, not once.*

*It wasn't until February 2, 2007 that we decided to make things official. Things went really well despite one small hang up: Deanna Reid. I had no hostility toward her, from what Travis said, she seemed like a very nice girl. But he made it clear that she could under no circumstances ever know about us because if she found out she would freak out and he was tired of dealing with her every time he tried to date someone. I was very understanding of this, as I had dealt with a similar situation in the past.*

*We began to progress to the point where the talk of marriage became more and more frequent. We often talked about family structure, baby names, how many children we wanted, boys, girls, etc. Each time he referenced the future, he included me in it. To me, this was a natural progression. In May 2007, I had to move out of my home in Palm Desert because I could no longer handle the mortgage. Travis insisted that I move closer to him so that we can have a more "normal relationship," although he expressed concern for Deanna's reaction, saying that if she found out it would be "World War III." As great as things were going, something just seemed off about the Deanna thing. I knew that he still loved and cared for her very much, and I thought that was admirable, but I didn't understand why he couldn't just tell her to back off. So in a snap decision I decided to move to Big Sur, CA instead. Travis was upset and hurt. I assured him it was temporary and that things would work out, but he wasn't happy that I lived even farther. So we began to make arrangements for me to move to Mesa. We had to keep it top-secret from Deanna. It was then I realized that if Deanna was happy, Travis was happy, and then Jodi was happy.*

*Sometimes things happen that seem like they're not part of the plan, but that is pure illusion. No matter how painful it is, we must trust that the hand of God is at work in our lives.*

*After Travis and I returned from a fun trip to Daniel's Summit, UT in June 2007, I acted on impulse and a gut feeling doing something completely dishonest. You see, I had been in a few relationships before when my partner was not being completely faithful, and there is a distinct feeling that comes with it. Travis had been interacting with some girls in my presence that gave me cause for concern. I knew he was the flirtatious type, and I had witnessed it on countless occasions prior to that point. I am not a jealous person, but something about the way he conducted himself that time caused me to question his level of commitment to our relationship and to me. The dishonest deed which I had mentioned was that I looked at the text messages in his phone. I thought to myself, he said he has nothing to hide, so why not? A flawed logic, I know. I fully expected to find a few mild flirtations w/ other girls, as this was his MO anyway, and he was not secretive about it. What I found, however, was far more, including several references made of the many, separate, intimate rendezvous he'd had with other girls including plans in the making for further associations of the same kind. I checked the dates to make sure I wasn't getting worked up over nothing, but as feared, they were well within the range of when we began dating "exclusively." I didn't freak out, I didn't even tell him. I didn't know what to do. We had another trip planned to Niagara Falls, the Sacred Grove and HuntingtonBeach, so I decided to sit on it, get through that and then make a decision. It ate at me, and as soon as we got home from Huntington Beach, it all came out. He was very apologetic. He said it was wrong. There was no way I couldn't forgive him. Despite his shortcomings, he'd been very good to me. However, there was also no way that I could trust him any longer. I decided we should just be friends on June 29, 2007. This was a very difficult decision for me because I loved him very much. It was especially difficult because he begged me to marry him that same day. He said things would be different. Up to that point, a proposal was expected any time, but once the trust is gone, it is hopeless. I'm not perfect either. I violated his trust by reading text messages that perhaps should have remain private. My justification was I had the right to know, I'm not saying it was okay. Fast forward 3 weeks to July 2007. I hesitated to fol-low through with plans I'd already made to move to Mesa, but Travis is a very persuasive man, and at the hand of his persuasion, I folded and decided to go. I used to wonder what it would have been like if I'd ac-cepted his proposal. But I don't think things would have changed. Here's why: About a month before I moved back to CA, March 2008 we decided to have a "come clean" conversation about everything, everything, every-thing. He confessed that most of time I'd been living there he'd been dating someone (Lisa Andrews). The subject of dating other people had come up all of 4 times between us while I lived in AZ, 3 of which he brought it up, and he stated that he wasn't dating anyone. I never had any reason not to believe him, because there'd be no reason for him to hide that from me. I'm not the type to have a crying emotional meltdown over something like that the way Deanna has in the past. In fact, I would have been happy for him. So the shock came not in the fact that he'd lied again, and cheated on yet another girlfriend, but that this time I was the "other girl." I felt very ashamed. My first thought was poor Lisa, I should tell her everything. But they'd long since broken up and Travis had taken a de-cided interest in Mimi Hall. Besides, talking to Lisa not only would have destroyed our friendship (mine & Travis'), but it would have cause a lot of unnecessary drama and pain. After listening silently for a few minutes while he continued gushing about Mimi, I could see in his eyes that he was very happy. I asked him how she felt about him, and he jokingly responded by saying that he doesn't think she even knows he's male. We both laughed and I reminded him of the charmer that he is and that it's only a matter of time. He rolled his eyes and said, "please, whatever you do, don't give me any dating advice. I get enough of that crap from Sky Hughes, I'm sick of it, I can handle this." I didn't say another word. If anyone knew how to win over a lady, it was Travis. So we left it at that.*

*But when it was my turn to come clean, his attitude change 180 degrees. All hell seemed to break loose. He lost his temper completely and flew into a rage. He began punching himself in the head so hard that he injured his neck and his back and could barely turn his head from side to side. I was afraid to get near him, but I wanted him to stop. Travis never hit me in the face, but he bruised other parts of my body. It was easy to shrug off a few visible bruises with friends. I could blame it on work or clumsiness. That only happened on 2 occasions. The second time was on a Tuesday, in early April 2008. Two men at the Tempe business briefing actually joked, "What is Travis beating you now?" We just laughed. Playing along with their joke was the only way to protect his reputation. I know it is common behavior for women in abusive relationships to protect their partner by covering for him (or her) and by making excuses, but I didn't see it so much like that. Travis and I were not in any kind of committed relationship at that point, he was not my "partner" any longer, and it was only a matter of days before I rolled out of town in a U-Haul truck. By putting several hundred miles between us, any further opportunities for abuse (not to mention immoral conduct on both of our parts) would be prevented. But even when I moved away, he didn't let up. I stopped to sleep in Hollister, still hundreds of miles from my destination in Yreka, and Travis call me in the middle of the night, angry that I'd moved, angry that I'd dated other guys. It was so confusing to me because I thought we were on the same page about me moving, and I knew how much he liked Mimi. We both knew we were never getting back together, but it was like he was determined not to let me off that easily. I really cared for him. His cruelty and abuse never made me angry. It only invoked pity and remorse. And shame as well. For he acted that way out of pain, and the last thing I ever wanted to do was hurt him. I know you all probably hate me even more than before you started reading this letter. Well hang on, because the plot thickens, and by the time you're done reading this, you most likely won't consider me worthy of your own spit. Travis told me that I'd hurt him more than the death of his father. He is not one to dramatize things, so I knew he'd been sincere when he said that. I didn't fully understand why he felt that way. How was it that he can date and have relationships but if I did so he branded me a whore? I knew he was hurting, but I didn't get it. Especially since he liked Mimi Hall so much.*

*Tanisha had made mention online that I was obsessed with Travis. Obsession would not be an accurate way to term it. But if obsessed means that I've cried everyday since his death, then maybe there is some accuracy there. If obsessed means that I couldn't stay away, then there is a bit of truth in that. I could not say no to Travis. He would not let me escape his influential grasp. He called me at all hours of the night. The reason I was at his house so frequently was because he invited me over. Most of the time it was in the late evenings when the "coast was clear." He would send me sweet text messages in the middle of the night, beckoning me to get out of bed and sneak over to his house. It was too hard to resist most times. If I didn't respond to his solicitations, they would be followed by a heavy and relentless onslaught of the ultimate guilt trip. I know I should've been stronger, for his own spiritual well-being and mine. Naturally, I was flattered that he was so attracted to me and wanted to spend time with me. Usually, the feeling was quite mutual. But it became obvious, especially after our behavior continued even after he met Mimi, that neither of us was going to be strong enough as long as we lived in such a convenient proximity. I've never regretted my decision to move back to CA. There are, however, some decisions that I do regret, and I cannot tell you how remorseful that I am for my inactions. Let me clarify by saying the following: I had a trip planned to Southern California and Utah the week of June 2-6, 2008. Travis found out and tried persuading me to come to AZ instead to visit him. I told him I just didn't have enough time. He acted sad and hurt and tried to guilt me into coming. I stood my ground though and said no, but I played up all of the positives, like his impending trip to Northern California. We were going to check off 3 more things on the list of 1000 Places to See Before You Die, which were Crater Lake (although he'd been there when he was very young, he wanted to re- experience it), the Oregon Coast, and the Shakespeare Festival in Ashland, OR. But he refused to be consoled and just said, "ok, whatever, I see how it is, you don't love me," just his usual rhetoric, guilt trip lingo, etc. We hung up the phone, and I could feel my heart once again being pulled in his direction. I knew that if I went we'd have fun. By the time I arrived in Pasadena, I made the decision to go to his house. I arrived in Mesa around 4 AM on Wednesday, June 4, 2008. He was already expecting me and was very happy to see me. So was Naps. I'd missed them both so much, it had been months since I'd seen either of them. Travis was awake when I arrived. He waited up all night for me. He and Naps were in his office and he was watching some silly video on YouTube.com, some kind of dancing robot girls or something. I was exhausted from driving, so after a few more YouTube videos, we went to sleep as the sun was rising. We slept until about 1 pm. When we woke up, among other things, we tried looking at photos from past Church History trips, they were on 3 cds that I had made a year prior, but they were pretty badly scratched, not to mention Travis' laptop had recently contracted a virus and it was difficult to bring up the disk drive. He had instant Quaker oatmeal for lunch. I remember him a clear as daylight sitting in his office chair, feet kicked up, in his pajamas eating oatmeal, waiting for his computer to accomplish a simple task, but having no luck. I sat on the floor next to him, petting Napoleon, looking around the room. The poem I'd written back in February was still on his whiteboard: "Roses are red, violets are blue, T-dogg's the best, forget all the rest, Napoleon's pretty great, too." Anyway, when we realized we weren't getting anywhere w/the pictures, we went back upstairs. I took pictures of him in the shower, but they were tasteful pictures. We were going for a sort of Calvin Klein advertisement kind of look. Travis and I and the rest of the Pre-Paid world new about the Cancun trip a year prior when it was announced, but those who were eligible weren't announced until early in 2008. When he found out he was going, he began working double-over-time on his body and by May & June was feeling very confident in his own skin. If it weren't for that fact he might have not agreed to do those shots, who knows? From this point on, things are blurred and confusing. I was sitting/kneeling on the floor next to the shower, going through the pictures I'd taken when I heard a really loud pop. I must have been hit on the back of the head because the next thing I knew I was lying next to the bathtub, my ears were ringing and Travis was screaming, but he sounded so far away although he was right next to me. I'm really sorry for this. I know you're going to hate me even more than you already do, but as hard as this is, I keep telling myself that if it were my brother, I'd want to know. When I came to, I saw 2 individuals standing near the bathroom in the bedroom right where the carpet and in the tile begins. They both began walking toward us. My only thought was to run into the closet, possibly by-passing them so I could get out of the room, via the other door to his closet. But as I reached the other door, I was stopped by a male pointing a gun directly at my forehead. I was made to get on my knees near the armoire and was told not to move. By this time I'd surmised that the other perpetrator, now standing over Travis, was female, but both people were wearing black ski masks, black gloves and dark clothing, with the exception of the male who was wearing blue jeans. He left the room, and without much thought I charged the female who was standing over Travis. I shoved her hard enough that she fell over Travis, who was conscious but quiet at this point on all fours w/his right hand holding his head. The girl had fallen near the left sink, close to the trash can in the corner. I pulled on Travis saying, "come on, come on!" He came forward lethargically but wouldn't stand up, and he kept saying, "I can't." I only got him about halfway down the hallway of his bathroom, I kept urging him but he said, "go get help, go to my neighbors." I didn't want to leave him, I felt like I was going to pass out, my whole body was tingling painfully all over, I just kept pulling on him. At that point I was crying and kept pleading, "come on, please!" and he said, "I can't, I can't feel my legs." The girl came at me w/ a knife but I was able to grab her wrists. I was already weak and I felt like I could hardly breathe. She tried kicking me repeatedly in the knees. I tried blocking her and holding her hands but she was making repeated attempts to stomp on my feet, landing her target a few times. I was at an unfair advantage because she had shoes and I was in my bare feet. At the time I didn't notice the pain, maybe it was adrenaline, but my left foot was later throbbing and bruised so I know she got me at least once, probably more on that foot, and she had caused two of the toenails on my other foot to bleed, which I didn't discover until later as well. Again, probably adrenaline. We struggled and I was able to throw her off of me again, but out of fear I ran as she was about to double back and come after me. Again I was stopped by the male perpetrator who had come back into the room. He yelled at her to stop. He said that's not what they're here for. (I'm sorry about my handwriting, I'm shaking as I write this). She argued with him, saying they should "do" me, too. But he said no. He asked who I was but before I could respond (I could barely breath by then, let alone speak), he grabbed my purse and began to go through it. I was on my knees in the bedroom, Travis was still midway in the hall of the bathroom, the female standing over him, yelling at the male. He got out my wallet and looked at my driver's license. He took the cash that was in it and besides gas receipts I'd accumulated up to that point of my trip, I had the registration to my car (which I no longer kept in my glove compartment because I'd cleaned my car out of all valuable items and paperwork, because it was going back to the bank any day). The registration has the address of my parents' house printed clearly on it. He said to me as he began to stuff things back into my purse, I know who you are and I know where you live. I know exactly how to find you, and I can find your family. Unless you want them all to die, you keep silent or I will silence you. I agreed, but the woman kept shouting and arguing with him. She was "shouting" as quietly as possible. He kept telling her to shut up, that that's not what they were "here for." He finally gave under the pressure because he held the gun to my head and tried to fire but nothing happened, just a click. I shoved past him w/ my purse which was then on the floor next to me. He seemed to make no effort to stop me, but as I flew down the stairs I swear I could hear footsteps behind me. I ran out front door, leaving behind my shoes, and slamming the door as some last ditch effort to create any kind of obstacle to slow down whoever was pursuing me. My rental car was parked in the driveway. I was shaking and hyperventilating and crying. I kept my eye on the front door as I backed out and drove away (awful, I know. I didn't look as I backed out. I probably should've never been driving in that kind of state. It wasn't heightened awareness, it was blind confusion). The front door never open. I don't know what time it was when left, but I'm guessing it was sometime between 4:30 and 6:30 PM, just don't know. There were 2 young girls outside playing. I don't know if they noticed me. One was maybe 9 or 10 years old, the other look maybe 13 or 14, I'm not good at guessing ages, they both had blonde hair and they were running west down Queensborough Ave. on the north side of the street. That is one of the last details that I remember of Travis' neighborhood. When I left, Travis was alive, although I he was hurt. My phone was dead, and as cowardly as this is, I probably wouldn't have called for help if I could've. I was racked with fear. I knew that if they were capable of doing what I'd seen them do, then they were capable of carrying out their threats.*

*I did not harm Travis. I did not take his life. But looking back on the way that I acted, I might as well be held equally responsible for his death. I have two brothers, two sisters, and two parents, but all I kept seeing was my dad and my youngest brother, and all I could think of was their safety.*

*A huge part of me regrets my last minute decision to go to Travis' house that week. Part of me has faith in the notion that all things happen for a reason. I wish I could give you more. I did not committ a murder that day, nor would I ever harm Travis. The evidence against me was presented to me by Detective Flores. There is a lot. The only explanation I have for that is this: I was there that day. I never committed a crime, therefore it never occurred to me that I would need to cover my tracks. Whoever did this came prepared.*

*All I can say now is that I am deeply remorseful for the pain you have been experiencing. If I could give my life in exchange for Travis' life so that he could live here again amongst the people that love him, I would do so w/out a shadow of hesitation. What happened that day was horrible. I'm so sorry that I didn't have more courage to stop it, or more power. My heart has ached to no end during this entire traumatic experience. Putting on a smile and pretending things were fine for my family didn't work out so well. I felt like I was a danger living near them and began to make preparations to move back to Monterey, where I'd lived 4 years ago.*

*I loved Travis very much as a friend. We had our fair share of arguments, but I would never intentionally hurt him. I did hurt him emotionally, and for that I am very sorry, too. But above all, I hope you can find peace. I know that his killers are still at large, and each and everyday I've been praying not so much that they are brought to justice, but for my family's safety and protection. At then end of the day I have to give it all to God. God is fair and just. And regardless of what the world believes, I am so grateful that it is ultimately His opinion that counts.*

*Again, I would never hurt Travis. He has shown me very little other than kindness and generosity. He would give me the world if he could. He assisted me in moving (to & from AZ), he let me store my books and artwork at his house when I had no room for them, he was constantly doing little things for me, just always full of thoughtfulness. We traveled to many places together, each determined to conquer the book 1000 Places to See Before you die. I hesitate even mentioning all of the little knick-knacks he'd accumulated that adorn his house as a result of our travels together or through gifts from me that he treasured and proudly displayed for fear that it would taint your opinion of those same items, which are no doubt now in your possession.*

*I know this letter may only raise more questions, but I hope it also answers others. Again, I know that God is just and fair. Ultimately, whoever did this will be held accountable. I think we can all agree on that much. Like I said, what prompted this letter is that I know you all deserve to know what ever information I have. I also feel like I should explain the following: There have been many comments made about my smile in my mug shot, which I was fully expecting. It was cocky, I know, but so was Travis. And anyone who knew Travis well enough know he was cocky also knew of his happy and positive outlook on life. I know of my own innocence, and so does our Father in Heaven. For this reason I cannot be sad. I also asked myself, what would Travis do? Barring the fact that he would likely not find himself and such an unfortunate set of circumstances, he would, no doubt, be flashing that smile of his that he always did.*

*Like you, I wish that I knew why all of this happened. Forensics can tell us what, but not always who, and nobody seems to know why. Detective Flores suggested a few possible motives, but to me they don't make sense. He said maybe I was angry or jealous. Travis has never done anything that would incite that kind of anger. As far as the physical way he retaliated during two arguments that we had, my own father has done worse to me as a means of discipline. The only other thing Travis has ever done to upset me was be unfaithful in our relationship, but nobody would expect me to be thrilled over it. I'd forgiven him long ago. Either way, he'd have to get in the back of a line of ex-boyfriends who are guilty of those same folly in relationships with me. The detective said that perhaps I was jealous that he was going to Cancun. As I mentioned, I'd known about that trip since last year. There is no way I could break up with a guy and then expect him to take me on a trip of that magnitude. The idea of accompanying Travis on a trip to Cancun was as short-lived as a snowflake in Mesa during the month of July. There was never any question or discussion of us going together.*

*I just don't harbor any hostility toward Travis, and I never have. I know that we both struggled to move on, but we both wanted the other to be happy. Travis was a good man. Our relationship was never perfect, but it taught me so much. Knowing Travis has been one of the greatest blessings of my life.*

*I know it would bring you a great sense of closure to know that his killers were brought to justice. Ultimately, the persons responsible will be held accountable. I, however, will not serve one day in prison for a heinous crime in which I had no part.*

*Travis lives. He is not far, and it won't be long before you can see him again. One day all of our questions will be answered. I just hope you can all find peace. My prayers are with you and have been since the inception of this nightmare, and so are the prayers of many.*
*With deepest sympathy and humble sincerity,*
*Jodi Ann Arias*
*"...and your sorrow shall be turned into joy." - John 16:20*

[See our copy of this letter at www.ourfriendtravis.com/letter]

You may want to take a moment to pick your jaw up off the ground! How diabolical is this creature? While the entirety of the letter is unfathomably disturbing, there are some things that stood out to me. Below I have addressed different parts of the letter by sharing thoughts that came to my mind as I read it. (Note: The following was therapy for me.)

"It is no longer about me . . ." It is always about Jodi. It always has been and always will be. I love that Flores told her that nothing she said would change the family's opinion about Travis. I'm sure this bothered her (obviously it did because she put it in the letter), because she wanted to upset and shock people—she was hoping she had a "Bombshell! Mesa, Arizona," as news commentator Nancy Grace often said while covering this trial. Little did she realize that some people knew that she and Travis had been fooling around, maybe not every detail and position, but people had a good idea. Both those who didn't know and those who did, didn't care like she had hoped they would.

". . . we discovered just a few things we had in common: traveling, the UFC, the 49ers, and the drive to create an amazing life." Really? The UFC (cage fighting)? When we first met Jodi, Travis, Chris, and I were watching UFC, and she went in her room because it was too "violent." The only thing she was "driven" to do before meeting Travis was to hack her boyfriends' email accounts, make up bizarre lies, try to become like her boyfriend's ex-wife, move from job to job, fight with her family, and stalk her boyfriend to the point he had to move out of the state. Unfortunately, she hung onto all of these "drives to create an amazing life" into her relationship with Travis.

Travis may have said, he had "never met anyone more prepared to receive the Gospel," but if he were alive today, he would probably say, "I have never met anyone as narcissistic, conniving, manipulative, evil, and chameleon like as you. You fooled me; you fooled lots of people. You have an incredible ability to forge yourself into someone you are not." In fact, he said something similar in their last fight.

Joining the Mormon church was something she did for Travis, and she led him to believe that her desire was genuine. The way she writes reminds me of her walking around my chaotic house while the boys and Travis wrestled on the living room floor, along with many other things going on, and she was reading the Bible. It was weird, forced, fake, and out of place!

"Things went really well despite one small hang-up: Deanna Reid" Can her jealousy of Deanna scream out for help any louder? No, it can't! The truth is, Jodi broke down many parts and pieces of Travis, even destroying some, but the one place she could not penetrate was the part of Travis consumed by Deanna. Jodi hated her for it. She wanted nothing more than to take Deanna's place and it would *never* happen.

"Travis insisted I move closer to him . . . In a snap decision I decided to move to Big Sur, CA." *What?* Her dream come true, and she turned it down? Five months of my life wasted listening to her whine non-stop about Travis not asking her to move to Mesa? Six months of crying, begging, and pleading with him in hopes he would want her to move to Mesa! He finally asked her, and she makes a "snap decision" to move farther away? Hmmm . . . I'm going to go out on a limb and guess he didn't ask her to move to Mesa. Mike Bertot heard Travis telling her that she had no business moving to Mesa.

"Sometimes things happen that seem like they're not part of the plan, but that is pure illusion. No matter how painful it is, we must trust that the hand of God is at work in our lives." Thank you, Mother Theresa (apologies to Mother Theresa). Did she come up with that on the car ride crossing state lines to romp on a guy after just having butchered another? She is *soooooo* spiritual and wise. This entire letter is shocking to me. This letter alone warrants the death penalty! Zero remorse.

". . . fun trip to Daniel's Summit." Fun? They fought the whole time, and he left for hours without telling her because he had to get away from her! While he was gone, she paced back and forth looking for someone's pet bunny to boil!

"I am not a jealous person." I won't waste any time addressing this. I think we all get it.

"I looked at text messages on his phone." She didn't just look. She studied five months back to when they "began dating 'exclusively.'"

"I decided we should just be friends." "I?" In other media interviews and in the police interrogation, she said that it was a mutual "breakup" because they each violated one another's trust.

"Up to that point, a proposal was expected anytime." In her dreams.

"I hesitated to follow through with plans I'd made already to move to Mesa, but Travis is a very persuasive man, and at the hand of his persuasion, I folded and decided to go." She is delusional. On his drive to the four-wheeling trip, Travis spent hours telling her that she had no business moving to Mesa! Not to mention the continued arguments throughout that weekend about the move he "persuaded" her to make! He never wanted her there, and he begged her to go home. This sounds a lot like him "persuading" her to visit him on June 4.

"I'm not the type to have a crying emotional meltdown over something like that the way Deanna has in the past." Ex-boyfriends of Jodi's claimed otherwise. They said she would have breakdowns, and a lot of them. And the "emotional meltdowns" continued into her relationship with Travis. She just has to keep picking at Deanna, she is so jealous.

"So the shock came not in the fact that he'd lied again . . . but that this time I was the other girl." She claims no knowledge of Lisa. We have already covered how we know this is a blatant lie! "My first thought was poor Lisa." Poor Lisa? You mean because "someone" scared her by opening the door to her house, knocking on the door and running off, slashing Travis's tires twice at her house, sending her a demented email about repenting and being a child of God, spied on her and Travis while they were on a date(s), and then slashed her tires while she was at Travis's house? I, and others, believe that had Lisa and Travis not broken up, Jodi would have killed Lisa.

"Please, whatever you do, don't give me any dating advice. I get enough of that crap from Sky Hughes, I'm sick of it, I can handle this." This actually made me laugh out loud. I thought it was funny that I bother her enough that she had to fit me into this letter that has nothing to do with me. Yes, I gave Travis a lot of advice, and yes, I bugged him, but he would always call and run things by me to either get advice, or an interpretation of why a girl blinked twice while drinking her water on a date. I was honest with him, and sometimes it wasn't easy for him to hear, but he kept calling and wanting more. But, it is very possible he said that.

"He lost his temper completely and flew into a rage. He began punching himself so hard that he injured his neck and his back and could barely turn his head from side to side." It is so hard to keep stories straight when you lie. During the trial, Jodi said that she told Travis about her dating another guy in March. He couldn't take it, and began "beating his head against a door." Can you say, "Whoops?" Someone needs to start writing their stories down; they seem to be getting "scrambled." In another interaction during the trial, Juan Martinez asked her if she was confused, she told him no, but when he, or someone like Travis, yells at her, it causes her "brain to scramble."

"Travis never hit me in the face." He didn't? She said during the trial that he hit her across the face in the car when she told him she was moving to Yreka. Evidently, she needed a few years in jail to come up with this story. It wouldn't make sense for him to get mad. After all, he had been begging her to move back to California since she moved to Mesa in the summer of 2007!

"Two men at the Tempe business briefing actually joked, 'What is Travis beating you now?'" Unfortunately these "two men" were unavailable for subpoenas, because they don't exist. They have had almost seven years to find one person who saw Jodi with bruises, a broken finger, or these two guys. She is making it all up!

"Travis called me in the middle of the night, angry that I'd moved . . . It was so confusing to me because I thought we were on the same page about me moving." Now she is confusing me! According to her, he hit her in the face because he was mad she was moving. Now she is confused because she didn't know he was mad that she was moving until after she left?

" . . . by the time you are done reading this, you most likely won't consider me worthy of your own spit." Bombshell, Mesa, Arizona! Jodi Arias told the truth!

"But if obsessed means that I've cried everyday since his death, then maybe there is some accuracy there." I have no words.

"He would not let me escape his influential grasp . . . He would send me text messages in the middle of the night, beckoning me to get out of bed and sneak over to his house." Interesting. There are plenty of texts of her soliciting sex, but not true coming from him.

" . . . especially after our behavior continued even after he met Mimi." It is fascinating how Jodi claims to have wanted to "protect" Travis's reputation and that she didn't care about these other girls Travis liked, but she wanted everyone to know everything that was going on with them. At the memorial, Jodi approached Travis's bishop and told him that she thought she should tell Mimi that she and Travis were having sex. The bishop did not see why that was necessary, and told Jodi that Mimi wasn't interested in a romantic relationship with Travis. Jodi also told Aaron Dewey she and Travis had sex. Jodi wanted people to know.

"I had a trip planned to Southern California and Utah . . ." Jodi does not mention Arizona, but when she called Darryl, her ex-boyfriend, to borrow the two gas cans (so that she could get in and out of Arizona without being caught on camera getting gas), she told him that they were for a trip to Mesa. Jodi claims she did not tell him that, even though Darryl said in his deposition that she did.

" . . . I played up all the positives, like his impending trip to Northern California." This was a trip that Travis kept putting off. Travis was trying to separate himself from Jodi. On the recorded call between Travis and Jodi that was used during the trial, Jodi said she was going to go to D.C. too, where Travis had already made plans to attend a business training. It's very obvious Travis wasn't okay with this. This further shows he was trying to break away from her.

"He was already expecting me . . ." Was he? Where are the text messages of him "persuading" her? Why are there no texts of him asking, "ETA?" "Are you staying awake?" "How close are you?" In the trial, she said she stood in the doorway of his office and watched him for a while before he noticed her. If he were expecting her, why wasn't he aware she was almost there? I don't think he knew she was coming, and I don't think he planned on having sex with her. I think once she got there, she said she wanted to apologize in person for their big fight, that she couldn't survive without being at least his friend, that she wanted him in her life, and he felt bad and let her stay. I think he told her that she could stay, but they could not mess around—that's why there was no sex that night. I bet she gave him a wakeup call the following morning he couldn't refuse, and once that was over, he thought, "Well, I messed up again, might as well have fun."

No need to address the two intruders story. She has admitted this was a lie. Once again, her family was threatened, which is a pattern we see in the "made up" life she shared with the world while she was testifying. The saddest part about this letter is when she describes what Travis was doing while he was being attacked by the intruders. It breaks my heart, because he probably did say he couldn't move his legs. Did Travis try to kick her in the knees as an attempt to save his life after he had been so badly wounded? Did he stomp at her feet while having his hands sliced? How much pain and torture did Travis have to endure? His defensive wounds tell us there was a lot. Not to mention, the emotional anguish it must have caused that this person he cared about, defended, and repeatedly threw away any chance at happiness for was butchering him. He had continued to show her kindness while she tormented and slowly tried to destroy him. This was the "nicest person he had ever met." The woman who "wouldn't hurt a fly," the woman who completely fooled him and countless others and the woman who butchered him.

Jodi didn't tell Detective Flores about the gun being held to her head and misfiring. This was something she added for effect during the interview she did with *48 Hours* and in this letter to the family. She had barely escaped with her life! So despicable. While she was in jail, she told Detective Flores that the intruders had written her a letter reminding her that they knew where she and her family lived, and that she wasn't to "talk." When Flores asked her for the letter, she told him she was so scared that she threw it away.

"(awful, I know. I didn't look as I backed out.)" Not, *Awful, I know. I left your grandson and brother there bleeding and dying and did nothing!* I know this isn't a real story, but her inability to realize what would be appropriate in this situation shows how callous, cold, and dangerous she really is.

"I never committed a crime, therefore it never occurred to me that I would need to cover my tracks." Jodi had put her plan into action before she ever left her house. She had it all figured out. From the moment she left Pasadena, she tried to cover every intention she had. She had three gas cans to get her in and out of Arizona. She had planned a trip to see Ryan, so she would have an alibi. She turned off her phone and didn't turn it back on until she was out of Arizona. She called and left Travis a message after she killed him to act like she was never there. She lied to everyone about where she was. She sent emails to Travis after she killed him to try to throw off the police. She lied in her journal entries. She made him a memorial video and posted it on YouTube, and created a memorial album dedicated to Travis! She tried to cover everything up, and she failed miserably!

"Whoever did this came prepared." This is the most honest thing Jodi has said since we met her. The person who did this *did* come prepared. Jodi came prepared to stab and shoot an amazing man, all because he was leaving her and taking with him the life and world that she wanted for her own. She was afraid that she would be exposed for the gruesome, diabolical monster that she is. She knew Travis was finally going to be happy with someone else, and she was not about to let that happen.

"I hesitate even mentioning all of the little knick-knacks he'd accumulated that adorned his house as a result of our travels together or through gifts from me that he treasured and proudly displayed for fear that it would taint your opinion of those same items . . ." This absolutely nauseated me. It's just so evil. Some killers take souvenirs from their victims; she wanted the family to know she left them some of hers. This is just so sickening! Why would she even bring it up? I do not see her point in any of this other than to just torment the Alexanders.

"There have been many comments made about my smile in my mugshot . . ." But there is only one word for it: EVIL. And no, Travis would not be "smiling" if he was arrested for slaughtering someone he cared about! He would be an absolute mess. He would realize how many peoples' lives had been changed forever by what they thought he had done. She was right that Travis would never be in that situation, because he was not like her. Travis had a soul, and it was good.

Talking about the trip to Cancun, she said, "There was never any question or discussion of us going together." This is not true. Travis took her off his reservation.

"I just don't harbor any hostility towards Travis, and I never have." Twenty-nine stab wounds, a slashed throat, a gunshot to the face, and left to rot says otherwise.

". . . we both wanted the other to be happy." Travis was headed toward happiness, and she couldn't stand it.

"I, however, will not serve one day in prison for a heinous crime in which I had no part." Now I know the meaning of "sweet justice" thanks to Detective Flores and Juan Martinez.

"I just hope you can all find peace." She will, and has thus far, done everything in her power to try to prevent that from happening. From her tweets, her blog, selling her artwork, saying Travis was an abuser and a pedophile, to her fundraisers for an appeal, she wants Travis's family to experience everything but peace. She wants to continue to hurt all of those who Travis loved more than he loved her.

Nice scripture at the end of her letter! She really is "soulless," as so many have described her.

CHAPTER 16

# Human or Hypocrite?

*Travis loved to eat at Costa Vida and to drink slushes from Sonic.*

Travis in Colorado before the last (or one of the last) trainings he ever did.

During the trial, the defense team created a smokescreen around the real issues of Jodi brutally murdering Travis by accusing him of being a hypocrite based upon the fact that he was both "Mormon" and engaged in premarital sex. This premise was so incredibly weak. As a reminder, Jodi was "Mormon" too and was also engaging in premarital sex. There are millions of people all around the world whose religion frowns on premarital sex who are engaged in it anyway. This does not make them bad, nor does it make them hypocrites, especially when they make the efforts that Travis was making to stop. This included breaking up with Jodi, compelling her to move away, and confessing his mistakes to the Lord and his church leaders and asking for their help.

There is a big difference between someone making mistakes and working to become a better person, and someone who preaches, condemns, and chastises others for doing the very same thing they are doing. The first is human, while the second is a hypocrite. The defense team started the fire, and the media fanned the flames. So much of the trial and the conversations surrounding the trial were about sex. Who cares? People have sex. Even religious people have sex all the time. Sex had nothing to do with Jodi butchering him. But it sure made for "great TV" and a distraction for the jury. The defense team had nothing, so they tried everything.

Travis would be mortified to see the way he has been portrayed by the media: "Good Mormon Boy Gone Wild." From a Mormon perspective, Travis was way out of bounds. He and Jodi violated covenants each made at baptism. And, Travis violated other sacred covenants he made in the Temple. He was "off the path," and he knew it. He was miserable about it, and he would certainly be heartsick if he knew what has gone on since his death. He would want people to know that following the teachings of his church were important to him. He would want people to know that he was trying to do what he knew was right, even though he stumbled and made mistakes. He would want people to know how sorry he was for traveling the paths he traveled.

Travis always tried to do his best. When he was "messing up," he did the things necessary to get back on track. In the Church of Jesus Christ of Latter-day Saints, we take the Sacrament every Sunday (similar to Communion in the Catholic church). We believe that one should be in good standing with God when he/she partakes of the Sacrament. So, if a person is not following the law of chastity, or the Word of Wisdom (code of health), etc. they should not take the Sacrament. I remember multiple occasions where Travis didn't take the Sacrament or participate in an ordinance that required a certain level of worthiness. There was no one there to tell him he shouldn't take the Sacrament or participate in an ordinance except his own conscience. I know a lot of people who will take it regardless of worthiness, because they don't want anyone to know they messed up or they are embarrassed, but Travis wasn't one of those people. Travis stayed outside of the Temple when Chris and I got married because he had stumbled at that time in his life. His bishop wasn't there to stop him from going in. Nothing more than Travis's integrity kept him out. Travis was certainly not a hypocrite.

We live in a highly sexualized world where human intimacy has become marginalized, degraded, and trivialized. I don't know of any religion that condones premarital sex. All the religions that I am aware of have a doctrine of abstinence prior to marriage. Some have chosen to be more lax in the observance of this commandment, claiming it is outdated, against our nature, or impossible to adhere to. The teachings of the Church of Jesus Christ of Latter-day Saints have never changed their position on sexual sin. Obviously, I'm not a spokesperson for the Church of Jesus Christ, but I know we are all imperfect, and God knew we would make mistakes. That's why He provided us with a Savior who suffered for our sins and died for each of us so that, according to Bruce Hafen, ". . . we may *learn* from our experience without being *condemned* by that experience." Jesus Christ provided a way for us to turn our "sins" from crimson to be "white as snow" despite our failures, mistakes, and shortcomings.

If we see a hypocrite as anyone who has a knowledge to live or act a certain way, but is not one hundred percent perfect in those actions, then are we not all hypocrites? I strive to be a good person, adhere to my beliefs, and do what I know is right, but I often fall short. I always try to do better and improve. According to dictionary.com, the definition of "hypocrite" is: *a person who pretends to have virtues, moral or religious beliefs, principles, etc., that he or she does not actually possess, especially a person whose actions belie stated beliefs.* If you look at the "pretends" and "actually possess" part of the definition, it is important to note that Travis, though acting against them, did actually possess the belief that sexual relations between a man and a woman are sacred and are only to be explored within the bonds of marriage. Otherwise, he would not have tried to stop the sexual relationship with Jodi, and he would not have spoken to his bishop. Travis was in turmoil. He tried to live the standards he believed in so strongly, and when he messed up, he would repent for it. This showed that he truly believed in the importance of his beliefs. Not only did Travis not hide Jodi from his friends, as the defense team insinuated, but he didn't hide her from his church either. Travis had spoken to his bishop more than once throughout his relationship with Jodi, and he was in the midst of a repentance and healing process when Jodi killed him.

Travis tried many times to stop the sexual relationship with Jodi and still remain friends, but without help from Jodi, this just wasn't going to work. On multiple occasions, Travis let Jodi know that he wanted to work on getting back on track, and that he would no longer be engaging in any sexual contact with her. I can only imagine she pretended to be completely supportive about this new agreement, only to show up at two a.m. to pounce on him while he was asleep. From what I was told, Jodi would make it near impossible for Travis to stick to his commitment to stop the physical relationship. Travis would give in to her pressure, then completely regret it afterward. He would tell her *no more! That was the last time! I don't want to live like this!* He would plead with her to stop coming over in the middle of the night, and on many occasions, he begged her to move back to California. They would refrain for a period of time, and I bet as soon as she saw him or read that he was moving on in his emails, she would seduce him again.

The relationship was not this ongoing sexual relationship that Jodi explained. I think it was periods of being "good" and withholding from Jodi, followed by giving into her relentless efforts during moments of weakness. Some people have no compassion for Travis in this situation, suggesting that he should have just sent her packing and been strong. To them I say you have never encountered a Jodi Arias. I even thought *he always had his choice*, but did he? He wasn't dealing with a normal person. She took conniving, manipulating, and deception to a whole new level! It's easy to stand back and say what Travis should or should not have done, but she was in his head and in total control, and I don't think he had any idea.

I was telling an expert on sociopaths about what I saw between Jodi and Travis, to which she responded, "That's the scariest thing about sociopaths. They have a way of entering someone's mind through manipulation until they have control, and the victim has no idea that they are no longer in control of their own life. They may think they are, but they aren't." I can only imagine that Travis felt like he was going insane. He would pull away, and through making him feel guilty about "abandoning" her or threatening suicide, she would reel him back in, begging for a friend. When she would reel him back in, they would agree not to "cross the line," and she would end up seducing him. Why do I think this? I know Travis. I watched her manipulate him more than once. We also saw it in the text messages. On January 18, 2008, they are "being good." During these times of "being good," Jodi would test the waters to keep him thinking about what could be happening between them. We all know that when we think about something often enough, we eventually act on it. Jodi sent the following text:

> "*The reason I was asking about later tonight is because I want to give you a nice BJ and I'd like a generous facial in return.*"
> Followed by something like . . . "*Or we can just grind.*"

People that are engaging in an ongoing secretive sexual relationship don't talk about "grinding," nor do they offer that as a back-up to sex. This screams to me that he was trying to break off this toxic physical relationship, and she was trying to push the envelope and see what she could get away with.

Travis wasn't "using" Jodi. Jodi was using Travis to get everything she wanted in life, and sex was her means of control. Travis felt used by Jodi, not the other way around. Travis was doing all in his willpower to resist her advances, but sometimes he gave in. Like most people in that situation, he went with it, made the most of it, and enjoyed it. In the countless text messages, it is Jodi who solicits sex or sexual acts from or for Travis, not vice versa! I thought there had to be times where he was feeling it and wanted her to come over, but there is no evidence of that. There are plenty of communications from Jodi initiating sex talk, requesting favors, and offering them, but very few, if any, from Travis. It's obvious that once they were together it was mutual, and they would both initiate physical activities. But, when they were not together and Travis was focused on moving on, she did the initiating.

There are those who want to paint Travis as a bad guy, or just a "guy," so, of course he is going to have sex if she is willing to. I don't believe we are giving Travis enough credit. Travis was not stringing her along, lying to her, nor getting her hopes up that he would one day commit and marry her. From the text messages and recorded call, it's clear that he was honest with her about their relationship and it not going anywhere. She led him to believe that she was okay with it. He was constantly asking her to move back to California. I just don't believe the nature of the sexual relationship described by Jodi. It was a constant battle between the two of them. Periods of abstinence followed by periods of giving into fantasies and sexual desires, which were followed by much sorrow and regret on Travis's part. This roller coaster was taking an emotional toll on Travis. He cared about her, but he hated who they became when they were together. She would be so sweet, then she would manipulate him, create drama, get into his email, follow him, cry, and bring him down, and he would want to be done with her forever. Then she would thank him for being so good to her and tell him how amazing he was, and he would hope she had or would change! It was an awful, destructive cycle. Without them completely cutting off all communication, it was just too easy to fall back into old ways, no matter what Travis had told himself he was going to do.

CHAPTER 17

# Pedophilia Accusations

*Of more than forty thousand people recruited into Chris's
business, no one started and grew faster than Travis. He still
holds the record for the fastest start in Chris's business. He
was a dynamic speaker. When he took the stage, he was in his
element! Speaking, loving people, and helping them change
their lives was his calling. It's what he was meant to do.*

IN 2010, A PRE-TRIAL HEARING related to Travis's murder was to be held
in Phoenix, Arizona. Shortly before the hearing, Chris and I were subpoenaed by the defense. Not long after receiving the subpoena, I received a call from Kirk Nurmi, one of the defense attorneys. He called
me because he wanted to share something with me that he said would
be hard for me to deal with. He indicated that he would rather I learn
about whatever this was while I was at home as opposed to being blind-
sided by it on the witness stand in front of a bunch of strangers. I told
him that if it was a naked picture of Travis that I really didn't need to
see it. He assured me it was not, and asked for my email address. He
told me it was a letter that Travis had written, and that it had been verified one hundred percent as authentic. He also said he had irrefutable
evidence to back up what was in the letter.

After receiving it, I opened it on my phone, but it was difficult to read because it was too small. I was able to make out a couple of a parts, one in particular, which read, "I want to blow my f***ing head off." Travis texted me a few weeks before he was killed that he had, "f'd up his life" and wanted to "blow his f'ing head off." He was so distraught over the things that he and Jodi had been doing, as well as the fact that he had ruined his relationship with Lisa. I later found out that Regan and Taylor, both friends of Travis's, also received similar texts. Upon seeing these words in this letter, the same words Travis had texted to me shortly before being killed, I immediately assumed this letter *was* written by Travis.

Struggling to read the small text, I sat down in front of my computer, so I could enlarge the letter. It was a letter from Travis to Jodi, dated January 21, 2007. This was about four months after they had met. Jodi was living in California and Travis in Arizona. I began to read the letter, and it was disgusting. I kept thinking, *This can't be true,* but I continued reading until the end.

*Jodi,*                                                                                          *1/21/07*

*Please give me a chance to explain what you saw. I know it looks bad. And honestly it is. Your probably the only person on the planet who has the capacity to understand and the compassion to even try. This goes back years. I have desires I can't explain. What is worse is I've acted on those desires. I have hurt children because of urges I can't control. I can't help it. I know it's pure evil but I can't stop. I've prayed about it repeatedly, I've gotten a blessing, but nothing helps. I have gone to my Bishop but I cannot tell him directly about it for obvious reasons. I had "toys" in the attic which is [why] I never let you up there to clean. Even after I said I was done I didn't get rid of them right away because I thought what if? What if I might need them again? I finally donated them. Enough is enough. I want to stop and at times I think I can. Other times it feels like I'll never be able to. I can only imagine that it's like a drug problem. I worry about getting married. I worry* *that my wife won't suffice. I worry about having kids. What if I have to adopt? If they are not my seed will it be too easy? I'm scared to be alone with a boy. I get unwanted thoughts and I don't want to act on them. It's true, kids can get annoying but the truth is I'm scared to be alone with them. I worry about going to the Hughes in the future because Ryell is getting close to that age. It would be so easy. I know you think this is sick. I am sick. I've had sex with boys and I don't know if they'll ever get past what I've done. The truth is I f\*\*\*ing hate myself! I want to kill myself! I want to blow my f\*\*\*ing head off! Sometimes I can't stand being alive. I'm sorry you had to see what you saw. Honestly you've helped me on several occasions without even knowing it. You've been an outlet frustrations via the fantasy enactments. It's one of the reasons I like anal sex so much. It's the reason for the boys underwear. Don't get me wrong I'm not gay. I'm not a fag. I've just had this inside me. And when I'm getting it from girls I desire boys less. I know this is evil. But this is not who I am nor who I am becoming. Jodi I don't want to be labeled a pedophile or a child molester. Do you understand what I am saying? Please just call me. I need to know that I can trust you. I know that I can trust you. I'll tell you everything, just call me. You have never judged me before. Please do not judge me now. Just call me when your done reading this.*

*T.V.A.*

*There is no way!* I thought, as I finished reading. Chris called and asked what the defense team sent me. I told him he needed to come home immediately, so he could read it himself. Numb, I sat in the front room staring at the letter. The only thing "irrefutable" would be videos or pictures. I was thinking, *How did Detective Flores not mention this?* Chris got home and read the letter.

"Anyone could have written this," he said.

I reminded him about the "irrefutable evidence." It was just so unbelievable. This wasn't Travis! We were both sickened, shocked, stunned, and at a loss. We knew Travis as well as anyone and this didn't add up. It was an impossibility! But the defense had "irrefutable evidence" and had verified it to be his writing.

While I was in college, I volunteered at the Children's Justice Center. It's a center for physically, emotionally, and sexually abused kids. We would review the case files and become an advocate as the child went through the court process and years following as they worked to recover from the abuse. It quickly became obvious that children are not abused by random strangers on the street, but by people who are related to them or close to the family. When we would work with families, I would watch mothers who were in complete denial that someone they knew and trusted would do this to their child. Some were in so much denial that they refused to believe the "irrefutable evidence" and their child. I promised myself I would never be like that.

I share this simply to illustrate where I was mentally. I sent an email to the defense attorney:

> *WOW! I knew he had issues—but not these. Thank you sooooooo much for your consideration in giving this to us ahead of time. We really appreciate it!!!!!*
>
> *Sky*

(The "issues" to which I was referring were his commitment issues.)

My emails to Nurmi in regard to this are absolutely NOT a reflection on Travis, but on my past experiences with sexual abuse victims, and our ignorance as to what was legal and ethical as far as the actions of the defense team. We were responding to Nurmi's lies, and it had nothing to do with Travis. It never even crossed our minds that it would be legal or ethical for an attorney to lie to us and even conjure evidence. Keep in mind this was way before everything was played out in the media, before we had a feel for what the defense team was all about, and the extent Jodi would go to continue to destroy Travis. I couldn't fathom anyone making up this sort of thing up under any circumstance . . . ever! And to do it shortly before we were to testify seemed illegal to us.

The more we thought about it and discussed it, the more confused we became. We were trying to wrap our minds around it. On the one hand, we knew Travis, loved Travis, and knew he would never do anything like this. On the other hand, we had an attorney, who is governed by the bar association and their rules of ethics, telling us this letter had been one hundred percent verified, and he has "irrefutable evidence" to back it up. In complete bewilderment and a confused state of mind, I wrote another email to the defense attorney asking for more information. My heart told me this was a lie, but the defense said they had "irrefutable evidence," and he said it had been verified one hundred percent as Travis's writing.

Convinced that there had to be "irrefutable evidence," because attorneys are bound by rules of ethics, including being truthful in their statements (AZ Bar Rule 4.1), we were just trying our best to process it all. Something else I learned at the Children's Justice Center was there is always child pornography involved in sexual abuse. If this handwritten admission were true (though my heart was screaming that it wasn't), I wondered why we'd heard nothing about child porn being on his computer. *If he was a child predator, he would had to have had child porn on his computer,* I thought. Every show and movie I'd ever seen about crooked cops flooded my mind, and I was thinking, *How could no one have told us about this?* It had been two years since Travis's murder! Jodi's attorney was *kind enough* to call more than once and apologize for being the bearer of such bad news and just to check if I was okay. *What a nice guy,* I thought. He also continued to remind me that the writings had been "one hundred percent verified as Travis's writing," and about the "irrefutable evidence" every time we spoke.

Still sitting in a stupor, I scoured my memory. *Had Travis ever tried to "groom" my boys* (which is something pedophiles do)*? Anyone's boys? Were there any red flags? Did he try to be alone with my boys . . . any of our friends' boys?* I was trying to be open to the possibility, considering this is how it happens more often than not, but there was nothing! Suddenly, it came over me . . . *This isn't true!*

I read the letter again, and this time it seemed as if I was reading a completely different letter. I think the initial shock and trauma numbed my brain to any sort of common sense! Suddenly, everything about it seemed utterly ridiculous—the when, the how, and the what. This just wasn't Travis! All my fears began to dissipate.

"This isn't true," I said to Chris.

"How do you know?" he asked.

"It's just not. There's no way it's true," I responded. "I'm calling Flores." I went into the kitchen to make the call.

As soon as he answered, I said, "So, Travis is a pedophile?"

"What are you talking about?" Detective Flores responded.

"Is there child porn on his computer? Did you find videos or pictures of him with kids?" I asked.

"No! No!" he said. "What are you even talking about? There's nothing like that!" Flores was totally confused.

I told him about the letter the defense attorney sent to us. Flores was shocked. He knew nothing about it! He said they had gone through Travis and Jodi's houses, and there was no letter! He told me he would call me right back. Moments later, a call came in from a blocked number.

"Sky, this is Juan Martinez with the Maricopa County Attorney's office. Tell me about this letter. How did you get it?"

I relayed to him the phone call from Nurmi, the email, the letter, my emails back, and the follow-up phone calls of "concern." Martinez was not happy. He didn't know anything about this letter.

Now we were mad! We were ready to fight. I had plans to go to a movie with my good friend, Shari. I didn't feel like going, due to the circumstances, but I needed to clear my head. I was telling her about everything and read her the letter while we sat in the parking lot of the movie theater, and she immediately knew it was fake. While we were sitting in the car talking about it, I got another call from Nurmi. He was worried about how I was dealing with the news. I put the phone on speaker, and the conversation went something like this:

"I just wanted to check and see how you are doing," he said, sounding concerned.

"Great!" I exclaimed cheerily.

"Great? How are you great? Your tone has changed considerably from your emails. What about the letter?" he asked.

"It's not real. There is no way Travis was a pedophile. There are so many things in that letter that are so unrealistic. So, I'm doing great," I said.

"Mrs. Hughes, it was verified by a handwriting expert to be Travis's writing, and what about the evidence that backs it up?" he asked.

"Well, then you may want to get a new handwriting expert. And what evidence do you have anyway? I don't think you have any evidence."

"I can't disclose that at this time, but we definitely have evidence that cannot be disputed," he said. He was obviously upset and even angry that I did not believe his ruse; I looked over at Shari and we both started laughing.

"Well, I don't believe you, and I am heading into a movie with a friend. Have a great night!" I hung up, realizing for the first time what this attorney was all about. There was no limit to how low this man would go in an effort to ruin Travis's good name. He further proved this with all the shenanigans that would come years later in the courtroom.

After returning home from the movie, Chris and I reconnected and were even more convinced the letter was fraudulent. Chris and I were both guilt-ridden for even thinking, even for a moment, that the letter was authentic! I think that the instinct to protect our kids, temporarily, until we stepped back and really looked at the situation as a whole, clouded our judgement. It was still hard for us to believe that it was legal for someone to make something like that up. We definitely learned our lesson. The defense never stopped slinging mud from that point forward, and we have not wavered in defending Travis's good name.

The following day, I wrote an email that I was going to send to the defense attorney. I wanted to make it abundantly clear that I responded the way I did in my email to him because of the lies I was told, and *not* because I ever felt this was true about Travis. Then I thought about the emails I had already sent to him and how he could twist them! So I decided to send it to Martinez instead, and he could forward it to the defense attorney if he wanted to. Before sending it to Martinez, I sent it to a friend, who said it was her opinion that the defense team was shady and suggested I just drop it. I took her advice, and I never sent it to Martinez, but I saved it. I pulled it out of my files to include it in this book, and I found it interesting that I wrote it on June 4, 2010, two years to the day after Travis was brutally slaughtered.

(This email was not edited)

*Mr. Martinez,*

*I was going to send this to Mr. Nurmi, but didn't know if I should send this to you first. So, if you see it appropriate, please send this to him.*

*Mr. Nurmi,*

*Yesterday when we spoke, you said, "Your tone has changed considerably from your emails." I was so shocked by what you sent me, because it just didn't work for me. Travis would never do those things! There is no way Travis wrote this letter. Travis does not fit the profile of a pedophile whatsoever! I racked my brain trying to come up with ANYTHING that would make this believable, and there is nothing! It is so unfathomable. And, after the initial shock of the email wore off, I began to realize just how ridiculous this letter was, for soooo many reasons other than the fact that he wouldn't do this. I am by no means a professional, but I have worked with abuse cases, and things show up in the lives of the perpetrator that validate the accusations, and with Travis nothing! Except a letter that surfaces two years after he is dead? When detectives have gone through his house, computer, and life thoroughly?*

*Jodi has faked emails, sent texts pretending to be Travis, broken into his email, made up totally unbelievable and impossible stories, and lied from the beginning—I don't put anything past her. She is a liar, it's what she does. This letter isn't any different than what she does—a lie.*

*If I was going to be put in prison for murder, you better believe I would be yelling from the rooftops that the person I killed was raping little boys, and I had proof. Why make up a ridiculous story about intruders when she has proof he was molesting/raping children? And why not mention it until she is about to be sentenced to death for slaughtering someone? If I were her, I would have pulled this card long before the "intruders" story.*

*The writing—Totally uniform, straight, nice. His "secret" life has just been revealed—not only secret, but despicable and illegal, and his life is about to be destroyed—he will go to prison for a LONG time . . . If it were me, my writing would be all over the place. I would be freaking out, and my writing would reflect that! Travis was a VERY smart guy. Who would put such atrocities in a letter to someone they knew for four months? Not a smart person.*

*"I had toys in the attic which is why I never let you up there to clean." REALLY? I have never, nor do I know anyone that has ever cleaned their attic. Maybe he had a useable attic, I honestly don't know, but this is a girlfriend he has known for four months, offering to go in the attic—more than once, it is just odd. It wasn't like she lived there.*

*"Never let you" sounds like there were multiple times she wanted to go in there. Just seems off to me.*

*What kind of person finds out after four months of knowing someone that they are raping young boys and doesn't turn them in to the police? But instead, they put on boy underwear and proceed to act out despicable and disgusting things (the "fantasy enactments" of the raping of children) thus feeding the appetite and need for more! Then hides this information from family, friends, and police when under investigation?*

*It seems obvious to me that this letter you have sent me that has been "verified to be Travis's writing by a handwriting expert" (your words) is nothing but a tactic by you and Jodi to demonize and obliterate the victim's, Travis Alexander, reputation, but this is nothing new for her! It is obvious that you are attempting to gain sympathy from the jurors that "this beautiful, sweet girl was manipulated and abused by a horrible man, and that she did the world a favor by ridding it of this heinous man." That portrayal of Travis could not be farther from the truth, but you already know that. It is disturbing to what extent people will go to keep a cold-blooded murderer from getting the death penalty that she deserves! Do you have no conscience? I know she doesn't. She tried saying that he was abusive, and that didn't work—the "intruder" story is a joke, so you guys have stooped to an abhorrent low by saying the good man she slaughtered, raped children—how convenient two months before the trial! Who does that? I was naive enough to think, wow, how considerate you were for sending this to us ahead of time, only to realize this was a shameless manipulation tactic. I thought it was illegal to conjure up evidence and trick someone into thinking something horrible to get what you want.*

*We will see you on the 17th. Sky*

[You can see the email at www.ourfriendtravis.com/email-to-defense]

We set out to do our own investigation to prove that Travis did not write that letter. Deanna Reid, who helped the Alexander family go through Travis's things after his death, gave Chris a box full of Pre-Paid Legal-related items, one of which was his first business journal. With his journal on the left and the letter on the right we began to compare the two.

The letters were his letters—exactly! But, the spacing and slant of the writing was not Travis's writing. Someone had forged it using something Travis had written. It was almost as if whoever wrote this letter, scanned something Travis wrote, and wrote this letter by cutting and pasting each letter of every word, or more likely, cut and paste words. A few days later, we called our friend Randy, who had recently retired from the San Bernardino Sheriff's Office after thirty years as a CSI (crime scene investigator). He, too, was suspicious about the letter and referred us to his friend, who was a former handwriting expert for the FBI. We called him and explained the situation. We told him that there was no original (which we discovered later), only a digital version sent to the defense team from an "anonymous source." He started laughing and told us that the defense had obviously not found a very reputable handwriting expert. "No expert can give even a fifty percent probability without an original document," he said, indicating that we had been lied to.

I think there were six or seven other letters that emerged with this one, but those all spoke of Travis's alleged physical abuse of Jodi. (Court documents which became available after the eBook version of this book was published, stated there were a total of ten letters.) And, in typical Jodi fashion, the letters, again, supposedly written by Travis to Jodi, talked about how amazing and talented Jodi was. If I remember correctly, these letters were dated from January 2007 to May 2007 (don't quote me on that). Some have argued that it's understandable that the wrong year was put on the January letter because it was near the year change … but by May, one would have that figured out. But, when Jodi testified, the first time she claimed she was "abused" by Travis was January 2008.

We would also learn that she had been caught with pens and paper and other contraband items in her jail cell. Jodi and her cronies concocted these letters. They were frauds, and this is why they never showed up in the murder trial.

Jodi was collaborating a "story" with who we, and many others, believe was Matt McCartney, her ex-boyfriend, and only long-term friend as far as any of us knew, as evidenced in the magazines with the secret messages that emerged the summer of 2011. During a jail visit from Ann Campbell, Jodi's jail mate pal and ex-convict, Jodi requested to have two magazines sent home with Campbell. The guard took them and scanned through them, but didn't see anything. She took them to her superior, and she didn't see anything. The guard had a gut feeling that something was going on and was not right. She took the magazines and looked through them under better light, and she saw something!

She found numbers written in one magazine, and messages on different pages in the other magazine. What are the chances? We are so thankful she listened to that voice within her. After showing her boss what she had discovered, her boss said, "Do you know who that is over there? That's Juan Martinez. He's Jodi's prosecutor."

Juan Martinez just happened to be in the jail *that day* at the *perfect moment!* The guard walked over to Martinez and told him about the magazines, and in a matter of minutes, he was able to secure a subpoena to intercept them. (I think little miracles along our journey of life is how God lets us know that He loves us and is aware of us. This was one of those miracles.) There were always the "what-ifs." What if people believe her? What if the jury believes her? What if the judge believes her? What if she is able to manipulate the jury and the public to believe the terrible accusations she made up about Travis? What if she gets off because of some technicality? So many "what-ifs." This was the first time since Travis was murdered that I thought, *Okay, there is no way her lies will work. This is the nail in the coffin.*

After securing a subpoena, Martinez was able to get to work on the messages. There were two magazines, *Photo Pro* and *Star.* (Ironically, the *Star* magazine had a cover story about Casey Anthony to whom many people have compared Jodi Arias. Casey was arrested the day after Jodi.) In one magazine there were page numbers, and on the corresponding pages in the other magazine there were fragments of sentences. It's generally believed that the secret message hidden in the magazines were meant for Jodi's buddy, Matt McCartney. It read:

"You f@$%&* up. What you told my attorney next day directly contradicts what I've been saying for over a year. Get down here ASAP and see me before you talk to them again and before you testify so we can fix this. Interview was excellent. Must talk ASAP."

Incredible, isn't it? Ironically, Matt is the only person on planet Earth who claims to have seen the "originals" to the "pedophile" and "abuse" letters. He was also the only person on planet Earth who claimed to have seen bruising around Jodi's neck and her "broken" ring finger on her left hand, both a result of, according to her, beatings by Travis. The message states, "What you told my attorney next day directly contradicts what I've been saying for over a year." Just "over a year" previous to this message hidden in the magazines, Jodi came up with the allegations of abuse, pedophilia, and that she killed Travis in self-defense.

As a point of interest, on July 16, 2008, Jodi talked in detail about the injury to her "left ring finger" during a police interrogation. Remember the masked intruders story? According to her statement during interrogation, it was the masked woman who injured Jodi's left ring finger, leaving it, in Jodi's words, "not the same." Then, February 11, 2013, while on the witness stand, she told an elaborate story of how Travis body slammed her (she gets body slammed a lot), and then kicked her in the ribs, breaking her left ring finger when she tried to block his kick. She told one therapist that this attack happened in January 2008, and she told another therapist that it happened in February 2008. What investigators believe really happened was while Jodi was savagely stabbing Travis, over and over and over again, her fingers slipped off the knife handle and over the blade, resulting in her cutting her tendon. This is common in stabbings. The downward motion of that much force (there were knife divots in his bone) causes the stabber's hand to slide down and be cut in the process. Not to mention how slippery blood is, causing her hand to slip even more. This explains how her blood was in her palm print found on Travis's bathroom wall after the murder. Over the years, the damage to the tendon would cause the finger to appear bent. She did not seek medical attention, because she had just butchered Travis. It wouldn't have looked good for her once Travis's body was discovered with twenty-nine stab wounds in it. Mark, a former cop and friend of ours and Travis's, reported that Jodi's fingers were wrapped when she went to dinner with the Pre-Paid Legal group in Utah the day after killing Travis. However, she adds yet another story to the mix. She told Ryan and the others that she cut her fingers on a broken glass while bartending. And, finally, when being grilled on the witness stand by Juan Martinez, in a brilliant barrage of questioning, he asked Jodi if she cut her finger while stabbing Travis. Without taking time to think about it and consider all her many stories, she said, "Yes." Oops!

Matt McCartney, the one and only person on the planet who had all the good stuff against Travis, was never called to testify in the trial. Interesting. He made a claim online that it was because of Jodi's respect for him and his new life with his new family. She was kind enough not to involve him. Good one. Or, perhaps, it had more to do with committing perjury and being arrested and thrown in jail? If your life is on the line and there is anyone, anywhere who can potentially save it, you subpoena them. Period. They never subpoenaed Matt, and we can all figure out why.

All of this took place shortly before a hearing scheduled on August 4, 2011. Though not subpoenaed, Matt was scheduled to appear. Matt was a no-show. I don't know if it was this hearing or a subsequent hearing when the messages in the magazines were addressed. Jodi found another inmate to take the fall for her, but the plan failed and ended in a complete debacle.

The other inmate, who claimed she was the one who wrote the messages, took the stand. Martinez presented her with a magazine and asked her to find what she wrote, but she couldn't. He told her what page to turn to and asked her what she wrote, what the code meant, and what message she wrote. She didn't know anything about the message, the code, nor how or where it was written. She even accused Martinez of switching the magazines. It was a beautiful disaster.

Jodi wanted to get the letters that she had concocted in as evidence that Travis was a pedophile and that he abused her. It's my opinion that her attorneys were as sure as I was that the letters were fake, and they wouldn't pursue the issue. This was when Jodi inexplicably fired her attorneys and made headline news, yet again, by announcing that she would be defending herself. The judge, however, ordered that the defense team stay on to advise her. She tried to get the fake letters in on her own, and it was denied because they were fake. She then rehired her attorneys and continued with the case. There were never originals to these letters, and to my knowledge, a source of these emailed letters was never revealed despite multiple requests from Martinez. Somebody had the courage to create false evidence, but not the courage to go down for it.

In the words of defense attorney, Kirk Nurmi, "Let's go back . . ." to the day when Jodi claimed she found out Travis was a pedophile. On the witness stand, Jodi testified that she was at Travis's house on January 21, 2008. According to Jodi, the year on the fraudulent letter was the wrong one. Shortly after leaving his house, she returned to retrieve something she left there. According to Jodi, she "ran up the stairs." (He would have certainly heard her had she run up the stairs, which were right next to his bedroom.) She burst into his room and over to the dresser to get what she had left. She turned and saw Travis scrambling to gather papers on his bed. Just then, one of the papers flew off the bed and floated back and forth until it landed at her feet. (If you have some extra time, watch this on YouTube. The way she describes the paper floating down is something you must experience.) She looked down. It was a picture of a young boy in his underwear. Oh ya, and Travis was allegedly masturbating to the pictures on the bed.

When I heard this, I thought, *What? Where did this come from? How is this legal?* Her story in 2010 was that she had been cleaning his attic and found videotapes and children's toys, to which Travis responded with this ridiculous letter explaining that he had been raping little boys. Now, the story was that he was masturbating to printed images of little boys. And, we can't forget the second of three stories she told to three different therapists—that she walked in and saw him sitting at his computer in his room, masturbating to images of boys. This story had a short life, because she learned that there was no child porn on his computer. Expert witness for the defense, LaViolette, was asked about this. She said that she must have been mistaken when she was deposed by Martinez and said it was a computer that Travis was viewing. And, apparently, all three therapists made a mistake in their notes and their depositions as well? Hmmm. What are the odds? I could go on and on. But, "let's go back . . ."

What really happened on January 21, 2008? In Jodi's testimony, she claimed she was devastated after walking in on Travis and catching him in the act of masturbating to pictures of little boys on his bed. She went home and puked, and then went to the LDS Temple visitor's center to pray (because she is so righteous). She testified that Travis kept calling her over and over again, and that she would not take his calls. That was what she said happened. If we look at what actually happened the day she discovered "the love of her life" and the man who "would be the most incredible father" (these were things she said to a friend *after* January 2008) had a thing for little boys, we get a completely different story.

January 21, 2008 Phone Calls and Text Messages:

3:53 pm- Jodi Calls Travis
4:09 pm- Jodi Calls Travis
4:29 pm- Travis Calls Jodi
4:53 pm- Jodi Calls Travis
4:54 pm- Travis Calls Jodi
5:11 pm- Travis Calls Jodi
5:20 pm- Travis Calls Jodi
5:38 pm Jodi Text Travis: I can't remember- am I coming in for you on wed @10:30am
5:48 pm- Travis Calls Jodi
5:53 pm- Jodi Calls Travis
6:41 pm- Jodi Texts Travis: Can we trade cars before FHE? [Family Home Evening—a church activity at the singles' ward.]
7:19 pm- Jodi Texts Travis: Never mind. One of the stores I need to go to closes @ 8pm. I'll just go tomorrow.
7:20 pm- Jodi resends above text
7:24 pm- Travis texts Jodi: I got a ride from some peeps in the ward now you can just go get it. Let me know when you made the exchange.
7:25 pm- Jodi texts Travis: I'm almost asleep. We'll see. Zzzz...
7:27 pm- Travis texts Jodi: You obviously don't need it that bad. I got a ride so you could go get the car. Now you are going to sleep?
7:29 pm- Jodi texts Travis: I fell asleep and a phone call woke me up. That's when I sent you the text.
7:36 pm- Jodi texts Travis: I have a really bad headache. I can barely move.
9:11 pm- Travis texts Jodi: Alright get it tomorrow then
9:16 pm- Jodi texts Travis: Can you talk right now?
9:17 pm- Travis texts Jodi: Not right now

Jodi said in her testimony that from the time she ran out of Travis's house he just kept calling and really wanted to talk to her. She said that she didn't want to talk to him until she finally gave in and called him. As you can see, this is not what the phone records and texts show. Travis does not call nor text her that day until 4:29 p.m. when he returns her two calls she made at 3:53 p.m. and 4:09 p.m. Their major concern is switching cars, not that she just found out he was a pedophile! And it's Jodi who wants to talk to him and Travis is busy. He obviously isn't dropping everything to speak with her, which seems strange for someone who, according to her, was so relentlessly trying to talk to her.

As if this isn't enough, Martinez provided her journal entries. From January 20 to January 24, there are no journal entries. Remember, the 21st was the day she "caught him." You would expect that in her very next journal entry she would tell the horrific story of walking in on Travis. Her first entry after "the incident" was January 24, 2008. "I haven't written because there has been nothing note worthy to report." Years later, in an effort to save her own life, she would claim that between January 20–24, 2008, Travis beat her up, strangled her until she passed out, and broke her finger, not to mention that she discovered he was into little boys. Those would definitely be "noteworthy" events in my life. But, since they didn't happen, there truly was nothing for her to report.

Here is what I know about pedophiles. They like little boys or little girls, but rarely, if ever, both. And, someone who is turned on by children is certainly not going to be involved in fulfilling sexual fantasies with a curvaceous woman with breast implants. It's either or, but certainly not "all of the above." It just doesn't work that way. A man who is engaged, as Jodi originally claimed, in having sex with little boys, would have zero interest in sex with Jodi.

While I was in Arizona to testify at a hearing, I approached Jodi's dad. Prior to my testifying, a tape had been played where Jodi said some awful things about her younger sister, Angela. I think Angela was about fourteen when this happened, and she idolized Jodi. I felt awful for Angela. She was just a kid. I wanted her to know that Jodi always spoke highly of her. Angela wasn't in court that day, so I approached her dad in the hallway.

"Mr. Arias, I was hoping you could let Angela know that Jodi always spoke highly of her. She loved her very much and always had nice things to say about her," I said.

"Are you a friend of Jodi's?" he asked.

Awkward! "No, I'm not. I'm a friend of Travis's. Jodi spent a lot of time at my house. My name is Sky," I responded, and I started to walk back to my seat outside the courtroom.

"You have a little boy?" he asked.

I stopped, turned around, and I nodded.

"In November 2007, Jodi told me she would always keep an eye on your little boy and protect him from Travis. I also saw bruises from where Travis had hurt her. She tried to cover them up," he said.

"In November 2007?" I asked, making sure I had the year correct.

"Yes," he responded.

"None of that is true," I said.

"You don't think so?" he asked.

"I know it's not," I said, and walked away.

Though I felt badly for him and his son who was with him, in my head I was thinking, *What? November 2007? Really? We kicked her out of our house in April 2007, and she wasn't around my kids after that. She didn't "find out" about Travis's "pedophilia" until January 2008, although the date on "Travis's letter" was January 2007. C'mon, Mr. Arias, I get that you are going through hell right now, and you feel the need to support your daughter, but you don't need to support her lies! And there is no way you saw bruises, or she told you he was a pedophile! If I were you, guess what I'm telling the police when they inform me that my daughter murdered her ex-boyfriend? 'Did you know he beat her and was a pedophile? I saw the bruises! She told me that she was protecting his friends' kids!' But, no! You didn't say that, did you? Instead, in your police interview, you said that Travis "was a pretty good guy from what I hear." Remember that?*

I know it's not popular, but I feel awful for the Arias family. I really do. It's so much easier to be on Travis's side of this whole thing. How do you reconcile in your head the abhorrent, evil, unthinkable things your daughter, sister, niece, cousin, friend did to another human being, all because he was moving on with his life? They have been attacked so much, which makes me sad, even though they seem to have recently crossed the line and now feel she was wrongly convicted. Some people think they deserve the attacks because of them being seen laughing in court, being rude to the Alexanders, and their support of Jodi's lies. Bullying at any level, for any reason, and in any form is still wrong. I don't agree with everything they have done, but my heart does hurt for them. I can't imagine enduring what they are going through. To critique their every expression, movement, and comment seems harsh, as I can only imagine they are just trying to hang on. They did not make Jodi this way. From what I have heard from many people who know the Arias family, they are really good people. They said Bill and Sandra are good parents, and they did what they could for Jodi. They didn't just let her run wild. According to Bill and Sandra Arias' police interrogation, Jodi has always been troubled.

We didn't know the defense's strategy and if they and Jodi would in fact follow through with their claims that Travis was a pedophile. We hoped Travis's good name would not be soiled by such despicable lies. With the letters being deemed fakes and rejected from the light of the courtroom, and Jodi's trying to fix Matt's testimony, we felt confident they would drop the whole nonsensical story. We were wrong.

One evening, I got a phone call from my brother, Zion, who had just finished an interview about Travis on the *Nancy Grace Show.* He told me that in his earpiece he heard them prepping a spokesperson for the *National Inquirer,* and that he would be talking about a letter claiming Travis was a pedophile that Jodi's mom had asked them to publish. My worst nightmare.

*What am I going to do? How am I going to protect him? How can I refute these lies?* I wondered. We weren't doing media. We were trying to lay low. Martinez told us he would not be calling us to testify, and we were confident that the defense wasn't going to either. We had never been deposed by either side. Upon their request, we gave the defense ten dates that would work for us, but they never followed up. We would destroy their case. Having us get up and talk about how we kicked Jodi out of our house a year before she killed Travis because we were scared of her wouldn't do much for them. Had they called us to testify, it would ruin the good thing they had going with the emails we had written back and forth with Travis in January 2007. Had they put us on the stand, we would be able to explain how Jodi manipulated the situation by lying to us and lying to Travis. The entire email would also be allowed in, which would give it context and meaning, and would have hurt them, not helped them.

They never told us we were on a witness list nor that we could not watch the trial. But, we knew they didn't want us there. In a pre-trial hearing, we were asked to leave the room after Jodi turned and whispered something to her attorneys. We knew they weren't going to call us. Prior to the trial starting, we were never instructed by the defense team, never deposed, and never subpoenaed for the trial. In fact, during a hearing, Nurmi reprimanded Martinez because apparently, Martinez failed to do Nurmi's job. Nurmi seemed to have thought it was Martinez's responsibility to make sure we knew the rules. If Nurmi put us on a witness list and didn't want us to watch the trial, it was his responsibility to tell us. He failed to do so. After sitting down in the gallery, following my testimony at a hearing during the trial, the defense noticed me and had me removed from the courtroom. They subpoenaed me on the spot. The subpoena requested that I show up to testify on a *Sunday*! There is no court on Sunday. The subpoena was not so I could testify, but so they could keep me out of the courtroom.

Back to the letter given to the *National Enquirer*. I knew Abe Abdelhadi was going to be on the *Dr. Drew on Call* show, which immediately followed the *Nancy Grace* show Zion was on. Abe is a character. He is smart, witty, bold, and really funny. Jodi would call and whine to Abe about how much she loved Travis, how amazing he was, and how she couldn't imagine marrying anyone other than him, nor anyone other than him being the father of her children. This was after she "found out" he was a "pedophile," and after he "beat her." Abe would ask her why she was so obsessed with him, since it was clear that Travis wanted to move on. Finally, he told Jodi that he was sick of her "high school drama" and wanted nothing to do with her. I had met Abe a couple of times before Travis was killed, but didn't really "know him." I had gotten to know him after Jodi was arrested. I called him. I couldn't even keep it together . . . poor Abe!

"They are going to say he is a pedophile!" I was losing it, but somehow Abe made out what I was trying to say.

I told him about the letter, the *National Inquirer,* and some additional background. I asked him if he would do his best to protect and defend Travis while on the *Dr. Drew* show. Abe was so nice about the whole thing. He was probably thinking I was a little crazy. When I called him that evening, the guy from the *National Inquirer* hadn't gone on Nancy, yet. It did not unfold how I thought it would. Turns out, the pedophile letter was too fake for even the *Inquirer.* The *National Inquirer* representative said how awful it was that Jodi was continuing to manipulate people, including her own family, from behind bars. He said Jodi's mom was crying when she brought the letter to him. Clearly, she knew what she was about to do to a good man, a good man her daughter ruthlessly mutilated and slaughtered. What she told the *National Inquirer* is telling. "Jodi wanted me to get these letters out to the public. I am only doing this because she asked me to." She didn't do it because she believed it. She didn't do it because "it was the right thing to do." She only did it because Jodi asked her to.

Where did Jodi come up with this idea of pedophilia? I went back and forth debating whether or not to include this information in this book. While I want to respect the privacy of the family that experienced this tragedy, it is vital to this story. I ran it by several people whom I trust and respect (some even know the people involved). The people

I spoke to were adamant about the importance of this information in clearing Travis's name, and showing how heartless and cruel Jodi is. On the same day Jodi was arrested, a family that was close to Jodi and Travis lost a son to suicide. The two events were completely unrelated. The suicide occurred before Jodi was arrested. In the note left by this young man, he spoke of being molested as a child and how he had the urge to do this to other children. He killed himself, because he didn't want to do to others what had been done to him. It is my belief that this was where Jodi got the idea for the pedophilia accusations.

So, let's recap. In June 2010, Jodi claimed that she was cleaning Travis's attic and found videotapes and little boys' toys. She also claimed that following that incident, Travis wrote her a letter claiming that he had had sex with little boys. She then told three different therapists that she walked in on Travis masturbating while looking at little boys on his computer. She later said that she never told these three therapists that, so I guess all three were lying. This is not the story she told during the trial, because his computer had zero child porn on it, so she had to come up with another version. She then told the jury that she walked in on him masturbating to printed pictures of little boys, but since there was no child porn, where did he get those? Lies! Lies! Lies! How is this legal? Why is it okay to murder someone and then murder their character with all manner of outlandish, unsubstantiated claims? How is this fair to Travis, the victim? What kind of a person must she be to even conjure up these various stories? She is evil, totally and completely evil. How is it that in our judicial system, you can lie about a good person, but you can't tell the truth about a cold-blooded killer?

[You can see the letter at www.ourfriendtravis.com/fake-letter]

Two excellent blog posts addressing this topic:

www.ourfriendtravis.com/blog1
www.ourfriendtravis.com/blog2

CHAPTER 18

# Trial Revelations

*The Ten Commandments* with Charlton
Heston was Travis's favorite movie.

JODI'S BEHAVIOR IN THE INTERROGATION room is something to see. The detective left Jodi in the room alone. She did a headstand, chastised herself for not wearing makeup, sang, went through the trashcan, and laid down. She was not upset. She was not crying. She seemed confident and at ease. I wish I could say that this odd behavior ended after she was arrested. How do you carry on with life seemingly unaffected after butchering someone? If the brutality of the murder and her odd behavior does not speak to how evil she is, I'm not sure what would.

During the trial, Jodi's lies seemed infinite. For example, when talking about Travis's treadmill, she said he would "walk" on it. Really? Anyone who knew Travis knew that he would go crazy on that treadmill! He would run his guts out for twenty minutes. So why did she lie about that? So she wouldn't have to explain how she was able to run away from him in the last seconds of Travis's life. If he "walked" on his treadmill sometimes, maybe the jury would think he wouldn't be fit enough to catch Jodi when chasing her around in his bathroom (which never happened). But if she told the truth, that Travis ran like a beast every day, it might cast a shadow on her "I outran him" story.

When Darryl Brewer, Jodi's ex-boyfriend she was living with for four months after she started dating Travis, testified during the guilt phase of the trial, it was obvious he had no idea that Jodi was moving on, yet Jodi told Travis, Chris, and me that it was a mutual breakup and that they were going in their separate directions. She claimed she broke up with Darryl the Thursday after she met Travis, but Darryl explained that in January 2007, he thought the relationship would continue.

On Travis's way to our house one night, he stopped by Jodi and Darryl's house. I asked Jodi about this the next time she came over. She told me that Darryl didn't mind if Travis came over as long as Darryl wasn't there. She said he knew she had moved on, but he still cared for her and didn't want to see her with another guy. I was blown away! I commented how impressive and mature that was, especially after a four-year relationship. Again, it was very clear from Darryl's testimony that he had no clue about Travis. According to Darryl's testimony during the murder trial, he explained neither one of them ever "broke up" with one another. As he said, "There wasn't a formal breakup conversation, as much as we both saw our paths going the other way. I was hoping that Jodi would be back with me after resolving the house issue, but it was an unsure time."

Jodi claimed that in October 2006, shortly after meeting Travis, he texted her a picture of his penis. There is no record on Travis's, nor Jodi's phone, that this occurred. The picture was on Jodi's computer. How ironic…Jodi just happened to have a penis photo and submitted it to the court as evidence to attempt to show Travis was a sexual deviant. Judge Stephens allowed the photo in as evidence. During the first trial, a person interested in the case, Kim Lapara, put together a comparison of Travis's fingers and the fingers in the picture. It was obvious that they were not Travis's fingers. During the trial, Darryl, Jodi's ex-boyfriend, didn't want his face shown while he testified. Instead, the courtroom camera focused in on his hands the entire time he testified. The same person who compared Travis's fingers to those in the "penis" picture compared the picture to Darryl Brewer's fingers. Legally, I can't say for sure, but it is my opinion that those fingers look more like Darryl's than they do Travis's. Compare them for yourself. People went so far as to compare the background in the pictures to the pictures on the Multiple Listing Service (where homes are listed for sale) of Jodi and Darryl's house. The similarities in granite and flooring speak for themselves (not shown in the picture below).

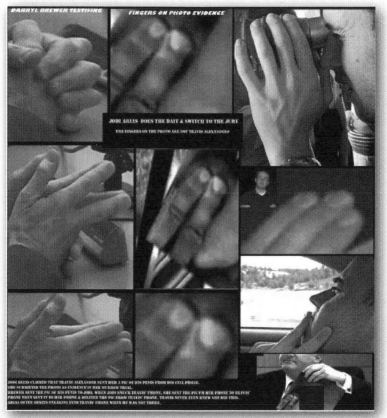

See a larger image of this picture here: www.ourfriendtravis.com/fingers

Shockingly, I have heard a few people question the premeditation of this crime. It really is shocking, but someone said to me just the other day that the gun that was stolen from Jodi's grandparent's house was "circumstantial evidence," and that there was no concrete proof that she stole the .25 caliber gun. While those with common sense can put two and two together, I guess some people need a little more convincing. A .25 caliber gun was stolen from the home Jodi lived in, and seven days later, Travis Alexander was killed and was shot with a .25 caliber gun. For those who need more, the Siskiyou County detective testified that this was a very odd burglary. The only things taken were a DVD player, the .25 caliber gun, and Jodi claimed $30 was taken from her room. The .25 caliber gun was in a cupboard with other guns, but it was the only one missing. Not only that, but there were stacks of undisturbed quarters on the counter above the guns. Why wouldn't a burglar take the money?

Chances are, Jodi didn't steal money from herself, so that leaves us with the gun and the DVD player. We know that she had the gun, so what happened to the DVD player? While Darryl was on the stand, he told the jury that he and his son had breakfast with Jodi on June 3, 2008. He gave her the two gas cans she had requested the week before. She left, but then she returned. Juan Martinez asked why she came back, and Darryl's response confirmed that Jodi staged the robbery at her grandparents' house. He told the jury that she came back to drop off a remote! The defense jumped to their feet with objections and asked to approach the judge. When Juan returned to questioning, he didn't pursue information about the remote. Why? Because Jodi forgot to give Darryl the remote when she gave him the DVD player she had stolen from her grandparents' house. It was too "prejudicial" for the jury to hear.

Jodi claimed during the trial that it was the initial trip to my house where Travis went into her room, and without saying a word, performed oral sex. Travis told me a completely different story. If you want to believe Jodi's ridiculous claims then you would have to believe that this relationship didn't follow the normal progression of a physical relationship. In Jodi's own words, on the recorded conversation between she and Travis played during the trial, Jodi asked Travis, "Do you remember the first time we grinded?" It was on a trip to Ehrenberg, Arizona, in October 2006, where they had met between California and Arizona. This was supposedly after "oral sex at Chris and Sky Hughes'." Who does that? Who goes in reverse? How do you have oral sex, and then "grind" for the first time down the road? It is nonsense. She wants the world to believe they had sex on this trip, and then he turned around and baptized her (which would require a certain level of moral cleanliness). Then after the baptism, she claims they went back to her house, and he "spun her around" and had anal sex with her. This is absolutely ludicrous! It's pretty obvious how made up it is, because on the recorded conversation, she is remembering the first time they did anything "significant," for lack of a better word, in their physical relationship. It was "grinding" in Ehrenberg. Not vaginal sex, not anal sex, not oral sex. Did they have a physical relationship? Yes, but it didn't start how, nor when, she claims it did. If we are all being reasonable, a near thirty-year-old guy who "grinds," and nothing more (or she would have brought it up on the recorded call), on a weekend rendezvous in a hotel room with a girl is a pretty upstanding guy. An upstanding guy does not do all that she is claiming he did, in the manner that she claims he did it in. Jodi didn't stop slaughtering Travis on June 4; she continued slaughtering him leading up to the trial, during the trial, and after the trial. She will continue to slaughter him after she is sentenced. She will NEVER stop, and that is something we will all have to live with.

She tried so hard to make Travis look like someone "living a double life" or lying to the world by claiming that she was not aware of the Mormon law of chastity, and that Travis lied to her about it. Jodi knew all about the law of chastity. The Mormon missionaries taught her about it. Travis taught her about it, and she and I had more than one conversation about it, so her playing dumb during the trial made me want to show up at court screaming what a liar she was, and rattle off the long list of everything she lied about, and it is a LONG list! Does anyone know a religion where sexual indiscretion is promoted or encouraged? I don't. So her saying she did not know, or she thought some stuff was okay, was another complete lie.

During the trial, Jodi claimed that Travis would ignore her in public. When they first started dating, Travis had just gotten out of a relationship, so he was trying to keep his dating Jodi private, because he was still in love with his ex-girlfriend Deanna. After our emails, Travis changed the things that were bothering Jodi. The media and Jodi's attorneys jumped all over this referring to Jodi as "Travis's Dirty Little Secret." There were even television shows with that title. Juan Martinez, the prosecutor, called Jacob Mefford to testify during the trial. Though many people had seen Travis and Jodi affectionate in public, Jacob had something that no one else did—a video. At a convention, in a crowded lobby, Jacob recorded Travis telling a story to a bunch of friends and associates about a night when he was held at gunpoint in an armed robbery at Mimi's Cafe in San Bernardino, California. In this video, Jodi was lying on Travis's lap, and then he put his arm around her. This was the same convention that Jodi was talking about in her testimony when she said he wouldn't acknowledge her in public, trying to get the jury to buy into the "dirty little secret" thing. Many people assumed that Travis was dating Jodi when he wasn't because they were always together—publicly. Chris's older brother, Tony, lived in Arizona and worked closely with Travis in Pre-Paid Legal. When Chris mentioned to Tony that Travis was considering getting married, he thought Chris was talking about Jodi. Tony didn't know anything about Lisa. All he knew was Travis was with Jodi "all the time." And Tony wasn't the only one. Many people thought they were together, which ruins the "dirty little secret" story. She might have been dirty, but she was no secret.

Initially in her interrogation by police, Jodi talked about her family lovingly, saying how great they were. As a way of providing "mitigating factors," suddenly her father had attacked her and her mother spanked her with a wooden spoon. (Many found this quite humorous because people from Jodi's generation were on the receiving end of much worse when it came to discipline and punishment.) After she was convicted of first-degree premeditated murder, she did an interview with Troy Hayden, an Arizona news anchor. She told him that her attorneys had advised her that she really didn't have any mitigating factors. She said there was no abuse in her home and no drug use. When the penalty phase had to be retried, we heard new stories from Jodi that she was abused and her father did cocaine and her mom smoked marijuana while she was pregnant with Jodi. On a TV interview, Patty, her childhood friend who she hadn't seen or spoken to in years, and the only person who has spoken about Jodi's childhood, spoke about what great parents Sandy and Bill were. She said they are really good people, and she loved them. This isn't the only thing that changed in Jodi's stories.

Many things changed before she was finally able to testify in the main trial. With investigators, Jodi said Travis was amazing and always very kind. After sitting in jail for an extended period of time, she was able to come up with new stories in an attempt to save her life. Jodi told her first therapist that Travis beat her twenty to thirty times. As time went on, and with future therapists, the number dropped to three. She was right when she told investigators that he was amazing and always very kind. The number of times Travis beat Jodi up was actually zero. The "having sex with little boys" changed to pictures of boys on a computer. It later changed again to printed-out pictures of boys on his bed with no computer. Incredibly, Jodi's own words completely annihilate the 2010 version of her story. While being interrogated, Jodi spoke about how good Travis was to her. She also said he didn't own a gun (which she claimed in her testimony that he did).

In 2010, Jodi changed her story from "two intruders killed Travis and tried to kill me," to "I killed Travis" in "self defense." She claimed she was taking pictures of him with his new camera and he attacked her when she dropped it onto a bathmat. He certainly had many bigger opportunities to lose his temper, but through texts and other evidence, we see the true Travis. He was kind, patient, understanding, and forgiving when she accidentally did worse things than dropping a camera, and even when she intentionally did things like slashing tires, stealing his journals, and stealing a diamond ring out of his drawer, he never attacked her! He responded kindly when she put his BMW on the back of a U-Haul and burned up the engine by leaving it in first gear. He told her that she could make monthly payments of $100. Jodi spoke about how nice he was about that. She spoke about how he was always nice. It's interesting to note that during a five-month trial and six years of investigations, the defense team could not produce one man, woman, or child who Travis had harmed in any way! There was, however, evidence of Travis being unkind to one person—Jodi. But these were rare instances and were in direct response to something crazy Jodi had done. In every instance, Travis's response was fairly mild compared to how most people would have responded. The defense team did a great job of taking a few incidents and hammering them relentlessly, so it appeared that these three incidents were how Travis was all the time. Travis would get upset over Jodi lying to him, invading his privacy, or harming him in some way, and then quickly forgive her. It was a terrible cycle fueled by Jodi's manipulation and desire for control.

Travis wasn't the only person Jodi lied to. She seemingly lied to everyone. Her boss at the Purple Plum in Yreka, California witnessed her lying. He reported a gentleman came into the restaurant, and Jodi began flirting with him. She told the man that she was new to town and asked him if he would show her around. Jodi had grown up in Yreka. Jodi was trying to pick up on this guy shortly after she slaughtered Travis. There were reports from coworkers that Jodi would ignore the female customers while focusing on the males.

I always thought it was the May 26 fight that triggered Jodi to kill Travis. But, during the retrial of the penalty phase, I wondered if she had been planning it much longer. Was moving away from Mesa part of her plan? I began to wonder this, because Juan Martinez displayed a text message dated May 2, 2008, which was a month before she killed him. It was a vile text. The text was from "Travis" to Jodi, and the defense had used it during the first trial to make Travis look like a pig! It spoke of an epic photoshoot the two of them would engage in. It was graphic, sexual and talked about him making her *feel like she had been raped, but she would have enjoyed it.* I couldn't believe Juan was showing this to the jury! I kept thinking, *Juan! At least cover that up!* It wasn't long before I realized where he was going with this.

He asked the computer expert on the stand who assigns the name to a phone number on a cell phone. The expert said that the owner usually input a name with a phone number. In other words, when I want to add a contact to my phone, *I* input the phone number and the name associated with that number.

The displayed text message was not like the other text messages we had seen displayed in the court room. The others were typed with a white background with different pieces of information broken up into different boxes, or fields. This message was several screen shots, or pictures, of the text. I thought *Oh my goodness! Travis didn't send this text!*

When Juan had Fonseca, a defense "expert" witness on the stand, she had talked about how she used texts from Travis to Jodi to learn more about the relationship. Juan displayed the May 2, 2008 text message and handed her a book of texts between Travis and Jodi that had been subpoenaed from the phone company. He asked her to look at May 2, 2008, to see if she could find this text outgoing from Travis's phone. She couldn't find it. He asked her to check the texts on the day before and the day after—it wasn't there either. Why would Jodi do this? Why would she relabel a number in her phone with Travis's name and send herself a text from that phone number? Was it to pretend that Travis wouldn't leave her alone? Was it to show off that Travis *really* wanted her? Or did she already plan on killing him and wanted something to show Travis was a deviant of some sort?

Travis didn't send those texts, yet the defense provided screen shots of them with his name at the top showing he sent Jodi the text. Jodi had to have changed the contact name in her phone and sent herself the messages! This was in the penalty phase retrial in 2015. This isn't the only disturbing thing Jodi did when it came to text messages. In 2013, Dr. Hiatt, who was like a father to Travis, said in a TV interview that Travis told him that Jodi would send herself messages from his phone! It makes me wonder, *What else is Travis being blamed for that he didn't write, say, or do?*

The list of her lies are endless, but I feel satisfied to stop here. Anyone who watched the trial knows, and anyone who has read to this point in the book also knows that Jodi lies. Jodi is a liar, and a vicious murderer.

## ALYCE LAVIOLETTE

Alyce LaViolette was the domestic-violence expert called by the defense to testify that Jodi was abused by Travis. As a caution, my feelings and opinions about Alyce LaViolette may not be popular, but this is how I feel. During and after her testimony, which people, me included, felt was slanted and one-sided, LaViolette was attacked on the Internet. Her book was attacked, she was attacked, and there were campaigns launched to get her public speaking engagements cancelled.

Alyce is an advocate for battered women, a very honorable cause. Battered women need strong and loyal advocates like LaViolette. When I heard that she was going to testify for Jodi, I called my aunt, a marriage and family therapist in San Diego, California, to see what she knew about LaViolette. My aunt made some calls and discovered that LaViolette was very respected in her field and had done a lot of work to help battered women. I don't think LaViolette is a bad person, nor do I believe she was ill-intentioned. I believe she was happy to speak for a woman who claimed to have been battered and abused. When testifying, she admitted to having been denied access to *all* the information. She was given what little the defense wanted her to have, and it was biased. She testified based on the information she was given and her limited time with Jodi.

She isn't the first to be duped by Jodi, and she certainly won't be the last. Speaking from personal experience, Jodi is good at getting in your head, and she is good at making you feel sorry for her. Jodi used and manipulated many people and continues to do so, even from behind bars. LaViolette was, and continues to be, one of her many victims. How can I be mad at someone for defending Jodi, when myself and some of Travis's closest friends did the same? LaViolette had very little time with Jodi, whereas Chris, myself, and other friends had much more time with her. Many of us were fooled.

She received death threats (as did we), and it's not cool, regardless of the situation. Travis wouldn't have wanted people to behave that way. Granted, she didn't have to testify, and she could have insisted that she speak to us about our emails and the women that she testified for without ever speaking to them. Us, nor the women she spoke for, that I know felt the way she said we did. She talked about these women being "vulnerable" victims of Travis. She said that Travis was abusive. She referenced portions of our emails taken out of context. She was giving a skewed snapshot of the facts, and she willingly gave her expert opinion that Travis was an abuser. Toward the end of her testimony, I think she realized that she didn't have all the facts, and she began saying things like, "Based on what I was given," and, "I looked at what they gave me." I don't even know if she had all of our emails, and from her testimony, it seemed that they heavily influenced her opinions about Travis.

Travis didn't tolerate violence against women. I know of three women, and there could be more, that Travis helped during a time of crisis. He helped them leave abusive relationships, and he had zero tolerance for the abuse of women. I'm not an expert, obviously, but I have studied enough about child abuse and domestic violence to know that sometimes children who are abused or witness domestic violence grow up to abuse. BUT, sometimes they grow up with zero tolerance for it, as Travis did. I have seen this as a high school teacher when a male student raised his voice at me and got in my face, and in nothing flat, another male student was between us and had the kid by the throat. The boy who came to my rescue was from an extremely abusive home. Travis was like this student, knowing that these women he cared about were being mistreated, and it did something to him at a very deep level. He was going to protect them no matter what. I think LaViolette would have liked Travis, because, like her, he was willing to defend and protect Jodi even when he shouldn't have. Even when she lied to them, manipulated them, and used them, they both defended her. I feel bad for Alyce LaViolette; it was her big heart and her dedication to protect women that blinded her to Jodi's evilness. She, like so many, was a victim of Jodi Arias.

In the early days of their relationship, Chris and I defended Jodi to Travis. She had us completely fooled, and we spent a lot more time with her than LaViolette did. She had mastered the art of getting what she wanted by any means necessary. She fooled a lot of people who cared about Travis, including some of his closest friends. Aaron Dewey and the Freeman family are just a couple on that list. Both defended Jodi even after she was arrested. Aaron eventually saw the light, but it took Dan Freeman and his family a lot longer. To be mad at him, LaViolette, or anyone else for being fooled by Jodi just wouldn't be fair of me.

All that being said, I think LaViolette's testimony was a terrible injustice to the real victim, Travis Alexander. She slandered him something fierce. I would like to think that if I were in her situation, I would refuse to testify unless I could look the parties in the eye and ask them about my assessment of their emails, texts, or whatever I was looking at, and find out if I was accurate in my assessment. I just really wished she would have interviewed us in person or even just called us. There is no way, knowing what I know about Jodi and what I know about Travis, that she could have possibly come to the same conclusion that she did. Had she just talked with us for an hour or so, she could have known too.

Earlier, I said that female victims of domestic violence need strong and loyal advocates, but this case made me realize male victims do too.

In the near future, I hope to have the opportunity to take LaViolette to lunch. I hope she accepts the invitation, so I can tell her who Travis really was. I owe that to Travis. LaViolette failed to see who the real victim of domestic violence was. She perpetuated the abuse he endured even after he was dead by continuing to slander him on the stand by misrepresenting us and others that she had never even spoken to. She diagnosed someone who she was never able to evaluate, with one of the worst possible diagnosis—batterer. It is my understanding that this is an ethics violation. Not to mention a slap in the face to all those she has worked so hard to protect and fight for.

# CHAPTER 19

# More Good Than Bad

*"When I despair, I remember that all through history the way of truth and love have always won. There have been tyrants and murderers, and for a time, they can deem invincible, but in the end, they always fall. Think of it—always."* Mahatma Gandhi

TRAVIS BEING MURDERED WAS ONE of the worst things I have ever experienced. It was traumatic and awful, and what his killer tried to do to him after killing him compounded that a thousand times. Alissa Parker explained it well. She is the mother of Emilie Parker, who was one of the twenty young children killed in the shooting at Sandy Hook Elementary School in December 2012. In an article she wrote for *The Huffington Post*, she said: "There have been times where I felt like I HAD to hold on to the dark things, like it was some responsibility I was supposed to carry. But Emilie's life was about color and joy, not about pain and suffering." She and her husband, Robbie, went about doing good in memory of their daughter. They put together a video called *Evil Did Not Win*. It's available online. Make sure that you have plenty of tissues if you watch it. I remember hearing a part of a speech that Alissa gave that moved me, and I wanted to include it in this book about Travis. She said, "Evil did NOT win that day at Sandy Hook." And evil did not win that day Jodi took Travis's life. Because of the incredibly good people all over the world, evil cannot win, no matter how hard it tries.

Travis wanted to change the world, and he has! So many people came together in support and love for Travis, his family, and his friends. Incredible friendships have been made and continue to be made because of him. He continues to touch lives because of the wonderful person he was, and he wanted nothing more than to be able to do this. So many people have written us expressing love and support, and they often apologize for feeling such a great loss and feeling like they "knew" Travis. I know there are so many people reading this book who feel the same way: awkward, weird, uncomfortable that they should have such strong feelings about him. That is Travis. To know him was to love him, and he loved people! Travis would not want us to dwell on the tragedy but to move on, become more, be kinder, be better, and help people. That is what he was all about.

Through this tragedy, there has been so much good, so much love, and so much kindness shown. I think it was a month into the trial when Chris received an email from a gentleman by the name of Michael. He was very concerned about Travis's siblings' financial standing having attended the trial every day. In his email, he did not pry for information, but rather, wanted to offer his help if it was needed. We had no idea at the time, but the stress level of the Alexanders was extremely high. They were struggling financially. Some had left businesses and jobs, and one was even demoted for leaving, but they were dedicated and were going to be there every day no matter what. Greg and Gary, Travis's older brothers, and their wives wanted so desperately to be there full-time, but because of their jobs, they just couldn't do it. Some of the Alexanders were out of money with no end in sight. Michael emailed us wanting to help with a substantial amount of money. We thought, *This guy might just be crazy!* He wanted to remain anonymous (Michael is a pretty common name, so I feel ok using it), so we called Sam and told her about this, but repeating over and over that it may not be real, and to proceed with caution. She was overwhelmed, saying, "If this is for real, you have no idea how much this will help my family!" We asked her to set up a bank account for the funds separate from her own (we didn't know if this was some kind of scam). She set it up, and within three or four days the money was there.

A day or two after hearing from Michael, we received another inquiry about how people could financially help the Alexander family. The administrators for the State vs. Jodi Arias Facebook Page, Nora and Elna from Australia, contacted us, saying several people had contacted them wanting to know how they could help the Alexanders. The response was amazing to watch. It was life changing to see the goodness of so many people come to the rescue of this family who was dealing with an incredible amount of stress, and complete strangers alleviated so much! The outpouring of donations, letters, cards, gifts, and love was overwhelming, and they were strangers no more.

We have appreciated all of the love and support we experienced. It was amazing to watch the acts of kindness and goodness. There was a group of ladies who got together and made quilts for the Alexanders. They even made one for Travis's (Deanna's) dog, Napoleon. There were people who sent the family "Travis" jewelry. Linda Ellis, author of *The Dash* and *Live Your Dash* (great books!) sent jewelry and a beautiful gift to the Alexanders. There were so many support pages on Facebook for Travis. People really buoyed up Travis's family and friends.

Through this tragedy, we were able to get to know several of Travis's good friends we had heard so much about: Taylor Searle and his family, and Lisa, the woman Travis wanted to marry, and her husband, Dominic. We have met so many amazing people through all of this. We met one of our favorite people in the world, Bill, a producer for the *Dr. Drew* show. He was a life-saver and we love him! Dr. Drew, his staff, guests, Shanna Hogan, Wendy Walsh, Beth Karas, the camera guys for HLN . . . all such great people, and so willing to go out of their way to help and be kind! The Victim's Advocates that helped the Alexanders were wonderful. Considering what the trial was for, the people we met and the support we received made it bearable. They gave us the strength to make it through and become stronger and (hopefully) better because of the experience.

Studies have been conducted about acts of kindness and the impact they have on the people involved. Any time an act of kindness is experienced, we get a surge of endorphins through our body. Endorphins may produce a feeling of euphoria. Researchers have discovered that the person doing the act of kindness is not the only one who receives an endorphin rush. The receiver of the act also receives a rush of endorphins, and anyone watching the act also gets the benefit of the good deed by the release of endorphins. But, it is the person providing the act of service or kindness that receives the biggest release of endorphins. Through this tragedy, so many people have been involved in the giving, receiving, and observing of kindness.

We have been able to experience so much good throughout this tragedy. We have become close to one man who just loves to give and help complete strangers! We have watched him pay for college, buy a car for a family in need, pay for a young man to go on a mission, help people get out of debt, help widows by paying off mortgages, and do amazingly kind acts for his friends. He even surprised us with a beautiful grand piano! There are no words to describe the good we have witnessed.

It has been life altering to see so much kindness in a world where the news only reports the murders, rapes, abuse, and cruelty that we, as human beings, impose on others. I found myself watching the news and similar programs a lot during this trial. It is so heartbreaking, dark, and depressing. It is easy to get caught up in that, brought down and depressed by the negative in the world, but there is so much more good than bad in this world. Travis was a beautiful example of that. His life revolved around making people happy, loving them, and helping them. We are all connected, and as long as we each do our part to be a little kinder, a little more loving, and serve a little more each day, evil will never win. It can't. This world is full of wonderful, good-hearted, caring people.

It is our challenge to you to not let Travis die in vain. We challenge each of you, and ourselves, to do more good every day. Even if it's something as simple as smiling at a stranger or saying "hello." Call your loved ones more regularly. Tell those you love that you love them—don't assume that they know. Make an effort to connect with people, and share that light that is in each of us.

Every year on Travis's birthday, July 28, we hope that everyone who wants to will participate in a Travis Alexander Day of Service. Travis loved to serve! You don't need to travel, and it doesn't need to be extravagant. You can do it right where you are. It can be any act of service, from planting a tree to feeding the homeless. You could take dogs at the shelter on walks or bring them treats. You can do anything that will better this world and bring a smile to people's faces. Desmond Tutu said, "Do your little bit of good where you are; it's those little bits of good put together that overwhelm the world." Travis always wanted to make this world a better place, and he did. We can keep the ripple effect of Travis Alexander going by continuing to make the world a better, happier, and safer place to be. By our acts of kindness and service, we can ensure that evil never wins.

## TRAVIS ALEXANDER DAY OF SERVICE

For the past couple of years on July 28, Travis's sister, Tanisha and the rest of Travis's family and some friends organized a "Travis Alexander Day of Service" in Phoenix, Arizona. One of the last things Travis and Tanisha did together was to deliver brown paper bags full of hygiene supplies to homeless people in Phoenix. The first year they got together in memory of Travis to do service was in 2013. They put together five hundred hygiene kits in brown paper bags with a picture of Travis and his quote, "The difference between a stumbling block and a stepping stone is the character of the individual walking the path." The second year they did it, they filled a moving truck full of clothes, shoes, and hygiene items, and created a buffet-style of things for families in need and the homeless. It is estimated they were able to help over a thousand people in need.

Travis's Siblings (From Left to Right): Steven Alexander,
Samantha Alexander, Hillary Wilcox and Tanisha Sorenson.

From Left to Right: Samantha Alexander, Angie Connor,
Tanisha Sorenson, Joilyn Owen, Stephanie Obolewicz, Tara
Kelley and London Owen. Front: Hillary Wilcox

# CHAPTER 20

# Forgiveness

*"Forgiveness is the fragrance that the violet*
*sheds on the heel that has crushed it."*
Mark Twain

NOTE TO READERS: THROUGHOUT THIS chapter, there are links to videos and articles. In order for the following information to make the most sense, we recommend you take the time to read and view the supplemental links in the order and places they appear.

For years after Travis was so brutally murdered, I thought I would never forgive Jodi. I was adamant that it wouldn't be in this life. My anger about this brutal, heartless, and heinous crime was overwhelming at times. I was fixated on the fact that Jodi worked hard to earn the death penalty, and there would be no justice if she didn't get it. I avoided crime scene and autopsy photos, because I knew once I saw those images, they would never leave me. I accidentally came across them on the Internet while looking up something else pertaining to the trial. I felt as if all life was being drained from me. I immediately became sick and threw up. My dear, sweet Travis was black and blue with a gaping slash across his throat. His hands were cut all over, evidence that he fought desperately for his life. What he must have gone through is unfathomable. Not only physically, but emotionally. The fear, terror, and betrayal that he must have felt knowing that this person he cared about, defended, and had taken care of was killing him would have been more torturous than the physical pain. Those images have now become the gate through which I must go if I ever want to remember Travis. Our good times, his laughter, and his kindness are now only available beyond that gate. Sadly, anytime I think of Travis, those images appear in my mind. I know this is true for Travis's family as well. Jodi was worse than I had ever imagined. What kind of monster does that to someone?

I often have conversations with Travis in my head, obviously not so much with him, as what I know he would say and how he would respond. There are ways he would have wanted me to act during this trial that I simply could not do . . . well, at least I thought I couldn't. I have spent years trying to avoid thinking about how Travis would respond, or how he would feel because it would just make me mad. I didn't want to acknowledge it. It bothered me how good, kind, and forgiving he would have been in this situation. When I think about how awful Jodi is, what she deserves, or how disgusting I think she is, I know what Travis would say. "Sky, she is your sister. Our Father in Heaven loves her. She is His child, and you must forgive her for your sake. The Lord will do what He needs to do, but *you* must forgive." This notion makes me mad. This whole idea repulses me. I want her to pay the ultimate price for what she has done. In the book, the Doctrine and Covenants, which Mormons consider scripture, there is a verse where the Lord says: "I, the Lord, will forgive whom I will forgive, but of you it is required to forgive all men." (D&C 64:10). *Forgive her? How? It's impossible!* Even if I didn't want to, I must, but I just couldn't see it happening any time soon.

I never thought there would be a day when I didn't feel complete disgust and anger for Jodi, but I have had a few of those days. I'm not going to lie, when I read her journal entries she wrote after killing Travis, when she tweets pathetic things, holds up a survivor shirt, or talks about helping others who have survived "domestic violence," I totally want to knock the teeth out of her mouth. As much as I wish she would stop and find some sort of human decency within that demented head of hers, I know that probably will not happen, but she can only bother me as much as I let her. Unfortunately, since 2008, that has been a lot.

It has been said that hatred is like drinking poison and expecting the other person to die. My hatred and disgust for Jodi has been so much more damaging to me than it has been to Jodi. I have allowed her to be a part of my everyday life. I have to forgive her, because I don't want her in my life that way. Hatred and disdain for her creates a connection between the two of us. I don't want that kind of connection. The only way I can sever that is through forgiveness.

I was worried about writing this chapter, because I didn't want it to "be used against [me] in a court of law." I think there is a big difference between forgiving someone and not holding them accountable for their choices. As Chris often says, "Forgiveness is separate from and unrelated to the demands of justice." What we do in regards to Jodi, and what God and the state of Arizona do with her are in no way connected. Jodi chose to murder Travis, and now Jodi deserves to be sentenced to death or spend her life in prison. Which one is more "fitting" is debatable. Has she met all the requirements set forth by the state of Arizona to qualify her for the death penalty? Yes. She isn't getting off either way, and she shouldn't. She is a danger to society. We asked her to never return to our home because we were afraid she was going to hurt us, our children, or both. She premeditated the murder of Travis Alexander. She should never be allowed out of prison—ever!

Can Jodi change? I believe most people can, if they choose to do so. But I don't see that she is willing. Certainly not right now. A key indicator of the probability of change is an unprovoked admission of the guilty act, a showing of sincere remorse, an effort to make restitution where possible, and incremental improvement over time. We are not seeing any of these things from Jodi. In fact, we have seen the complete opposite. I don't think Jodi "feels" the way most of us do.

This isn't to say she is mentally ill to the point where she didn't know what she was doing. She knew what she was doing, and she knew it was wrong because she planned it out. She knew she had to "cover her tracks" there and back. Like others who murder and deserve the death penalty, something is definitely wrong with her wiring. She didn't want to apologize to the Alexanders in her allocution because she didn't want them to "win." She clearly feels no remorse for what she has done. A normal, feeling person who kills in real self-defense feels immense guilt. Jodi only feels for Jodi. What am I hoping my anger will bring?

I think, like Alissa Parker, that I felt like I needed to be angry and be in that "dark place" of "anti-Jodi," because that showed how much I loved Travis. But that wasn't Travis. Instead of being "anti-Jodi," I need to be pro all that Travis loved and stood for. I cannot do both. I came to the point where I had to choose. Martin Luther King Jr. said it best, "Darkness cannot drive out darkness; only light can do that. Hate cannot drive out hate; only love can do that." How can I be a disciple of Christ with so much anger? I can't. I have to let it go, so I can be a better person than I once was. Anger makes us weak and miserable. It gives the person our anger is directed toward power over us. I don't want Jodi to have any power over me.

Forgiveness allows me to release the anger and the pain. So much of my energy has been focused on making sure that she pays for what she did. This has taken time and energy away from my family, service, happiness, and being able to focus on Travis instead of his murderer. She has been such a big part of my life for way too long—no more.

There are so many inspiring examples of forgiveness. There are powerful examples for us to follow so we can all be better. If victims of the Holocaust can forgive the guards who tortured them and killed their families, then I can forgive. If a father can forgive the drunk driver who killed his wife and most of his children, then I can forgive. I recently watched a video about a family whose mother was killed in a car accident by a young father who was high on drugs. It was the most amazing story. This family, understandably, were rocked and shocked by the sudden and senseless death of their mother. But even still, they found it in their hearts to forgive this young man, and both the young man and this family were all saved in the process. When the young man was released from prison, he named his new baby after the mother who was killed. (You can watch this story here: www.ourfriendtravis.com/forgiveness)

Bad things happen every day, and it is up to us to decide whether we will blossom or wither with bitterness. As Travis's and Chris's late mentor, Jim Rohn, often said, "The same wind blows on us all. The difference in where you arrive is not the blowing of the wind, it's the set of your sail." Lest I end up dashed on the rocks, I have decided to set a new sail, the sail of forgiveness.

Earlier, I said there were things Travis would have wanted me to do, but I didn't do them. I don't know if all murder trials are strange and scary, or just this one because of the media coverage. We were so afraid of "doing something wrong" that I don't think we did things right—things that Travis would have wanted us to do. In our defense, our fears were justified. We were so afraid that something we said or did would be taken and twisted by the defense, because that was what they did, repeatedly. They were constantly looking for a reason to file for a mistrial, and did, unsuccessfully, many, many times. So we were always on edge. Not because we had anything to hide, but rather because we knew that the defense team were experts at making a mountain out of a molehill. I feel like I have been watching the defense juggle air. There is a lot going on, but nothing there. They were the masters at distractions.

I saw a *48 Hours* episode that really touched me. A high school senior, Lauren Astley, was killed by her ex-boyfriend, Nathan Fujita. After the boy was convicted, Lauren's father, Malcolm Astley, went over to the Fujita family and hugged the parents of the boy who had killed his daughter. Wow. What an amazing example! How beautiful is that?

That's how it should be, where possible. In the courtroom of Jodi's trial, there was a very obvious chasm between the two camps resulting in an us-versus-them feeling. It was scary and very uncomfortable. I realize, looking back, that we can't let these horrible experiences remove our humanity. I wish that I was a big enough person to say, "Who cares what the defense does, who cares what people think, I am going to do the right thing." I may have gotten punched in the face, but Travis wouldn't have wanted it to be like it was. They were suffering, we were suffering, and there was a palpable tension between the two sides.

James E. Faust told a story about an Amish community that went through a terrible tragedy. A gunman came into a schoolhouse and tied up ten young girls. He shot all of them, killing five and wounding five before killing himself. The community came together. They forgave the man who had killed and wounded their children. They reached out to the widow of the man who had killed these girls with love and support. Half of the people at the murderer's funeral were Amish. What a beautiful example these good people are.

Dr. Sidney Simon, a recognized authority on values realization, has provided an excellent definition of forgiveness as it applies to human relationships:

"Forgiveness is freeing up and putting to better use the energy once consumed by holding grudges, harboring resentments, and nursing unhealed wounds. It is rediscovering the strengths we always had and relocating our limitless capacity to understand and accept other people and ourselves" (*Forgiveness: How to Make Peace With Your Past and Get on with Your Life, 19*).

James E. Faust said:
   *Most of us need time to work through pain and loss. We can find all manner of reasons for postponing forgiveness. One of these reasons is waiting for the wrongdoers to repent before we forgive them. Yet such a delay causes us to forfeit the peace and happiness that could be ours. The folly of rehashing long-past hurts does not bring happiness.*

*Some hold grudges for a lifetime, unaware that courageously forgiving those who have wronged us is wholesome and therapeutic. Forgiveness comes more readily when, like the Amish, we have faith in God and trust in His word. Such faith "enables people to withstand the worst of humanity. It also enables people to look beyond themselves. More importantly, it enables them to forgive."*

*All of us suffer some injuries from experiences that seem to have no rhyme or reason. We cannot understand or explain them. We may never know why some things happen in this life. The reason for some of our suffering is known only to the Lord. But because it happens, it must be endured.*

*Of course, society needs to be protected from hardened criminals, because mercy cannot rob justice. Bishop Williams addressed this concept so well when he said, "Forgiveness is a source of power. But it does not relieve us of consequences." When tragedy strikes, we should not respond by seeking personal revenge but rather let justice take its course and then let go. It is not easy to let go and empty our hearts of festering resentment. The Savior has offered to all of us a precious peace through His Atonement, but this can come only as we are willing to cast out negative feelings of anger, spite, or revenge. For all of us who forgive "those who trespass against us," even those who have committed serious crimes, the Atonement brings a measure of peace and comfort."*

(You can read or watch the whole talk by James E. Faust here: www. ourfriendtravis.com/healing. It is life altering).

While I was working on this book, and avoiding writing this chapter for the fear of being stoned by all those who love Travis, and the many more who have come to love him through this trial, I kept thinking, *How can I share this message without upsetting people?* Inevitably, this is going to make some people mad, and I guess I just have to be okay with that and remind myself why I am writing this book: it's for Travis. Trust me, I understand you more than you think I do. I've spent years being angry with Jodi. I was even mad at Travis, because I know this is what he would want. But while I was avoiding it, it seemed like every time I turned on the TV or was on the Internet, a story of forgiveness would pop up (that's why I have included so many). I don't think this was a co-incidence. Each story moved me and taught me so much that I wanted to share them with you. The following is another *48 Hours* show called "Live to Tell." (Can you tell I watch too many *48 Hours* episodes?) This was the story of two incredible women. One, like Travis, was the victim of a growing trend we are seeing called "break-up violence." Her story is too eerily similar to Travis's except she survived.

Melissa Dohme was stabbed thirty-two times simply for breaking up with her boyfriend. Her hands looked like Travis's hands—gaping holes from trying to defend herself. She was all her boyfriend had. She was very sympathetic toward him. She wanted him to feel loved and accepted. As the relationship became more toxic, she tried to get away from him on many occasions, and he would threaten suicide. He called her late one night and told her he wanted one last hug, and he would leave her alone. She met him on the driveway, gave him a hug, and he attacked her. They don't know how she survived it.

During her healing process, she met a woman named Audrey Mabrey. Audrey was separated from her husband who was a New York City detective. In 2009, he bludgeoned her with a hammer, then used a candle and gasoline to set her on fire. She was severely burned on over eighty percent of her body. She was twenty-six years old with two small boys. Audrey talked about how her abuser could not rob her emotionally nor mentally, because that belonged to her; it did not be-long to him. She said that she was sent to Melissa to teach her about the next chapter in her life, which was forgiveness. She said that she forgave her attacker and encouraged others to do the same. She said, "Forgiveness wasn't the first choice I made, but it was the most impor-tant one because it allowed me to be free."

Audrey forever changed Melissa's life, and all the lives of those who choose to let her story help them. Melissa said, "When you choose to forgive those who hurt you, you forever take away their power." The stories of these two beautiful women are incredible. They have both faced their attackers and forgiven them. They have dedicated their lives to inspiring and helping others. I really hope I can be this good of a person someday and experience the healing power of forgiveness that they have. (You can see their stories here: www.ourfriendtravis.com/melissa.)

I don't want to be too preachy, but I do want to share with you what took me from "I will not forgive her in this lifetime," to, "It's something I have to do, I am commanded to do, I can do and I want to do." In all of the stories above, if you watched them, you can see the happiness that forgiveness brought into the lives of these people. It's a joy that can be achieved no other way. While I know that forgiving is something Travis has done and would want me to do, much more importantly, it is something I know my Savior would want me to do. For some of you who are not religious, I hope you will not find this offensive. Whether you are Muslim, Buddhist, Agnostic, Atheist, Pagan, New Age, or just love Wayne Dyer . . . whatever your beliefs, I think we can agree that there is some force, some energy, "Light" . . . something that governs this universe. For me, it is God, who is my Heavenly Father, and His son, Jesus Christ.

If you do not believe in God, stick with me, because though my intention is not to force you to conversion, I hope you will find what I share to be good advice regardless of the source or my personal beliefs. (Tangent: If you are anti-religion, I understand. So many horrific things have been done in the name of "religion." But I would venture to say that one hundred percent of those were because someone was not following their religion. Take Christianity, for example. If people would have applied the following scriptures, many of the atrocities, modern day and historical, would never have been committed in the name of "God" or "religion." If all of us were abiding by these things, our world would be a much better place.)

Over the years, I have looked up many scriptures on forgiveness, maybe with a little hope that somewhere it said, "Forgive unless the person is a murderer." I didn't think I would find it, but there may have been a little hope deep down inside me. Here are the scriptures I found:

Ephesians 4:32
32 And be ye kind one to another, tenderhearted, forgiving one another, even as God for Christ's sake hath forgiven you.

Matthew 18:21–22
21 Then came Peter to him, and said, Lord, how oft shall my brother sin against me, and I forgive him? till seven times?
22 Jesus saith unto him, I say not unto thee, Until seven times: but, Until seventy times seven.

Matthew 6:14–15
14 For if ye forgive men their trespasses, your heavenly Father will also forgive you:
15 But if ye forgive not men their trespasses, neither will your Father forgive your trespasses.

I don't know about you, but I need to be forgiven often, which means I must forgive. After reading these scriptures, I began working on this chapter. I wrote about how I need to forgive, for me, but how that didn't mean I needed to like her or be her best friend. But then I had to go back and rewrite this chapter because of the following experience.

I was asked to teach a lesson in church a few weeks ago. You will not believe the topic I was assigned: "Love and Concern for All Our Father's Children." I thought, *Oh, this will be easy!* Boy did it challenge me. It started off with a beautiful quote by Joseph Fielding Smith, "I think if all men knew and understood who they are, and were aware of the divine source from whence they came, they would have feelings of kindness and kinship for each other that would change their whole way of living and bring peace on Earth." I thought, *Wow! I agree with that! That is so true!* And you would probably like to know that knowing not just "who" you are, but "whose" you are was something Travis was big on. Then I got into the scriptures:

Matthew 22:37–40
37 Jesus said unto him, Thou shalt love the Lord thy God with all thy heart, and with all thy soul, and with all thy mind.
38 This is the first and great commandment.
39 And the second is like unto it, Thou shalt love thy neighbor as thyself.
40 On these two commandments hang all the law and the prophets.

Matthew 5:16
16 Let your light so shine before men, that they may see your good works, and glorify your Father which is in heaven.

John 14:15
15 If ye love me, keep my commandments.

John 13:33–34
33 Little children, yet a little while I am with you. Ye shall seek me: and as I said unto the Jews, Whither I go, ye cannot come; so now I say to you.
34 A new commandment I give unto you, That ye love one another; as I have loved you, that ye also love one another.

Matthew 5:44
44 But I say unto you, Love your enemies, bless them that curse you, do good to them that hate you, and pray for them which despitefully use you, and persecute you;

Why was that so difficult for me? Because those scriptures teach us that there are two great commandments that everything else is built upon: Love the Lord, and love my neighbor. Who is my neighbor? Every human being on this earth. How am I supposed to love them? ". . .That ye love one another; as I have loved you, that ye also love one another" (John 13:34). How did He love me? He suffered and died for me, and that is how I am commanded to love everyone, including Jodi Arias, as Christ loves me. As He loves each of us. The thought of loving Jodi the way Christ loves us puts knots in my stomach.

The thing that stuck out the most while I was preparing this lesson for church was that there are no "unlesses." Many of us know we are supposed to "love our neighbor," but we do it with stipulations. I will love them "unless" they are black, white, rich, poor, overweight, too thin, gay, Muslim, alcoholic, addicted to drugs or pornography, Mormon, atheist, Buddhist, depressed . . . it can be anything. In my case, it was "unless she is a murderer." And that is not God's way. He does not give us an "unless" clause. He was very clear that we are to love *all* people the way He loves us, which leaves no room for bullying, racism, bigotry, or hatred of any kind. He does not ask us to "tolerate" our neighbors; it is so much more than that. He said to love our enemies. I would certainly consider Jodi an "enemy."

Forgiveness and love are powerful. They can change lives, especially the life of the one who chooses to forgive and love. I look forward to the day when I can say that I completely forgive Jodi. I know that is what Travis would have done, and what he would want me to do. More importantly, it is what I have been commanded to do by God. Who am I to say whether or not she "deserves" it? That's not what I was commanded to do. Though daunting and overwhelming, for my own wellbeing, it's something I need to do.

CHAPTER 21

# Friends of Travis

WE THOUGHT THE BEST WAY for you to get to know Travis better would be through the words, stories, and experiences of his friends. We have included those for you. We hope you enjoy reading them as much as we did!

Travis skydiving in 2008. Five months before he was killed.

# DUANE TOLMAN:

We met Travis in 1989. Our son, Nolan, used to visit Travis's family once a month. Travis later told us that he would stay in his room and just listen to the messages shared by Nolan and his companion while they visited with his grandmother. Nolan and his brothers, Aaron and Jerald, were always friendly with Travis at school and that made a big difference. He was more comfortable going to church since he knew some of the young men. I remember when Aaron received his mission call. Travis had received his the day before and was called to serve in the Denver, Colorado, South Mission. Our son was called to the Denver, Colorado, North Mission. They would be going to the Missionary Training Center at the same time, and they were thrilled!

Aaron Tolman and Travis Alexander

There are many things in life that defines a person to whom and what they are. This is what we call character, and often a person's true character will show itself in a time of trauma, danger, and stressful situations. Other times, these attributes will manifest by actions when no one else is around. It was one of those stressful and dangerous times that I had the opportunity to see the character of Travis Alexander in action.

Each week, we would attend a business briefing in San Bernardino, California. At the conclusion of that meeting, we would have what is called "the meeting after the meeting." This typically would take place at Mimi's restaurant a short distance away from the briefing where we would socialize and share stories and business tips with each other.

On one of these occasions, Elsa (my wife) and I joined many others for this event. We were seated in the back room at the furthest table. Elsa sat at the end of the table, where she could see the front area of the restaurant. I was engaged in a conversation with our friends and associate when Elsa caught my attention and said, "We are being robbed."

It did not sink in yet, and with confusion on my face, I said, "What?"

Then, with greater intensity, my wife loudly whispered, "Guys! We are being robbed!" I do not think the best choreographers could have planned the next few seconds better. Most of the people suddenly just disappeared under the tables. I made sure that Elsa was safe under the table and tossed my cell phone under there with her. There was no room for Travis or myself on that side, so we proceeded to the other side where no one was. I managed to make it under, but not without the perpetrator seeing where I went. Next thing I knew, there was a gun pointed at me and a demand for my wallet. I remember thinking how trivial my wallet was in this situation and freely just tossed it out. By this time, Travis was face down on the floor in the aisle just a couple of feet from me.

The thug demanded Travis to surrender his wallet. Travis kept telling him that he did not have his wallet with him. The tensions were building rapidly, and the gunman pressed the gun to the side of Travis's head. I was praying to God that I would not have to witness this type of harm to my friend. Travis surrendered his cell phone, which satisfied the gunman.

It was interesting to see a video account by Travis later on describing this experience and what he was thinking at that time. I remember that Travis remained calm, and shortly after he borrowed a cell phone to call his phone. He engaged in a conversation with the perpetrator and attempted to negotiate the return of his phone. It was noted that the thug did not seem to be the brightest bulb on the tree.

As I mentioned earlier, that character will manifest itself during the times when a person is alone. Otherwise, what does he do when no one else is looking? I will say this, "You know someone by the fruits of their labors." Travis had become a self-help guru, and you do not achieve that status by watching sitcoms, sports, and news for hours on end. It took a lot of face time with books, tapes, seminars, and good associations with a strong desire to be the best you can.

Travis and my older sons grew up together. Elsa and I would marvel as we observed the good character on all those kids as they associated and worked together to make a positive contribution in our world.

## LISA STEPHAN:

My husband, Jeff, and I first met Travis when we were with Pre-Paid Legal (now LegalShield) in 2002. He was such a young kid, but we could tell within twenty minutes that this kid was going somewhere big! We were impressed with him. Chris Hughes was our mentor, and he is the one who introduced us.

I couldn't get over how motivated he was, and I was instantly hooked. We saw him at weekly meetings and conventions, and we soon became friends.

We were having dinner after one of the weekly meetings at Mimi's Cafe in San Bernardino, and there were only about ten of us lingering, including Travis, when men came in and robbed the restaurant. Everyone was ordered to the ground, but we had been sitting in a circular booth, and I didn't make it out in time to hide. One of the men put a gun in my face. Travis had a gun to his head while he was lying on the ground. Travis locked eyes with me and told me to just keep looking at him, that he wasn't going to let anything happen.

We ended up getting out okay. I was shaking and crying, and Travis came over and hugged me and asked if I was all right. I really do think he kept me calm enough to think clearly, and I really feel as if he saved my life.

We stayed friends after that. We saw one another at meetings, but Jeff and I drifted away from PPL due to a change in our life including health issues and having to move. We lost touch, and by chance, I stumbled across a Facebook post I believe Chris Hughes had written about Travis being killed. It was a year after it had happened, and I had not heard about it. I remember screaming "no" at the top of my lungs, and collapsing to my knees. I called Jeff at work hysterical.

I have followed the trial and was even approached by Nancy Grace and Dr. Drew to talk about the robbery, but unfortunately, I had personal issues at the time, so I was unable to talk about it.

I truly want justice for Travis, because he was an amazing man, mentor, and friend. I will forever love him as a dear friend who, in my mind, saved my life.

I miss you, Travis!

## JULIE HASLEM:

I met Travis while we were both building our Pre-Paid Legal business in 2005. I admired how effortlessly he presented to hundreds of people and was so relatable. One minute you were laughing hysterically, and the next minute you were crying like a baby (men included). He would always end with, "And I am single." Ladies would run up to him afterward with all kinds of questions because they had a daughter, sister, friend, or granddaughter they wanted to line him up with. We all wanted to find the right person for Travis. He lit up the room when he walked in. He was someone who you could see as part of your family; I know he was part of mine.

Travis and Julie Haslem

Whenever I would see Travis, he would say to me, "Hey, I brought you something," to which I would reply, "Really?" Then he would flex (he had some big guns) and say "Bam!" That still makes me laugh. He *always* did this. I can't think of a time when he would come to my house or we would be leaving for a trip when he didn't say that.

When Travis would come to Utah, he stayed at my home quite often. My kids loved him! He was the comedy relief. One time, he came to stay and brought a couple of friends with him. They were attending our church's general conference that weekend. When it came time for him to leave, there was a gift with a note thanking me left in his room. That was Travis. Never did he stay here and take it for granted. He was always gracious and kind. We would stay up late into the night talking about life and God. This was pretty much the "norm" when he stayed with us. His testimony of the Gospel always strengthened mine. I remember vividly one of our late-night talks.

We were talking about life, ups and downs, and how you don't have to be a victim of your circumstances, being a "Mormon," and what a blessing it is to have the knowledge that we can live with our Heavenly Father again, that there is a life after death. And this is what I remember so vividly (which I have reflected on many times since his life was taken so short). He said to me, "I'm not afraid to die. I'm ready to meet my Savior." Those words have both haunted me and comforted me. I know at that point in my life I was nowhere ready to die or meet my Savior, and I'm still not. I was so shocked and almost jealous that he was in that position. Travis was forever a missionary!

I had the opportunity to stay with Travis too. We had a Pre-Paid Legal event in Arizona, and I had just had surgery. I wasn't planning on going because of the surgery, but Travis had a way of making you feel like you were going to miss out on the greatest thing ever. Needless to say, I went and I'm so grateful that I did. Of course, there was a house full of people, food, and laughing. He offered his home to several out-of-town people that weekend and bodies were on couches, love sacs, and the floor. He insisted that me and my friend have his room. He wanted us to have privacy and knew that I had just had surgery and didn't want me to be uncomfortable. He even bought new towels for us to use. How sweet is that? His home looked like he hired a professional designer to decorate. I teased him about his feminine qualities, and then proceeded to ask him how he made his walls look like suede. He made it sound so simple, but I can assure you it wasn't. I attempted to do the same on the walls in my bedroom and failed.

Whenever I was feeling down about how my business wasn't growing fast enough or just life in general, I would pick up the phone and call Travis. He always had the right set of words that I needed. I miss that! I miss his big laugh. I miss his big smile. I miss his big hugs. I miss our late night talks. I miss hearing "bam!" I miss my friend. But I take comfort in knowing that Travis is in a better place, and that I will see him again someday.

I love you, Travis!

## AARON DEWEY:

(This is an email that Aaron sent to a member of Travis's family. He gave it to me to include in this book, because it expressed how much Travis means to him.)

I first met Travis through Pre-Paid Legal in 2005. I only knew him as a superstar from Arizona who came up to work in Utah from time to time. At that time, I was going through some very serious personal and financial challenges. I had recently come out of the closet as being gay, and I was struggling big time to reconcile that with the church. In addition, I was drowning in over $50,000 of credit card debt (don't ask me how I managed to rack that up as a BYU student!). Needless to say, I was constantly depressed and saw no way out of my situations.

Fast forward to the summer of 2006. I was at our PPL retreat at Daniel's Summit when Travis debuted his alter ego Eddie Snell. To this day, I don't think I've laughed as hard as I did when I saw that routine. I was doubled over and crying from laughing. I couldn't help but think "Who is this nut job up on stage?" Then a few hours later, Travis came back out, and for the first time in a public setting, he shared the stories of his childhood. I'll never forget the story of Grandpa Vic, and hearing Travis tell everyone in that room that we were special with the same conviction that Grandpa Vic had told him over and over as a child. Again tears filled my eyes, but for a very different reason this time.

While Travis was speaking, I was moved to reach out to Chris Hughes for help. After talking with Chris and Sky about my situation, they suggested that I get in touch with Travis. Travis had some empty rooms in his house and was looking for a new roommate. And I was looking for a fresh start with a clean slate. I told Travis everything that had been going on in my life. I didn't want there to be any secrets. I remember him telling me, "Dude, I'm the most homophobic guy you will ever meet, and I'm a little freaked out about having a gay guy live in my house. But Chris says you're a good guy, so I'll help you out any way I can." Less than a month later, I had packed everything up in Utah and made my way to Arizona.

Over the next year and a half that I lived in Travis's home, he mentored me, helped me regain my confidence, and opened opportunities for me to get my career and life back on track. More importantly, Travis became a very special friend. He never judged me, never made me feel bad for who I am or the situation I was in. He let me be me, and through his example, he helped me to become the best *me* I could be. When my car broke down and I couldn't afford to fix it, Travis let me drive his BMW so I could still get to work. When I didn't have enough money to buy groceries, he opened his cupboards to me. He was always lending a helping hand to anyone he saw in need.

Slowly but surely, things started to transform for me. I finished college, I now have a great career, I own my own home, and I've paid off all of those old credit cards. Everything good that has happened in my life over the past seven years I owe to Travis. Travis gave me hope when I was hopeless. He was a friend when I felt like I had none.

Travis taught me to not believe in regrets, but if there are two regrets I have in life it is these: 1) Somehow with all the time that I spent with Travis, I never took a picture with him. I didn't realize that until after he was killed. 2) I never fully expressed my gratitude to him for all that he did for me. At his funeral, and every time I have visited his grave site since then, all I could do was say "thank you" over and over again, but it never felt like enough.

When I was first asked to do an interview with the media regarding the trial, I was terrified. I didn't know how I was going to get on live TV and talk about Travis without completely breaking down. But I soon realized that by going on TV and telling the world about the *real* Travis Alexander that I knew, in some way I would finally be able to repay him. Travis did more for me than almost anyone else in my life, whether he realized it or not. I will always cherish the books he gave me, and I still often reflect on the things that he taught me that continue to shape my life today. So I hope I have made him proud by telling the media what an incredible man he really was.

I will never be able to fully understand the pain your family has gone through in losing Travis. But please know that Travis was like a brother to me. Although nothing that happened in court yesterday will ever bring him back to us, at least it is somewhat comforting to know that our brother's killer has finally been brought to justice! As the verdict was read, once again I was crying, both tears of joy, as well as an overwhelming sense of gratitude for the great man that Travis was.

## CLANCY TALBOT:

I met Travis in October of 2005. Travis would lighten and liven up any room he entered. He had an amazing appetite for life! He was both hilarious and inspirational. I remember one of his trainings in particular when Travis dressed up as the infamous "Eddie Snell." He had the entire room laughing so hard we were crying. Then he took a break, came back in the room in his suit and gave the most inspiring, uplifting and amazing talk I have ever heard. It made me cry. He was so incredible that way. Travis had a way of making each person feel like they were special. He wanted each person to feel that they could accomplish any and everything!

Chris Hughes, Clancy Talbot, Travis Alexander, and Julie Haslem

Some memories:

Travis loved the outdoors, as do I. Some of my favorite memories of Travis were our 4-wheeling and snowmobiling trips. On one of the snowmobiling trips, we were jumping our machines over a road and having a blast! Travis had to outdo himself each time, striking a pose when he was off the ground in the air. On the 4th jump, he overshot the landing and went rolling down the mountain, rolling his snowmobile! There is a video of the after math but which shows Travis jumping up after rolling it, climbing the mountain, snow up to his knees with each step. The four of us were standing there with our hearts in our throats, anxiously watching him climb and waiting to see if he was okay. He reached the top and Chris Hughes asked him, "What happened?" Travis responded with, "I was cruising along and said to myself, 'Self, you're a man. You can go up this too!' So I did and did a barrel roll, like Top Gun, Maverick style. The thing fell, landed on me and didn't break a thing 'cause I'm unbreakable like Bruce Willis." We all laughed so hard. In the video I can hear myself laughing in the background. Laughter was guaranteed whenever I was with Travis.

Another snowmobiling trip, Travis was jumping a river that was half frozen. However amazing Travis was, he could not walk or ride on water, but that never stopped Travis. He had to try. Needless to say, the snowmobile ended up in the river and they had to go into the thigh-high freezing river and fish it out. Travis, of course, was laughing and joking the entire time.

Four-wheeling was my favorite of all the outdoor memories with Travis. Travis was such a character. He would ride his four-wheeler like Superman, lying on his tummy with his arm stretched in front of him, his hand in a fist like Superman. I loved every moment of those memories! Travis, as always, made everyone laugh each and every time.

As I said before, laughter was pretty much a given whenever I was with Travis. His "signature move" was the "BAM!" He would walk up to me, or anyone, including strangers, and hold up his arm, flex his bicep & say "BAM!" Usually there would be a comment before like "how are you?" I would say "fine" and he would do his "BAM" and come back with "how about now?" He had hundreds of sayings prior to the "BAM" If one arm didn't get you to laugh hard enough for Travis, he would do both arms at the same time.

Our conventions and events for work were so much fun because Travis was there. He was full of life and made sure all of the people around him felt happy. Another fond memory was Travis doing the chicken dance! He kept going until everyone was either joining in or laughing.

Travis truly was an amazing, kind hearted, funny, empowering, inspirational, compassionate and caring spirit. He was the most exceptional friend and possessed enormous personal character and integrity. I will love and miss him forever.

# MIKE BERTOT:

I had the pleasure of meeting Travis Alexander, one of the greatest people and friends that I've ever had, in June 2004. I and my wife at the time had started working with LegalShield (Pre-Paid Legal Services then), and Travis was a member of the support team responsible for training us. What started as a business relationship quickly turned into a friendship that I will cherish for a lifetime.

We spoke many times over the phone, since I made my home in Utah and he lived in Arizona. We finally met in person at a company convention in Las Vegas that September. I'll never forget how charismatic Travis was, and how people were drawn to him. His personality was magnetic. We spent a lot of time that weekend hanging out and getting to know each other. It didn't take long to find out how much we had in common, like the fact that we were only four days apart in age. From then on, he truly was my "brother from another mother." Over time, our friendship and business relationship grew. If there was ever anything that I needed, Travis was there. When times were good, he was there. When times were bad and I faced challenges in life and in business, he was there. Travis had lived a great and sometimes challenging life, and because of that, he could always relate in some way to the events I was experiencing in my own life. He was always a voice of inspiration and motivation.

I would see Travis several times each year at company conventions and retreats. He would travel to Utah to work with and train our sales associates. He spent time at my home, and I at his in Arizona. We took vacations with groups of our friends, which are some of my favorite memories of Travis.

Wherever Travis was, he was always the center of attention. I have never met someone who was so unafraid to be himself. I heard him best described once as "a walking musical." He was always singing, laughing or "mugging" for the camera when someone was taking pictures. There was never a dull moment when he was around.

Chris Hughes, Mike Bertot and Travis Alexander

The last night I saw Travis was in April 2008 in Oklahoma City at a company convention. It was one of the most hilarious nights I'll ever remember. After the events of the convention had concluded, Travis, myself, and many of our friends spent the rest of the evening into the very early hours of the morning just hanging out laughing and telling stories of funny things we had experienced in our lives. At one point during the night, we were waiting for the elevator to go down to the hotel lobby to continue socializing with everyone when Travis decided to push some large chairs into the opening of the elevators to keep the doors from closing, therefore rendering the elevators useless. After taking the stairs down to the lobby (since we couldn't use the elevators either due to Travis's brilliant idea), we all continued laughing and cutting up about our genius-level prank. Shortly after reaching the lobby, we noticed the hotel security guard heading to the stairs. A little while later, he reentered the lobby from the eleva-tor. Apparently, he had been alerted to the fact that none of the el-evators were working. We all had a good laugh at his expense, and we figured we should keep the good times rolling. So, for the next couple of hours, we would peel off in groups of two or three to keep block-ing the elevator doors, each on separate floors of the hotel, and then casually returning to the lobby to rejoin the group so we could watch the security guard head, once again, for the stairs. Childish, yes, but funny nonetheless. It was so hard for us all not to burst out laughing every time he walked by. Travis, myself, and two others were on what turned out to be the last "mission" of the night when we received a text from our group in the lobby. Our friend the security guard was on his way upstairs ahead of schedule, so obviously the gig was up. The folks in the lobby decided that they had better leave at that point, and we decided to do the same. We all said our good-byes and quickly went our separate ways, taking for granted that we would all see each other again.

I'll always have friends in my life, but I will never have another friend like the one I had in Travis Alexander.


## FITA AND STAR NISA:

It was a Super Saturday (training event) in Hawaii for LegalShield (Pre-Paid Legal then), and in the craziness of getting things situated for the event and getting some last-minute requests Mr. Katoa had for our guest speaker, Mr. Dave Hall, I happened to walk in on the middle of Dave's training. I sat on the back row to catch some of his teachings. Two rows in front of me, I noticed a young man dressed in a three-piece pin-striped suit sitting by himself away from the crowd. He stood out looking as sharp as he did, and no one in Hawaii was wearing three-piece suits, yet. Every time he moved around, the more I got curious and excited because I didn't get the memo that Brian Carruthers was gonna be joining us as well, and I was the regional manager of Oahu! Brian Carruthers was, and is, one of the very top money earners in our company.

I approached Travis during a break thinking he was Brian Carruthers. That was the beginning of what turned out to be a long-time friendship with Travis Alexander. "Actually Brian Carruthers looks like me" was Travis's response when I introduced myself and told him who I thought he was. We both laughed, and he later thanked me for the compliment. This would be one of many trips to Hawaii that Travis came on, always with his friends Chris Hughes, Dave Hall, and other top executives of the company.

Travis was a great presenter, fun trainer, and a humble speaker. What we loved most about Travis was that you could feel how authentic he was when you spoke to him, in his handshake, and in his hug. He was real! Even when we saw him at the yearly conventions, he'd always holler at us to say hi from across the hall or run over to give us a hug. Once a friend, always a friend and brother in Christ.

He is truly missed! RIL (Rest in Love) Travis!

## Debbie Ihler Rasmussen:

I had been at an early morning church meeting where I did not have my phone. When I got to my car, I had ten texts—Patrick had texted me twice so I called him back.

His first words, "Are you okay, Debbie?"

I thought, *Why wouldn't I be okay?* I was running a training that night for Chris and Sky because they were in Cancun. I had taken over Systems Training for Chris and Sky a zillion times. So I answered, "Yes I'm okay, why?"

"Well, Travis."

"What about Travis?"

"He's been murdered."

I literally could not breathe for a few seconds, but the first words out of my mouth, "It was Jodi."

Patrick responded, "That's what everybody thinks."

I felt sick.

No need for me to elaborate any more on that. As they say, the rest is history. But what needs to be said is this book. I knew Chris and Sky would write it one day—they just needed time.

I had associated with Travis in less formal settings, mostly with Chris and Sky at their home, and of course, I had seen Travis train on stage many times. But, the first time I saw the side of Travis on stage that was not a typical training was in a program at Daniel's Summit, Utah. He wore some ridiculous wig, cutoffs that were way too short, and he put on a skit that had everybody rolling. I still do not remember the skit, but the character he portrayed was unforgettable, just like Travis.

I am a lot older than the "kids" I hung around with in LegalShield (then Pre-Paid Legal). Most of them were the ages of my own kids, so when I refer to Travis as a kid, that is exactly what he was to me. A totally delightful kid. Some of the jokes Travis told and the characters he portrayed made me laugh until I cried. His quick wit and the totally innocent looks he could conjure up on his face were his trademark. And he was a ladies' man—all the women loved Travis. He was an incredible speaker too. I loved to watch him on stage. His story was heartwarming, and his knack for motivation remarkable.

But there was another side to Travis. The deeper, spiritual Travis. He was not perfect, I'm sure, although I have no immediate knowledge of that—only that he was human. But he was sincere. He had a deep love of God and for the gospel. When he let us peek into his vulnerability it was there—the wounded Travis—the one who had fought to be on top against all odds and he had won. His past is what drove him, at least that is what it appeared. He was confident and sure of where he was going. And he went there, fully pushing himself in every sense in the business he loved.

He was a good friend. Many, many people can attest to that. Even me—the mother figure—he was respectful when I was around. He would sometimes joke about something, and because I was around, he would look in my direction and say, "Oh, sorry." And then we would laugh. It was never anything that offended me. A year or so before he died, at the request of Sky, I had a one-on-one talk with Travis and suggested that he could do a lot better than Jodi. He said he knew that. I told him his friends were worried about him, and he said he knew that too. I don't think any of us really honestly realized what this girl was capable of, least of all Travis.

Travis Alexander was an amazing person. Was he perfect? Not even. Was he a good kind and warm human being? Absolutely. At the very least of his numerous accolades—but for sure the most important—Travis was, and remains, our friend.

## TAMI JOHNSON:
Alexander the Great-

I had the pleasure of calling Mr. Travis Alexander a mentor, colleague, and friend. As a mentor, he made himself available for coaching and training. He inspired all who heard him as a speaker and motivator. His story brought me to tears many times.

As a colleague, Travis was someone you could count on to give a hand and assist any colleague who reached out to him. As busy as he was with work, he always took your call if he could or returned your call. He had such great patience with those who didn't understand our business.

As a friend, he was more like a bestie. Someone you could count on in your time of need. If he knew you were having a challenge, he didn't wait for you to ask for help; he would always ask if he could help with this or that! Someone who cared and was there for you to celebrate, and in your time of despair to offer any support he could.

Travis did not have children, but yet my son, who was at the time in his pre-teen years, looked up to Travis as an uncle or cousin. Either way, Travis made a large impact on my son as a positive male role model. My son loved the suits Travis would wear, bold in color, sharp, and a strong look. My son called them "Zoot suits!" When I shared this with Travis, he was clearly delightedly surprised. He said he had no idea he had that impact on my son, but thought it was cool. We had a few work-related potlucks at Travis's home in Queen Creek, Arizona. I was a single mom and usually brought my son with me. Travis welcomed my son and made sure he had something fun to do while we were at his house. Of course, playing with Travis's dog, Napoleon, was a given.

Another time, the day I was to travel to our annual company convention, my then other half got into an argument with me, decided not to go to the convention, and cancelled our hotel reservation. I phoned Travis and told him of the development. "I'm on my way with no place to stay!" His words were, "I'm on it!" Within a half hour, Travis called me back with details of a hotel room for me to share with another woman. He checked on me with concern throughout the convention, and personally included me in all our team activities and breakouts for meals. When the convention was over and we were back in Arizona. I had a rippling effect with my other half that now put me in a financial disposition. One of the times Travis checked to see how I was doing, he found this out and offered to assist me financially without thinking about it. I declined, for I had already made arrangements for my two children and myself, but it sure was nice to know someone would and could offer that type of assistance.

All my interactions and memories of Travis Alexander are happy fond ones. He was so giving, you wanted to do anything to help him and give back in any way you could. He organized, ran, and managed our weekly business briefing and training for many years. His last two-plus years, I assisted him as a host handling the registration every week. It was one small thing I could do to help him. Travis was so absolutely appreciative and always made sure I knew it. This young man always had a smile on his face. I've never known him to be any way less than fun, happy, joyous, positive, caring, and genuine! He had a large love of life. He told me about this book he had, *1000 Places to See Before You Die.* He was well on his way to accomplishing that feat! I personally plan on visiting all one thousand places in his memory!

Alexander the Great, we love you and keep your fond memories close to our hearts. I personally take your recommendation to pursue and achieve my goals!

## D'Ann DaBell, "Girlie":

I was apprehensive to stay with Travis at his home in Mesa after being introduced by a mutual friend in 2004. We worked in the same industry and traveled to Phoenix quite a bit for business, and staying with him would save money on hotel expenses. I am so glad that I stayed that night and many times each year. Travis was always charming from the start and very hospitable, giving up his bedroom suite to myself and another female business partner.

That started a close friendship where he would instant message me as he saw me online. He'd write, "Hey, aren't you too old to be online? Just kidding." "Hey girlie, isn't a bit too late for you to still be up?" He would tease me about being older (seventeen years older than him), and I'd tease him that he needed to find someone and settle down as he was too old to be single. He cued into my personality right away and called me "Girlie."

One of my favorite memories of Travis was when I invited him to Park City where he gave a business overview at a luncheon. He was professional, polished, and personable. Travis always shared his personal development with me and others. After the meeting, a friend stayed longer and asked him about himself. Religion came up, and Travis bore the most amazing testimony to her of his beliefs in the Church of Jesus Christ of Latter-day Saints. I know he had a relationship with our Heavenly Father and Jesus Christ. Afterward, he toured Main Street and at the Family Tree Center, he started looking up his family, in particular his grandfather's genealogy. Family was obviously important to Travis. It was a fun few hours of research and flirting with the Sister missionaries there.

I regret that I don't have any pictures of me with Travis. I was always too uncomfortable to be in pictures. That has taught me that pictures are important, and I don't hesitate to be in them anymore.

Travis was genuine, and I am grateful for the four years of knowing him, and look forward to a continued friendship after this life.

## ALAN SHUMWAY:

Travis was someone I knew about throughout my teenage years, but I really got to know him more as a young adult in our early twenties. Travis was always a very confident person, as well as charismatic. My memory among many was when we were attending a bachelor's party. I think it might have even been at my own bachelor's party, but I can't remember for sure. After dinner, we were leaving the restaurant, and I noticed that Travis was stranded on the side of the road in his BMW. I offered to take him to the gas station to get a gas can. He said no to that idea. So we proceeded with his plan, which was to have me push his car with my truck. So for about a mile or two, we locked bumpers and when we got close enough to the gas station, I slowed while he got some distance. As he rolled to the pump with enough momentum, he gave me a wave with a huge smile. That was the last time I saw Travis before his passing. He was a fun guy and truly cared for others.

## SHANNON PETERSON:

My dear friend Travis changed my life. He was a voice of reason in my life, reminding me that I deserved the best out of life at a time when I needed it most. He wasn't afraid to say exactly what he was thinking. I loved that he didn't have that filter, because he always told me what

I needed to hear. He was the most flattering individual I have ever met. He knew how to make everyone feel welcomed and loved. He was always about uplifting and making everyone around him better. He was generous beyond belief, even when he didn't have much, he would have given it to anyone. His bellowing singing voice was my favorite. Sometimes, I would answer my phone to just very loud singing. Made-up songs, classic songs, it didn't matter. But one of my all-time favorite things Travis did, as I am sure many remember, was ordering his food. For years, I had the privilege of eating dinner with a group that included Travis once a week. He would talk to the waiter or waitress like he knew them his whole life and they were best friends. Nobody could resist smiling while he was in the room. He always ordered water with lemons. "Actually, would it be all right if I got a whole plate of lemons?" And he always did. He is missed each and every day by so many.

## TANISHA MORGAN:

So, Travis used to attend our work functions, and his favorite line after giving his two-minute bio would be, "I live in a four-thousand–square-foot home, I drive a BMW, and I'm single, ladies!" The first time I heard him say that I thought "this white boy is crazy!" And crazy he was. He was a fun, spirited young man who was always laughing. When we first met, he told me he had a sister named Tanisha, and I called him a liar. I rebutted that she had to be adopted because in all my years I had never met a Caucasian woman named Tanisha. Clearly, his parents were hiding something. He laughed and confirmed that she was the "black sheep" of the family, always doing what she wanted, and making their parents mad. That became our bond. He was technically a brother in my eyes from then on, because he had a "sista" named Tanisha. I was then his "sista" from another mother. He brought a certain flavor to our company, and helped many young men learn to dress professionally, as well as carry themselves as gentlemen. Over the few years we interacted, we always had laughs and good times. He will always be missed, and I think about him often, especially because we teamed up to do a co-ed presentation just the week prior to him leaving us. I only wish that I could have seen him grow into the great man I know he was creating inside. And to Travis I say, "Quit watching me shower, I know you always wanted me!" Love you, man.

## KARLA RAYPON SEVERSON:

Travis truly had a servant's heart and an infectious joy that permeated wherever he went. He impacted my life and many others. So thankful to have known him, even for a short while.

## EMILY SALTER ARZOLA:

I met Travis when he was dating my best friend in Riverside, California. Even after they stopped dating, we kept in touch. We became very close and good friends. We would talk on the phone for hours every day. He would also come and hang out at our house a lot. He lived on the complete opposite side of town, but you wouldn't know it, because he was always around. He started out just being friends with me and ended up being friends with several girls from my ward. He was close to my sisters, Amber and Angela, as well. He and I were always just friends, but we would go on group dates together and hang out a lot. When he was a teenager he had an obsession with Taco Bell. We would go to different Taco Bells in different cities to compare which was better. One time for a group date, he took me to Taco Bell. I was a very small and petite girl. I was five-one and weighed ninety pounds. He got a kick out of my fast metabolism and how I could eat so much. On this group date, he decided he was going to see how many tacos I could eat. He kept buying more and more. If I remember correctly, I got up to like fifteen. He raved about how crazy that was for years afterward.

Travis loved to do little things to make you feel special. We lived twenty to thirty minutes away, but he would always be there. I remember one time there was this song I really loved. I told him that I loved the song, and a day later my family got a ding-dong ditch and there was something on our doorstep. He had bought me the CD (which were not cheap at the time), wrapped it in tin foil (which was funny cause it was random), and put it on my doorstep and left. He did little funny things like that a lot.

Travis loved the gospel of Jesus Christ. I attended pre-missionary training class with him for a few years. He was so excited to be a missionary. He loved to share the gospel with random people in the mall, or different places we were hanging out. He wasn't shy about his beliefs. I remember one time he was hanging out with my sisters and I, and he called into a radio station that was asking what qualities we wanted in a man to marry. He kept calling and saying, "An R.M," (which means a return missionary). He really wanted them to say it on the radio. He kept calling until they finally did. Travis wanted to proclaim the gospel from the rooftops. A good scripture for Travis was:

D&C 24:12: "And at all times, and in all places, he shall open his mouth and declare my gospel as with the voice of a trump, both day and night. And I will give unto him strength such as is not known among men."

His missionary Scripture for his missionary plaque was Alma 29:1–2:

> *1 O that I were an angel, and could have the wish of mine heart, that I might go forth and speak with the trump of God, with a voice to shake the earth, and cry repentance unto every people!*
> *2 Yea, I would declare unto every soul, as with the voice of thunder, repentance and the plan of redemption, that they should repent and come unto our God, that there might not be more sorrow upon all the face of the earth.*

I have a great picture that he sent me while on his mission of him standing on a hill with a cityscape below him. He is holding the scriptures and outstretching his other hand like he is proclaiming the gospel to the world. He wrote his missionary scripture on the back.

Travis loved to be the center of attention. He loved it when he could get my sisters and their friends and I laughing. He was always pulling funny faces and making funny voices. He was always so much fun to be around. He was a big flirt, and would make several women feel special at once. Somehow, he had a talent for making you see your true potential as a daughter of God.

Travis was always great at making sure that you were staying on the straight and narrow. He would lecture me if he was worried I was going to go a wrong direction. Sometimes, he would frustrate me because he would tell me things I didn't want to hear, but I think it really helped me out during those important teenage years. We would sit talking on the phone for hours. Back then, it was just the home phone, and our families would get mad that we were always hogging up the line.

I have so many great stories that I could share about Travis. It is really hard to sit down and think of exactly what to share. I just want to tell you how he always made you feel special. Even if he was lecturing you about something . . . it was because he cared. He was very passionate about life and about the gospel. He was full of life. It was sad to see his life cut short. I think he would have done so many more great things.

## Dawn Ella Tate:

My dearest friend, Travis Victor Alexander, reminds me of an inspiring country song. After conversing with him, you always felt inspired, lifted up, and motivated to change. It is no surprise that he was a successful motivational speaker. He was not given the most ideal situation as a child. Yet he would not let this define him.

Travis Alexander is a person who will be marked in my mind, heart, and soul throughout my life. I came across Travis at a much-needed time. I was roughly about fifteen years old and a member of the Church of Jesus Christ of Latter-day Saints. I was the only member in my family and found it very difficult to get through such a wonderful church that held family at their upmost level. I did not fit in the "norm." We collaborated as a group in order to find comfort and support. There is one particular time Travis encountered a picture of the Savior in my house and he busted out in a song dedicated to Him. At this moment, I knew Travis had a relationship with his Savior. He prayed to Him and saw Him as more than just a being that once lived, but a being whom still lives and gives comfort and inspiration to those who seek Him out. Pretty remarkable for a sixteen-year-old!

Like all country songs, we have a broken heart to talk about . . .

There are many stories I can share with you that give details and explain what a treasure this world has lost, although one in particular wraps him up the most for me. I had come home from college one summer totally broken-hearted. I mean I was lost, my world was shaken from top to bottom, and I honestly did not think I was going to recover. Travis happened to be experiencing the same thing. We had thought we found the one; we started planning our lives and getting excited about the next level. Unfortunately, both of us had the door slammed shut and our souls were sad. We decided we needed some fresh air, and Big Bear was the place we would find it. There is something about nature and the beauty that surrounds it; one can find perspective and allow the hurt to flow through. I cannot tell you what exactly was said up in those mountain terrains, but I can say that we left our hurt down below. We laughed, joked, threw mud at each other, and lived a beautiful day. In that day, we found beauty amongst all the sadness. We were happy to be in this world, despite all the stuff thrown our way. Regardless of the madness below us, we would still sign up for this life. Why? We knew that this life was not the end, but just a journey that would allow us experiences to grow. Travis had a love for life and, despite his obstacles, he lived many days like the one I just described. Yet, again, too young for one to have such a perspective.

The inspirational country song he leaves us with . . .

I was recently inspired to go back to school to become an elementary school teacher. And, as I read Paulo Friere and Macedo, I often think Travis is one of the children they refer to in their pedagogy, children of the oppressed who need teachers to guide them.

My dearest friend Travis,

You are a remarkable person who has inspired so many, but I want to let you know that even though you're off to greater duties, you still affect many in this world, and because you have inspired me, you will affect countless children whom I will teach. You are a dear friend, and I am certainly better off because of knowing you.

And though some country songs end in a sad way, some may think that yours has ended in such, but I know, Travis, that your country song has just left the intro. And you have and will still inspire many.

Until we meet again, Travis!

~ Dawn

Travis was an example of any tune that one may listen to, which inspires one to make a change in the world for the better. We can all learn to be better tunes to our fellow beings.

## TAYLOR SEARLE:

I met Travis in 2005, and he was quite the character! He had this way of saying "word" when he agreed with something, but it's hard to describe how he actually said it. It was not in a regular voice, and he didn't just say it. Imagine a bellowing electric guitar mixed with the "most annoying sound in the world" from the movie *Dumb and Dumber* belting out "Wooooorrrrd!" This could be in many variations. A quick "word word," or "word to Big Bird, you big nerd," or "Word to the mother bird!" Travis wasn't just a funny guy; he was classy and incredibly charismatic. I have many wonderful and cherished memories with Travis.

Travis came over for a Sunday dinner with my family. I have a large family, so there were several people around the table. Imagine a full table of people with a nicely prepared meal. Like a good religious family, we started the meal with a prayer. Everyone around the table bowed their heads, and as someone in my family was giving a prayer over the food, Travis started rubbing my leg with his hand in an attempt to get me to laugh during the prayer. It was classic, irreverent Travis.

On another occasion, he was over at my house and we snuck into my brother's room while he was asleep. I hid in the closet, and Travis went and sat in a rocking chair in the corner of the room. I started making noises so that my brother would wake up. That brother had never met Travis before, so when he woke up, he saw a strange man sitting in the corner of his room just rocking in the chair. Travis said, "What's up?" and just kept rocking in the chair. My brother just went back to sleep, but I started laughing so hard that I couldn't contain it.

We double dated quite a bit. This time, we took our dates to a restaurant. When the hostess told us that there was going to be a thirty-minute wait, Travis flexed his biceps in front of the woman's face and asked if she wanted to touch it. Then the woman touched it and said how impressive it was, and then he asked, "So how long is the wait now?" When she laughed and said it would still be thirty minutes, he turned around and said, "You can touch my butt if you want to." In most situations, this would be horribly embarrassing and inappropriate for everyone involved, but with Travis, people loved him for it. There was never a dull moment with him around.

Travis and I became really close as we navigated the ups and downs of dating and relationships. We planned businesses together, and often talked about our futures. Travis planned his life without limitations. He pushed me to be and do better. He was convinced that with the help of God, he could achieve anything that he set his mind to. His entrepreneurial spirit was contagious. It saddens me that those aspirations were never actualized to the extent that he was capable. Looking at all the good he did, and all the joy he brought to those around him, I often wonder what he would have accomplished with more time. With his passing, he took a part of each of us with him, but he left a piece of him in return. It pushes me to work harder, be kinder, never give up, achieve my goals, and love more. Travis wasn't just a friend, he was family. He had a big heart, and loved to help others and do good. He also loved to have fun and make people smile and laugh. I definitely miss his big laugh. I look forward to the day we will see each other again.

## JAMIE SIMKO:

Even though I only knew Travis for a short time, I think it's important that the world remembers him for who he truly was, rather than the manipulated version that the media wants you to believe. He was a really compassionate dude who wanted nothing more than to better himself and help others to do the same. Any time I was around him, he would always share funny and inspirational stories about his life in the hopes that anyone who was listening could benefit in some way. Travis knew much struggle and hardship from his childhood, which made him very passionate in his later years about personal development and overcoming his personal battles, which he did. He lived the last few years of his life to the fullest, and he will always serve as a reminder that anyone who truly desires to change their lives for the better can do it. RIP T-Dogg!

## Marysia Hertz:

Travis was a colleague, a mentor, and over a short amount of time he became a treasured friend. His voice, charismatic way, and stage presence is unforgettable. Every time I hear Neil Diamond's "Sweet Caroline" or "Coming to America," I see Travis in our meeting room on the stage belting out every word and note as if he wrote the song himself. Travis loved to laugh. He taught to serve and love greatly, to dream big, to never look back, and to always know where you are going. Friends forever, Travis—miss you.

## Elisha Schabel:

I have a drive to succeed in life, help others and inspire others, just like Travis, who has ultimately helped me become who I am today. I now have a successful photography business, and I am building a doTerra business. I believe that we become who we are based on all the people who show up in our lives, and, most importantly, who we keep around to stay in our lives. We really truly are the average of those with whom we associate. Travis was an amazing person with whom to associate. I knew it the second I met him and saw him speak at an event I attended, in Utah (while living there) over twelve years ago. He was a rising star and someone to pay attention to.

Travis and I had a unique relationship/friendship. Because we were both single and available and in the same LDS "single scene," if you will, we shared a bond, much like the rest of the "single scene" in our LDS community. It was and still is a love/hate relationship with being single. We found comfort and solace in each other and our friendship. We helped each other "lick our wounds" and gave each other pep talks, like, "He's a loser, move on, you can do so much better," to, "He's not the guy for you," and, "Maybe you should be careful with that one," etc. I would also offer my advice back to him and tell him to not be such a flirt with *every* girl. I think we both had this sort of chemistry that we liked each other to the point of just flirting and allowing the fun flirtation to happen. But there just never was a real romantic connection or feelings for Travis on my end. And therefore I never saw him as an option to date or pursue, even though he might have seen me as one for him. We had a friendly yet flirtatious relationship until the end. We never did date or kiss. I loved having him as a friend, and I wasn't going to let a little flirtation get in my way. After all, it was so innocent, and Travis was always very flirtatious, but always respectful of my boundaries. I miss that flirtatious guy. A lot.

Because I live away from home (in Oregon, Ohio), and having lived out West since I was nineteen, I have relied heavily on my friends who have always become my family. I soon found family in Travis. I relied on his friendship and on him always being there for me. He always said he would be there for me no matter what. If I wanted to go grab a pizza at our favorite Venezia's Pizzeria in East Mesa, he would go with me, even just to watch me eat, when he was dieting. Because he became my family, I was his family too. It was mutual. I would always be there for him when he wanted to talk to me about a date gone wrong. I was his shoulder to cry on and listening ear. He was a home base. He was family and pretty much one of the first few souls I ever knew in the Mesa area. Still, to this day, there's such a tremendous loss that I feel now that he's gone. I think of him in that house as I drive past or on the freeway, and wish so much he were there, so I could pop on over and chat into the wee hours of the night, about anything and everything.

For thirty days, I shared his bed. Please don't get the wrong idea of me. Nothing *ever* happened, ever. Every night, I would make a pillow barricade with his stuffed lion on top, so it would make sure nothing ever did. It was his idea to share his room. Originally, he said I could have his bed and he would take the floor. Well, I wasn't going to let that happen and felt silly doing so, since it was a huge king-size bed and I'm a skinny gal who always hugs the end of the bed, not moving the entire night anyhow. He wanted to protect me from anything happening to me outside his room. It's a long story as to why I was staying there. The short of it is, my car broke down from Tucson to Mesa when I came up to get certified for massage therapy in Phoenix and to meet a few guys from online while I was up here. I'm a very practical gal, and I love a "kill a few birds with one stone" type of deal. Well, plans changed when my car broke and I had no money to get it fixed. With no way to go back to Tucson, I just decided to stay at his place while I figured something out, and long story short, I decided to move and just stay in the Mesa area, find a job, save up to fix my car, and eventually go back to get my things at my sister Gretchen's place. My dear, sweet, older sister and I moved here together. I moved here from Utah and she from New Mexico, four months prior to my car breaking down. I had always wanted to move up to Mesa the second I found out what a small town Tucson really was, and all the "hot guys" to date were up in the Mesa area. Travis was truly the only person I knew who lived up there. That was ten years ago. I now have a lot of friends, but still miss Travis deeply, because he felt like home and family to me, even now.

In those short yet very long at times, thirty days, Travis and I got to know each other really well. You tend to get to know someone at a hyper speed when you share their bed and talk all night long every night until the early morning hours. We really never slept. We talked and talked and talked. It truly was a fun time, and we learned everything about each other during that time.

On Sunday mornings, we would get ready for church together; he at "his" sink, and me at "mine." I watched him shave with his fancy brush he would sweep so delicately across his face with his shaving cream, as if he were someone doing it to him. He liked the luxurious things in life. He loved his fancy suits and ties and shoes, and wooden hangers. I would help him choose which suit to wear and which tie and which pair of shoes as he gave me options. Looking back now, I felt at times we seemed a lot like a married couple. We sang church hymns together while I put on my makeup and curled my hair.

One of my favorite memories of Travis is him whistling songs or hymns while he, for lack of a better word, urinated in the toilet closet,

I would call it. Just a toilet in a room that looked like a closet. He would whistle so as to cover up the sound. I laughed and smiled *every* time without fail. That's the thing about Travis, he was always smiling and always laughing. We, together, were always smiling and always laughing. He became my best friend at that time. I remember sitting on that bathroom floor, talking to my dad on the phone, begging him for help. I remember relaying to my dad where I was living at the time and who I was living with. I shared stories of Travis's generosity to take me to and from work every day and share his food with me and his bed and his house. Travis never asked for a dime in return. Not once. I didn't want to be a burden. I begged my dad for funds to help me get my car fixed and to be able to rent my own place, so I could be out of Travis's "hair." I didn't want to overstay my welcome. Travis never complained, not once. In fact, he was saddened by me having to leave so soon. I remember getting teary eyed and sad myself, on packing/moving day. I even thought my pink slippers his sweet pug puppy, Napoleon, chewed on, were endearing, and I was going to miss living there so much!

I found a place with a gal down the street. It's literally around the corner from where I now reside. I have come full circle in ten years. She lived across the street from that church building, which I now attend every Sunday. It had been ten years since I had been back to this building. That first Sunday back, it was really difficult to sit there and not shed a tear. That same ward house, Travis and I sat next to each other and pointed at the "hot" guys and girls we each thought the other should date or get to know. No one ever seemed good enough for me in Travis's eyes, even when I got married to my now ex-husband. The last memories I have of Travis were December 2007. Just eight short months after I was married, I was crying to Travis about my abusive ex-husband and my failing marriage. Travis was very upset and protective like a brother, and yet had to make sure to get "I told you so" in. I had texted him what had been happening and that I was separated from my ex. Travis was still his flirtatious self, and said, "Hey, we can finally have that kiss now." I said "Oh, Travis, I'm still married!" He said "I know, can't blame a guy for trying, right?" I realized then that being flirtatious wasn't so much trying to "hook up" with me, as it was trying to just make me smile and laugh. Something Travis always succeeded at making me do. He always knew *just* the right words to say to get me to smile and not stress about my problem at the time. He was such a blessing.

There were so many times that Travis had talked about selling his house in Mesa, Arizona, or even renting his house and moving back to the Riverside area. I remember saying, "Don't you dare. I don't want to lose you." I told him I would feel a tremendous loss. And I knew I wasn't alone in thinking that. There was such a security knowing he was around. Even when life got busy later on and our own personal and dating lives took over and changed, he was one of those friends that no matter how much time had passed since we last spoke or interacted, we picked right back up where we left off and it was as if no time had passed.

What I loved most about Travis was his work ethic, his smile, his laughter, his testimony of the gospel of Jesus Christ and the truthfulness of our church (The Church of Jesus Christ of Latter-day Saints), and of course his positivity and his generosity and his spirit. I loved our gospel-centered chats at night. Those were my most favorite chats! Our spirits meshed well, and we shared in having a strong testimony and also in the same temptations and struggles in life. So that's why we connected on a deeper level. We understood each other and had a spiritual bond. We helped each other. Being single and chaste, was and is difficult. We were each other's cheerleaders! We all need people like that in our lives. I knew by reading his books I borrowed even more about his weaknesses. He had highlighted, underlined, and dog eared, the parts of books that meant a particular something to him. I know Travis was trying really hard to make his weaknesses become his strengths. We all fall short, and we all need time and the application of the grace of God in our lives. Travis was no different. He was actively trying to repent and apply that saving grace in his life, and I know that for a fact.

Christ suffered and died for each of us, because we could not make this journey without Him. Travis was not perfect, and would be the first to admit that. At his spiritual core, he was humble. I'm honored that he let me in and allowed me to see his truth. He was only just beginning to tap into who he could become and his full potential. It's truly sad to me that we won't get to experience that in this life. My hope is that his legacy will continue and positivity will arise from his death. The world already knows about him, because of his death. And in that, there is positivity to be found, and that's my desire to help spread his positivity and share his legacy with the world and those who may read this book.

His drive to succeed was inspirational to me. After my day job, he would work closely with me at my "night job," which was working with Pre-Paid Legal, now called LegalShield. Travis and I were on separate teams, and he had no personal monetary gain from working with me, whatsoever. That's the kind of guy and friend Travis was. He gave me all his tips and tricks to succeeding in that business and would even allow me to sit there, while he was on his phone speaking to potential clients, his downline, and team. He was very successful at such a young age, and yet he was just beginning. Today, I have two of Travis's favorite books. I hold them dear to me. They are the only possessions I have that were his. One of them is *How to Win Friends and Influence People* by Dale Carnegie, and the other was *The Miracle of Forgiveness* by Spencer W. Kimball. He had a vast library of which I was envious. He allowed me to borrow any book I desired. I borrowed those two before I moved out and I still have them; he told me to keep them, because he had duplicates of each. I will always remember him as I read them and see his highlighted and underlined words, knowing he held these books in his hands. I find comfort in that.

To this day, I still speak to Travis. Our spirits are still connected. I know it may sound funny to some. I'm not concerned with how it may sound. Travis's spirit is very much alive. He's up "there" still cheering me on. I could feel his strong presence during the trial and when I was interviewed on national television. I can feel his presence now as I type these words in his honor. I know he is very much alive and doing good and big things where he's at. I know he's smiling down on his friends, and is still being that supportive friend and brother to us. And I know I will see him again someday, after this life. What a joyous reunion.

So, to honor him and his legacy, I will end with these (tearful) words:

I love you, Travis. I'm so grateful I met you. I'm beyond blessed to have known you. Thank you for being real and authentic. You are my brother, my friend, my family. Thank you for loving me. Thank you for being my biggest fan. Thank you for believing in me when I didn't believe in myself. Thank you for showing me and telling me what I deserve in this life and what I'm capable of achieving. Thank you for being a great example to me. Thank you for not judging me and always being positive and reminding me of my worth and making me feel beautiful and comfortable in my own skin. Thank you for teaching me so many wonderful things by example. Thank you for helping me to become the strong woman I am today. Thank you above all for your generosity and helping me strengthen my testimony of the Gospel of Jesus Christ, while you were on this earth and even more so now that you are gone from this earth. As I wrote in the book at your memorial service, I'll say it again . . . This isn't good-bye, Travis, this is, "See you later, my friend. I love you forever. Until we meet again" . . . Love, your forever friend, Elisha J. Schabel.

## JARED AND HEATHER BARNARD:

Admittedly I wasn't as close to Travis as many other people you may have seen on TV or read about here in this book. However, I do consider him to have been a great friend and confidante. We never went four-wheeling or snowmobiling together. We never went on camping trips or to church events. I met Travis through Pre-Paid Legal (now LegalShield) in late 2002. My wife, Heather, and I later became closer to him through our friendship with Chris and Sky Hughes, mostly over late night chats and late morning breakfasts in their home. We would visit them a few times a year while they lived in California, and more than once Travis would be there visiting or passing through. Heather keeps telling me, "You have to talk about eating breakfast at Chris and Sky's with Travis in his money pajama pants!" That is indeed a very fond memory. Travis had these great pajama pants with $$$$$ all over them. Their home holds many of our fondest memories of Travis. That's where we had the most one-on-one time with him.

Of course I always hung out with "the gang" when we were at conventions for PPL, too. It was late in the evenings, after our meetings, where we would talk, tell stories, laugh and get to know one another better. Travis was always the life of the party. He was so funny... and animated. (You were always guaranteed to laugh around Travis.) He also had an amazing ability to draw people to him, not just because of his wit, but also because of his leadership. He often turned a group conversation into a mentoring session, just as if he was living the life of his mentor and idol, Jim Rohn.

Travis was...and *is* incredibly persistent. He loved sharing his religion, but never shoved it down your throat. Having grown up in Salt Lake City, I was raised in a Mormon environment, but stopped following the LDS Church somewhere along the way. Travis was so funny about trying to get my wife and I involved. More than once while he was visiting Temple Square in Salt Lake City, he filled out a referral card to have the missionaries pay us a visit to our house. (He did always preach the value of "being system dependent.") They showed up one day and let us know it was Travis who sent them, and of course they kept coming back. It eventually became a bit of an inside joke, but he was persistent, and not because he wanted to bug us, but because he was so intent on sharing his love of the LDS teachings. Two years after he died, we moved to the United Arab Emirates. While in a hotel just days after our arrival there, I was wearing a Utah Utes t-shirt when we ran into a family wearing BYU shirts. (BYU is a private university owned by the LDS church.) "It's a sign from Travis!" we joked. Months after that we were invited to start attending the Mormon church—in the Middle East of all places. Again, my wife and I smiled at each other. "T-Dogg's at it again!"

He was a big kid, always playing a part to make people laugh. You couldn't help but be mesmerized by his grandiose personality. At the same time, he was so vulnerable. You know how sometimes people look like their "tough" on the outside but they're really just a big, tender kid inside? That was T. I remember him telling stories when he was training at Pre-Paid Legal events. He could make himself so vulnerable in front of a crowd, bringing himself and everybody around him to tears. He always talked about how "If your 'Why' doesn't make you cry, it's not a big enough 'Why'." His upbringing was his "why," or his motivation to seek a better life, and he was never shy about letting others know what it was like for him growing up. And the beautiful thing was, that he was somehow grateful for his past. He never played the part of the victim, but rather portrayed every abuse he suffered as a stepping-stone to the man he became (and the one he was working hard to become). Everything he did was focused on being better. He obviously made some mistakes along the way and ultimately got distracted by something that ended his journey, but he never stopped trying, and he never stopped encouraging others to work to be better themselves.

I'm lucky to have a constant reminder of Travis in my home. My son has a favorite stuffed animal, "Lion." Travis was with me at the MGM Grand hotel in Las Vegas when I bought Lion as a gift for my son's second birthday. He still sleeps with Lion every night, and I'd like to think that a little part of T has traveled with Lion and us around the world on our adventures.

Travis' passing saddens me, knowing what he could have done with his life, but I also smile knowing what a positive influence he was on so many people and the amazing things that he *did* do with his life. Travis would want us to celebrate his time here and learn from his mistakes, the same way he learned from his parents' mistakes. Travis would want all of us to work every day toward getting better, just like he did.

We love and miss you, my friend. Every day. We're grateful to have known you.

## C.A. Murff:

What can I say about my friend Mr. Travis Alexander? I guess I can start by sharing the fact that his phone number is still a permanent fixture in my phone, despite losing him tragically over six years ago. He is someone that I never want to, or will, forget!

Travis and Murff

From his easy, warm demeanor, to his ability to make anyone feel good about themselves, he was definitely someone special. I had the pleasure of sharing four-wheeling and camping trips with him and the rest of our close friends and family on several occasions. He shared his talents by coming to our Las Vegas community and sharing information and training about our company as only he could. Those evenings would be followed by long, enjoyable, philosophical conversations at my home.

My understanding of the depth of Travis's character culminated in one special evening at Daniels Summit in Utah. It was there, at a team event, that Travis took the stage as a Rock Star in tight, cut-off blue jean shorts, ripped-sleeved T-shirt, and a puffed-out mullet wig. He was wailing away with some crazy song, and had the whole audience in tears laughing hysterically at his antics. He had complete control of the room, and you could tell that he had thrown all inhibitions to the wind and was LOVIN' entertaining the audience.

Act II. Travis left, then came back on stage in "regular" clothing, and began to share with the audience intimate details of his family, his troubled upbringing, lifestyle, and bad choices that he had made in life. In an instant, it seemed, the same person who had us crying with laughter now had us crying with emotions. The only constant was the fact that Travis was still in control of the room. He was a skilled trainer and orator. From the heights of his showmanship to the depths of his raw transparency, he was truly something to behold. I miss you, my friend.

## TARA PAUSTENBACH:

Travis was one of those guys you just liked the moment you met him. He didn't wear a façade; he wasn't surrounded by walls he'd built up over years like so many, and he didn't live his life through filters based on who he was with like so many of our twenty-something population tends to do. He was just . . . Travis.

I first met him at a business event. I happened to be the person on stage that evening, and when we finished, Travis came to introduce himself and let me know he enjoyed my talk. Now, as a thirty-something woman at the time, it wasn't uncommon to have men come up and introduce themselves. However, what was uncommon—and SO refreshing—was that Travis brought no "vibe" with him other than gratitude and sincere conversation, laced with humor. We became friends.

Over the next several years, at all our business events throughout Southern California and our international events in different locations across the US, I spent quality time having great conversations with Travis. He was such a good person. He had such a good heart. He really, truly desired to make a positive difference in the world . . . and he was on track to do it. He had a spirit that just naturally attracted people. Bumping into Travis surrounded by a crowd of people (who were holding their guts, laughing uncontrollably) wasn't out of the norm. He made me laugh. He made us ALL laugh. I'll never forget "Paustenbalm" (You had to be there to experience Eddie Snell).

In 2004, I experienced a pretty significant personal transition in my life. Travis called me every day like clockwork for three months. He didn't miss a day, even if I missed his call, and even then, he'd leave a voicemail for me to let me know I was whatever outrageous adjective he could think of to make me chuckle. I wasn't even one of his best friends, but at a time he knew I needed true friends around me, he stepped up like a champ. Travis really touched my heart during that time, and he did it just to give.

It's nearly impossible for me—for any of us—to discuss Travis, think of Travis, or brag about what a stellar human being he was without feeling so cheated by how the world was forced to say good-bye to him. When Sky and Chris asked me to write a contribution, my only hesitation was in wondering, *How do I end it?*

So, as I write this on my birthday—my one day of the year I only do exactly what I want to do—I have decided that Travis's story just will not end. His heart, his spirit, and his humor will live on through all of us as long as we're here to share great memories and great times with Travis Alexander.

Love,
Tara

## Charlie Ethington:

The first time I met Travis was when I moved into an apartment with about five other guys in Riverside, California, in 1999. At the time, he literally had like three jobs. He seemed to be gone all the time either working, on dates, or at school. He seemed well liked in our singles' ward at church, but it took a little time before we really met. I remember he was a little goofy. He loved music like punk and ska, and drove an old beater blue truck. I remember seeing him from time to time in the apartment. I remember him always stealing my socks, or I would catch him wearing my clothes. This was how we first met, but fast forward a few years later.

I had been married a couple of years and we heard that Travis was doing well for himself. I was confused, because when I knew him, he had three jobs and was working around the clock. We soon got into business together with Pre-Paid Legal, and he became a mentor to us and helped us get started. It was from this point on that we became a lot closer. I remember him one time sleeping over at our house and in the morning, I saw him sitting in sweats making calls and he was wearing a Rolex watch. I thought that was odd. There had been a transformation from when I knew him before. I respected where he had come from and how he changed his life. He introduced me to personal development, and we became great friends as we set goals and worked our Pre-Paid Legal businesses. He was there when our first two kids were born and became like an uncle to them. We hoped that one day he would meet the right girl and be able to start a family of his own. I will always be grateful for the things he taught me and the friendship we shared.

## Autumn Ethington:

The first time I met Travis he was fresh off his mission and came to our apartment to have Otter Pops after a young adult activity. The whole time he was trying to get ten names of people I knew he could contact about the church. I laugh about it now, but at the time I was annoyed at this guy preaching to me. We started calling him "Preacher Man."

When our first baby was born, we had a lot of friends and family come to the hospital to meet our baby boy, Dylan. Travis and Deanna came really late one night to see him, and when it was Travis's turn to hold our baby, he was so nervous he would break him. Awkwardly, he sat and held him, and started telling him stories about Uncle Travis and how big and strong he was. I think I remember him showing Dylan his muscles.

We set a book out at Dylan's first birthday and had guests write in it. This was what Travis wrote:

*I'm your Uncle T-Dogg, and I've got really big muscles. So just in case when you are old enough to read this and I am fat. You'll know I was a BUFF guy. The reason you live in a big house and have nice cars and get to see the world with your parents is because right now as I write this your parents and I and a lot of other people at your first birthday party worked really hard to build our dreams so that you and all of our kids could have a better life. So now as you are old enough to read this and you have a lot that others don't have, know it is because your parents were brave enough to do things others kids' parents weren't willing to do. Now it's your turn to follow your parents' example and make the world a better place because you are in it. Travis Alexander*

Halloween 2006, Travis came to our house to hang out and showed up in a partial tin man costume, and asked a few of us to help him finish his costume. As Deanna and I were taping his butt and crotch with duct tape, we looked at each other, thinking, *What did we get ourselves into?* He left for his party, and I heard his costume was a hit! He had a great time until he realized he had to pee. This was something I loved about Travis; he loved to make people laugh even at his own expense.

# MIKE CHAPMAN:

Travis Alexander is one of the best friends I will ever have. We became friends when he was about seventeen years old. He attended a class I was involved with that our church offered for young people who were interested in serving as a missionary. My role in the class was to help these young people be prepared to teach the gospel of Jesus Christ, something that can be a little challenging for most at that age. Travis was unlike the others who attended. He possessed a confidence in himself and in his beliefs that I have rarely seen in others, especially someone so young. Travis was loud and proud about what he believed in, and he flat out didn't care what you thought about it. He dedicated two years of his life working seven days a week in Colorado, telling others about Jesus and the way the Savior had changed his life for the better. The many people he touched in Colorado know the truth about Travis and the kind of person he is.

After his mission, we reunited when he came to work for me. He had a hunger and a drive for success that was inspiring. He quit a job where he was making considerably more money to go to work for me because I told him I would help him learn how to run his own business someday. Travis had vision, and unlike most, he was not afraid to think big! Ironically, it wasn't long before Travis had come to me to announce that he had fulfilled his goal of going into business for himself, and I ended up joining efforts with him in his business. We worked together just about every day for years. Travis was younger than a lot of the people we worked with, but that never mattered. He was a true leader and because of his ability to lead, Travis inspired so many people. As his business grew, he had more and more opportunities to reach out and help others, which was what he was all about. The many people who he helped in his business life know the truth about Travis and the kind of person he is.

More than anything, Travis and I were friends. We were both very busy, but he always had time for me and my family. Here is one example of how Travis was always there for us. When our daughter was turning five, my wife and I made plans to take her to Disneyland. It was going to be a special day all for her. At the last minute, the family member who my wife had made arrangements with to watch our three-year-old son had something come up and could no longer watch him. For weeks, I had told our daughter how special she was and how we were planning a special day just for her. She didn't know where we were going, but she loved the idea that her little brother wasn't getting to come because it was "her special day." Prior to that day, my wife flat out refused to leave our kids with anyone except a handful of family members, so when I somewhat jokingly mentioned that Travis had offered to watch our son, I was rather surprised when she immediately replied that she would be ok with that. I questioned her to make sure she was really comfortable with it, knowing how strongly she felt about who watched our kids, and she replied that she trusted Travis completely.

At the time, Travis was only twenty-five years old, yet he was the one person she felt comfortable to leave our little boy with, and Travis went out of his way to make us feel like it was no big deal. When it came to his friends and family, Travis was willing to drop everything and help out however he could. His family and those of us who were blessed by his friendship know the truth about Travis and the kind of person he is. Like the rest of us, Travis was not perfect, but as someone who spent countless hours with him, day after day for years, I can tell you the truth about Travis Alexander.

Travis is a man of high character who genuinely strived to learn, do, and become better each and every day. He had a habit that was typical of the kind of person he was. Each day he would write out his goals for the day on a three-by-five card. Some of these goals would include big things, but usually they were just small and simple things like exercise for thirty minutes, call so and so to see how they were doing, read ten pages of an inspiring book, help so and so . . . He would go to work each morning on these written goals, checking them off as he completed them. Some days, he'd complete them all, and some days he wouldn't, but in either case he'd do it all over again the next day. No big deal, right? Well, if you think that it's no big deal, I challenge you to try it for one hundred days. Buy a pack of three-by-five cards and every day for one hundred days write down the most important tasks you feel you should complete that day, and then check them off as you accomplish them. Do this, and you will gain a true insight to the kind of person Travis really was and is. Then, remember he did this for hundreds of days without fail because he truly desired to progress and be better. And Travis, I have no doubt you are still at it, brother. Still learning. Still growing. Still becoming. I think of you often, my friend, and look forward to the day when we will meet again.

## KATIE LORSCH:

(This is from her blog http://thekatiedid.blogspot.com)
My dear friend Travis Alexander passed away a couple days ago. This is my post dedicated to an amazing man who I will never forget.

Oh Travis - I love you. I told you that all the time, because I really do. There isn't ANYONE out in the world like you. That's probably why I was sucked into your exciting world soon after I moved into the ward.

You gave me the sweetest and most sincere Christmas present ever. I had absolutely no money for Christmas, so I always planned on writing you a letter telling you how much I love and admire you. You were always a "Words of Affirmation" kind of guy. How I wish I had given you that letter. I would randomly remember all through these months and promise myself I would do that for you the next Sunday, or Saturday morning. All of my time is gone to tell you exactly what I think of you, so this will have to suffice until I see you again.

I remember the first time I really talked to you was bowling after Family Home Evening. You kind of intimidated me because you were hilarious, good-looking, knew everyone, and were liked by everyone. I mean, the coolness that you were oozing all over the place was enough to make me intimidated! But you approached me and we began a very "Travis-like" conversation about life, and how each person has the ability to be whoever they want to be. I'd like to say that at that moment, some of my best life lessons were learned.

Man you like to talk. I knew that if I ever started talking to you, we would end up talking for hours. It was very dangerous, but I love talking with you. I would always talk about how we needed to write a book based strictly on your life experiences since they were always so crazy and hilarious. For someone who craved compliments and kind words, you always had something nice to say to me. You boosted my confidence ten-fold, and made me feel like I was the coolest person in the world. Probably because I was friends with one of the coolest people ever.

I will never forget sitting upstairs on your love sacs and watching you do yoga in your PJ's. It was seriously outrageous. I remember trying not to laugh, but then I would let out a giggle, since the whole idea of this grown man doing yoga in front of me was just hilarious. I will admit, your flexibility surprised me, but you looked seriously goofy. :) Oh Travis, I miss you.

We had the best time ever on our road trip to Utah for General Conference. It really says something about a person when, after being with them continually for 4 days straight, you like them even more. I found out you are one of those rare people who are always enjoyable to be around. I craved your friendship, wisdom, and stories after that trip. On this trip I found out you could make the best wolf face I have ever seen. I mean, when you started snarling at that restaurant I almost died laughing. My obnoxious laughter might have almost brought the building down, but you looked exactly like a snarling wolf. I'm picturing those wolves off of *Beauty and the Beast*. That's probably where you got your practice anyway. :) I think the funniest part about your wolf impersonation is that you did it in the middle of a nice restaurant during dinner. You are so fun and spontaneous. Seriously, I never had a dull moment with you. You would always do outrageous things that would embarrass everyone but yourself. Oh man, remember that time you commented on the guy's picture in Jack-in-the-Box because he looked like a child molester? And then we found out he had passed away and the plaque was in memory of him? Foot in mouth moment Travis. You had tons of those.

You are the most generous person I know. So many cookie nights at your house where you spent hours baking and we only ate 1/6 of what you had made. Whatever did you do with all of those cookies? And then your brunches in-between conference sessions. Those were amazing, and of course you supplied all of the ingredients and most of the work. UFC will always be special to me now. You introduced me to the world of tight shorts on strong men with rippling butt muscles. I will never be the same. And I still can't get over you laughing at me when I watched the first one and was frozen in horror and anticipation.

Ugh, I don't like Napoleon. Thankfully, we had an open relationship about that. You would monitor the dog around me, but nonetheless, I always left your house with dog slobber all over me and a missing shoe. Who is going to take care of Napoleon?

I am so sorry I chastised you about being late. I tend to be a woman sometimes and I like to nag. It was so impressive to see you on-time and even early to church after that. You are always up for a challenge. Maybe that's why you aren't here anymore. I know you are having the adventure of a life-time right now.

Thank you so much for being passionate with me. We both love *Joe vs. the Volcano*. Oh dang, you quoting the "flibbertigibbet." Meg Ryan was outa control. And Atlas Shrugged. Oh, we loooove love, love that book. I still remember when I found out you loved Ayn Rand. Actually, you kinda found out first. We were driving in the car and you grabbed my book to see what I was reading. When you saw that it was Atlas Shrugged you interrogated me to see if I was reading it for a school assignment. Once you were sure I was sincere about my love of Ayn Rand and her philosophies, we had a bonding experience unlike any other. We talked about that book and her Capitalist ideas forever. I still remember your plan to have a huge statue of a man shrugging an atlas off of his shoulders in the entrance of your dream home.

You saved my life so many times by taking me out to eat. You were just so generous and I never had any money. I wish so badly I could pay you back. And that time on our road trip when you paid for everyone's dinner at that nice restaurant. So generous. And you really really don't expect anything in return.

I have been so excited about helping you write your book, "Raising You." The title is ingenious and your philosophies are amazing. I still have your hand-written draft of the introduction in my file. I don't know why you worried so much about it. You are an amazing writer all on your own.

Dude, you dress well. I loved complimenting you. The way you would receive them made me feel so good about myself.

Thank you so much for having the courage to be yourself. This allowed me to be completely open around you, which is how you met the real Katie Barnes.

You are one amazing interior designer. I was planning on having you be my personal consultant once I owned my first house.

I will never forget when you read your affirmation to me. The Enya music was so intense and you have the perfect speaking voice. Seriously, you should have done commercials or advertisements or something. But you instilled in me a desire to create my own and do what you do. That is, make myself a better person every day.

You see, you made me realize that in order to truly work on being a better person, I needed to consistently monitor my progress and have goals. I admire your self-discipline and strict daily schedule of productivity. Pray, read scriptures, exercise, learn Spanish, read *Ensign* article, write in journal, work on book, listen to self-motivation tape, work, paint the baseboards, read scriptures, shave my entire body, be a good friend. Yes, you are amazing. And I'm sorry, but I can't bring myself to shave every inch of my body. It's just not natural!! :)

You would always talk about the Greats; Abraham Lincoln, Alexander the Great, etc. You would tell me, "Katie, if you want to be great, you can do it. You have that same power that Ol' Abe did. You are great. You are amazing. Now go live up to your potential."

Travis, you are one of the Greats. I would like to say, the greatest. Who is honest Abe anyhow? Did he know Yoga? I don't think so. You strived to be the best you could be, to be that son of God who had divine potential. Travis, you are a legacy. You will always be remembered. You have touched so many lives, and the things that you taught them will be passed to so many others. You will live on and will be a Hero in thousands of lives. Travis - you are Great.

I will never forget you. Not ever.

'Til We Meet Again

Love,
Katie


## Brint Hiatt:

I remember vividly my first impression of Travis Victor Alexander at an event in Long Beach, California, years ago. He seemed so self-assured and confident as he got up on stage and spoke to a room full of people, and he was playing the crowd. If anything, I thought that he was cocky, being so young and apparently successful, and he was not at all ashamed of it. Later that night, I got to know Travis better at a nearby restaurant, and I realize now that Travis was larger than life. In everything he did, he really tried to live up to his nicknames, Victor and Alexander the Great.

I could not have appreciated then just how extraordinary he truly was. I didn't know then what I know now about his history, his character, or the odds that were stacked against him growing up. I just saw a young man only a couple years older than me, so how could he be so far ahead? I admit that I was jealous at the time, but now I recognize that he did all that he could to maximize his life in every way.

A few weeks later, he came to the Phoenix area for another event, where we hung out again both during and after the events. He spoke of wanting to move out from California, and he reached out to my brother and me about being his roommates. It didn't take me long to warm up to the idea. I knew that we were becoming friends, but I never realized that I would gain another brother from the arrangement.

Our house was still fairly close to my parents', so my brother and I would go back to my parents' every Sunday for family dinner. As we were leaving that first Sunday to go home for dinner, I noticed Travis hanging out. It could have been my imagination, but it seemed to me that he was feeling kind of lonely. So I invited him to come with us, not really expecting him to say yes, but he did. I'm forever grateful that he did, and I know that my family agrees.

Over the years that followed, Travis became a full member of my family, coming with us on fishing trips, to our cabin in the mountains, to Mexico, and many other places. He mercilessly teased my sisters, flattered my mom and dad outrageously, and he became my big brother, never letting me get away with being less than my best. "First class" became a motto for our house, one that he propagated for all of us living there, and while we sometimes fell short of the ideal, we never stopped striving for it. Travis certainly had his shortcomings, but not trying hard enough was not one of them. In his head, he had already eclipsed whatever goal he had set out to accomplish, because he would never give up on being Alexander the Great.

I would do almost anything to hear his crazy, maniacal-sounding laugh, see him flex his biceps, quote Christopher Walken, Will Ferrell, or Conan O'Brian, or just to see him do "the sprinkler" dance on the dance floor. He never cared what others thought of him. Like I said before, at times he almost seemed larger than life. Most days, I just laugh when I think of that laugh, or the pranks he pulled, or the pranks we pulled on him. Other days, it's still hard to smile, because I still miss my friend. I love you, Travis my brother, and someday I'll see you again.

## DEANNA REID:

I am usually a very private person. I always have been. I just want my personal memories of Travis to be just that, personal. I cherish our memories together and want to keep them for myself. But, I do want to say a few things about my friend. I want everyone to know how I feel about Travis and how my life has been affected by him.

When Travis' life ended mine was halted. Our lives were so intertwined that I wasn't sure how to move forward with my life after his death. He is and forever will be my best friend. The experience of losing him and then the process of seeking justice for him tested the limits of my strength. Although it seemed to me that I was at my breaking point...I did not break. It changed me. It changed me in ways I would have never expected. I developed a closer relationship with God. I was able to see his hand in my life guiding and protecting me. I have felt His holy spirit with me comforting and strengthening me in my times of need. It made me better. I have had so many experiences since that summer in 2008 that have made me stronger, more loving, more patient and compassionate, more service minded, and more grateful. I love and appreciate Travis more now than ever before.

Travis was a good man. We loved being together. It was easy and natural. I could just be myself around him. We were very young when we first meet and started dating. We had so much fun together. He was always a romantic. He loved music, especially sappy love songs. He also liked to read and write poetry. He was a good boyfriend from the start and I like to think I helped make him an even better one. It was important to him to be a good boyfriend. He would really listen to any criticism or advice I had for him and then actually follow through on it. He made sure he made time for me and was very attentive and sweet. He was sensitive to and cared about my feelings. He wanted me to be happy.

Travis had a genuine love for learning. He was very inquisitive. He wanted my opinion on all sorts of things. I always felt that he appreciated what I had to say and respected me and my point of view. He made me feel like my opinions mattered and that he really wanted to hear them. Travis was a good listener. He paid attention and had a great memory. He would remember my likes and dislikes. He would remember small details about our past conversations and experiences together. This (in my experience) isn't very common in most relationships. When I was with him I felt special and cared for.

Travis and I were alike in many ways but also very different. Our sense of humor was very similar and we made each other laugh all the time. We both like reading and learning, music, movies, church, etc. Although we both had a positive/optimistic outlook on life, I tend to be more skeptical and cautious. I am much more of an introvert than he ever was. He was so brave when it came to doing what he knew was right. He had no fear when it came to helping others and standing up for the little guy. I don't think he would've seen himself as being brave, just doing what needed to be done. But sometimes it takes bravery to be kind and to me Travis was very brave. Travis was the epitome of a dreamer. I came to really adore that about him. He trusted and believed in people. He was a true "people person". He was such a good conversationalist. He was an amazing story teller. I loved watching him in a group of people or at a party. He was so animated and sincere. Which made him good at light-hearted conversations and small-talk with strangers, but also very good at deep or serious conversations. Travis' love for life and his ambition was infectious. He truly did motivate people to want to do more and to be better. It makes me so happy that he continues to inspire and motivate people.

When talking about Travis I feel like I should say a few words about his dog Napoleon too. Travis loved Napoleon. Napoleon loved Travis. Travis loved and worried about him as if he were his child. As a puppy, Naps (as Travis often called him) ran out into the street right in front of a car. Travis screamed at the top of his lungs as he ran after him. Luckily nothing happened to Napoleon but Travis was pretty shaken up by the incident. Travis taught him tricks, gave him treats, took him on road trips, and spoiled him like crazy. They used to race each other up the stairs and play wrestle. Napoleon followed Travis everywhere like his little shadow. Naps lives with me now. Ever since Travis was taken from Napoleon I have been caring for him. But really he is the one who takes care of me. He is now my little shadow. He is such a blessing. He brings so much peace, love, and comfort into my life. He is best buddies with my nieces and nephews. He is my little cuddle pug and I love him so much! He's getting older now. He has a lot of gray and sleeps a bit more these days. It makes me realize that he will pass on someday. That will be very hard for me and I pray that I will have much more time with him. But it is good to know that when that time comes, he will be going straight back to Travis. What a happy moment that will be for the both of them.

I feel so blessed to have known Travis. He brightened my life in so many ways while he was here AND since he's been gone.

I always loved him and I always will.

Deanna Reid

# Epilogue

THE JODI ARIAS MURDER TRIAL lasted five months. Jodi was convicted of premeditated first degree murder on May 8, 2013. After the penalty phase, the jury could not come to a unanimous decision regarding the appropriate penalty for Jodi. On May 23, 2013, they came back hung. Eight of the twelve jurors voted for the death penalty. When this happens in Arizona, the prosecutor's office has the right to default to the decision of the judge to determine whether she will get life with the possibility of parole, life without the possibility of parole, or they can retry the penalty phase of the trial and go for the death penalty again. If the jury cannot decide on death a second time, it goes to the judge for sentencing. They opted to retry the penalty phase of the trial. One would think this would take less time than the actual trial, but unfortunately we were wrong.

The retrial of the penalty phase began on October 21, 2014. It has been a whirlwind of distractions from start to finish. Accusations of prosecutorial misconduct continued. The defense claimed witnesses refused to testify in public. This included Jodi. The judge closed the courtroom, which is a violation of the Constitution of the United States, so Jodi would testify. The Arizona Supreme court ordered that the courtroom remain open and the proceedings be made public, after which the murderer who sought out reporters and even had an interview scheduled immediately following her first-degree murder conviction refused to retake the stand. The defense's entire mitigation case was about slinging mud at Travis and trying to destroy him with lies and manipulation. We heard very little about any "mitigating factors" needed to save Jodi's life. Jodi had told Troy Hayden, a Phoenix news reporter, that she had no mitigating factors. She told him there was no abuse or drug use in her home, yet she got up on the stand in the penalty phase retrial, behind closed doors, and told the tale of abuse and cocaine use by her father and marijuana use by her mother. Samantha Alexander, Travis's sister, said, "I'm disgusted with the way her defense attorneys drag my brother's name through his own blood. She is evil! She has no remorse! If she did, she would have told the truth, not these made up stories about him being abusive and a pedophile."

On March 5, 2015, the jury came back hung again. Eleven jurors voted for death, but there was one hold out. In an interview with the Jury Foreman done by Jen Wood from Trial Diaries, he told her that they looked for the alleged abuse that took place. From December 2007 to January 2008, Travis did not make one mean comment to Jodi. He felt they had been misled and was shocked about the portrayal of Travis. (You can read the interview here: www.ourfriendtravis.com/ foreman.)

Jurors reported that Juror 17 refused to deliberate. When she finally began participating after further instruction from the judge, she was referencing the Lifetime movie about Jodi Arias. She said the movie made Jodi seem like a monster and she didn't get that sense from her in the courtroom. The jurors made the judge aware of this. It was reported that Juror #17 only wanted to look at Jodi's journals. According to the other jurors, she didn't seem interested in any of the other evidence. In a final effort to reach a unanimous decision, Juror #4 put the pictures of Travis's mutilated body in front of her, and asked, "If this doesn't warrant the death penalty, what does?" She had no answer. All eleven jurors felt that juror #17 had an agenda from the beginning. All eleven, not one or two. On March

6, news broke on social media about what that alleged agenda may have been.

In a tidal wave of tweets, Facebook posts, and news releases, it was reported that Juan Martinez prosecuted Juror #17's then husband and sent him to prison shortly after she married him. The man Martinez prosecuted is now her ex-husband and she is remarried. Shortly after the verdict, the first, middle, and last names of all jurors except #17 were posted on a pro-Jodi website. Juror #17's name was released via social media. This is against the law and is also being investigated. Juror #17's life has been altered as the lone holdout in this case. She has been subjected to online bullying which is never ok. Jodi's defense cost Arizona tax payers about three million dollars. Jodi was sentenced by Judge Sherry Stephens on April 13, 2015 to life without possibility of parole.

Travis,

We miss your smile, your laugh, your kindness, your compassion, your zest for life, and your love for people. We miss your unique ability to be true to who you are no matter how embarrassing it may be and no matter what people may say. We miss watching you flirt with every female that crossed your path. We offer you this book as a gift to your legacy, and as a record of what really happened. We know that were the roles reversed, you would have done this for us. It's the least we could do for you. You have touched countless numbers of people in life and in death, and you will continue to do so every, and any, time someone reads your story. Thank you for the gift of your friendship, your love, and your example of kindness and compassion. We love you!

In Love and Gratitude, Chris and Sky Hughes

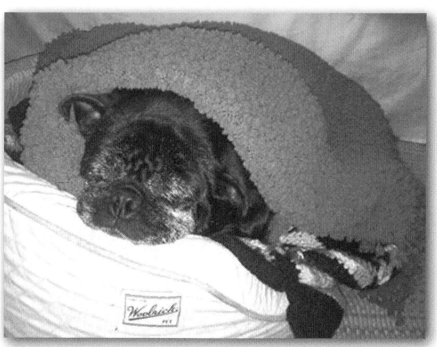

Travis's baby, Napoleon. (Deanna takes such good care of him!)

# Getting Better

THE FOLLOWING WAS WRITTEN BY Chris.

Travis was never able to finish the book that he began writing. There were several fundamental principles that he wanted to share with the world. It was these principles that changed Travis's life. Had he been allowed to live, we know he would have completed his book. Since that opportunity was taken from him, we want to honor him by doing it for him.

## WHEN YOU CHANGE, THINGS WILL CHANGE FOR YOU

One of the many things Travis and I had in common was the fact that we were both experiencing a bad financial situation that we desperately wanted to change. We found that in order for things to change for an individual, the individual must first change. I find it interesting that change, *the one thing* that is a constant and a guarantee in our lives, is so violently resisted. The thing that people oppose is the very thing that could set them free. Nido Quibaine, the CEO of the Great Harvest Bread company, said, "Babies in wet diapers are the only ones who want change." In large part, he's right, but there is a very small percentage of any population who expect change, seek change, and embrace change. These are those who enjoy the real richness of this existence.

Business philosopher Jim Rohn taught that when *you* change, everything will change for you. I believe that. In fact, I know it's true. I've not only experienced it myself, I've taught this concept to others and watched the miracle of unfathomable change unfold in their lives. This final chapter is devoted to the topic of change: how to change so that we can enjoy a higher quality of life, more peace, love, joy, success, freedom, income, and fulfillment. This was the "stuff" that changed my life and Travis's life, and it can change yours, too, if you're open to it.

Travis with his mentor Jim Rohn.

## PERSONAL DEVELOPMENT

During Travis's trial, I came to learn that there was such a thing as a "trial watcher." I had no idea there was a subculture of people in the world who follow trials as a hobby. Coming to this realization was similar to another realization I had several years earlier. I spent many years of my life feeling badly about myself because of my lack of success and progress in life. I had no money, no degree, very limited experience, no plan for the future, and was painfully single, wanting so badly to share life with someone I loved and who would love me. As I struggled in silent desperation, I discovered that there was an entire industry, the self-help or self improvement industry—a $10 billion a year industry, which is devoted to helping people like me, and all types of people, live a better quality of life. I had heard of "self-help," but was completely ignorant of what it meant. I can remember being in a bookstore one day and seeing the "self-help" section and wondering to myself, *Who is so messed up in the head that they would voluntarily buy this stuff?* Boy, have things changed.

The terms self-help, self-improvement, personal growth, and personal development can all be used interchangeably. I learned this in 1997 or 1998 when I was hired to do inside sales for a personal development company. Although I never sold anything for the very short time I worked there, in theory, I was supposed to be selling annual passes to a once-a-month networking event where local business owners, salespeople, and entrepreneurs could come to enjoy hors d'oeuvres and engage in business networking. The night concluded with a seminar given by one of the biggest names in the industry. Today, I would go nuts for such a thing! But then, I can remember attending my first seminar and thinking, *Who are these people? Who comes to this stuff?*

I've discovered that arrogance and ignorance have a tendency to travel together. That was me: arrogant and ignorant. I didn't know what I didn't know, and everyone knew it but me. Fortunately, I discovered personal development and the rest, as they say, was history.

Wikipedia defines personal development as: activities that improve awareness and identity, develop talents and potential, build human capital and facilitate employability, enhance quality of life and contribute to the realization of dreams and aspirations. In short, personal development is the practice of taking specific actions, which will help us reach our goals, whatever our goals may be.

When I first learned of this concept, it came to me with a short list of activities that will make all the difference in anyone's life, again, no matter what their goals and aspirations are. That list has evolved over the years as I experimented with them in my own life. Today the list looks like this.

1) read good books
2) listen to positive, educational, and motivational audios
3) attend seminars, classes, and workshops
4) apply the strategies, techniques, and principles you learn
5) associate with positive, successful, supportive people
6) disassociate with people who are negative, toxic, caustic, or otherwise unsupportive

As Shakespeare wrote, *the world is your oyster* for anyone who consistently does these half-dozen things throughout his or her life. I was taught that anyone who voluntarily engages in an *accelerated learning curve* for a period of six years can go from wherever they are to where they want to be. Any six years. Eighteen to twenty-four, twenty-four to thirty, fifty to fifty-six, or seventy-five to eighty-one. Any six years. I was further taught that if six years is too long, do it for five. Can't wait for five? Try four. Four years too long? Give it three. Don't want to give it three? Give it two. Can't do two? Just do one! Do this for one year, and you won't recognize yourself just twelve months later. The change will be wonderful, and your life will be renewed! So I did it. I committed for a year. Committed to what? What is an accelerated learning curve, and what exactly did I commit to?

An accelerated learning curve is simply learning a great deal of information in a very short period of time, and I committed to do it, for at least one year. At the end of that year, I was unrecognizable! I was so thrilled with the results in my life that I kept up the process and continue it today, even after all these years. I realized that there are no plateaus in life. If we're not growing, we're dying. Sadly, I was dying most of my life.

It's these concepts that both Travis and I learned and then began to do individually in our lives that allowed us to walk away from lives of poverty and despair. I did it. He did it. And if you're interested in making life better for yourself and those around you, I know you can do it too, whatever "it" is for you.

## READING GOOD BOOKS

Mark Twain has been credited as having said, "The man who does not read good books, has no advantage over the man who cannot read them." If you *can* read, and you *don't* read, you're a volunteer illiterate. This was tough medicine for me, because it was true. I could read, but I didn't read, so I was, by default, a volunteer illiterate. As a result, my quality of life was little better than your average literal illiterate. Once I discovered personal development, however, and learned that there were books written that would help me excel in any area of my choosing, I was actually excited to read them. And once I started, I couldn't stop. The fact that I was reading books, and excited to do it, was a miracle! I never read as a child, and I rarely read in high school and college.

Whether or not what I was learning was working, or would work, was yet to be seen, but I was feeling better about myself and about life, so I didn't really care what the end result would be. I was happy with the benefits I was already receiving. One day I went to my brother's house and told him about a book I was reading, *Think and Grow Rich*, by Napoleon Hill. He said, something like, "Those people only write those books to make money off stupid people like you." He may have been kidding, or not. I don't know. It didn't *feel* like he was. At first, I felt embarrassed and ashamed that I had gotten suckered, that I was one of those "stupid people" the author was making money off of. But then I remembered how the book made me feel as I read it, and I experienced a sudden surge of confidence. Rather than walking away dejected, I said, "You may be right, but I like the way it makes me feel." I am so thankful that I didn't succumb and allow myself to be derailed from the most incredible season of personal growth I'd ever experienced up to that point in my life. I was blessed to have walked away with my belief still intact.

I continued reading every day. I finished one book after another. With each completed book, I felt a boost of confidence. There was not much else that I was accomplishing in my life at that time, so to finish a book was a big achievement, and my self-esteem increased with each one. By the end of one year of reading, I was different . . . vastly different. I was beaming with optimism. I was living with expectancy. I was looking in every direction for blessings, because I just knew that life was about to get really, really good for me. It was about this time that I would learn about Pre-Paid Legal and start my own business. From that point forward, my life got better in every imaginable way! This was not coincidence or serendipity. It was cause and effect. When I got better, things got better for me. When you get better, no matter how "good" you may be, things will get better for you. Period.

It's incredible to me that countless numbers of people have lived full, successful lives, overcoming every conceivable obstacle, who then write a book to share their story, and make it available for purchase for only $10–$20. That amazes me! For an insignificant sum of money, anyone who is willing can gain a lifetime of knowledge and information from some of the world's most successful people in any area of interest: finances, spirituality, relationships, music, business, or virtually any other subject. And that's the point. All of us live in our own little villages, among our own little tribes. In most cases, few, if any, in our tribe are living the life *we* want. In other words, most of the people most people know don't know how to be successful and fulfilled in life, yet they teach their children and others in the village everything they know anyway, which results in yet another generation who lack the proper information to live a truly remarkable life. That's when the books (and audios, seminars, etc.) come in. Reading these good books allows us to learn from other tribes from other villages, giving us an infusion of information that can make all the difference in our lives.

I was raised with the belief that money is bad and it doesn't grow on trees, that relationships don't work out, that you can't teach old dogs new tricks, that if you want something done right you have to do it yourself, that the secret to success is hard work, and that no good deed goes unpunished. These philosophies, or beliefs, were spoon-fed to me and came with a label of "truth" on them. As little children, we believe that whatever our parents and teachers tell us is true. It's inconceivable to a little mind that our parents, teachers, and caretakers would lie to us, or could even make a mistake. But as we all know, teachers and parents misspeak all the time. They might be telling an untruth, while feeling certain they are telling a truth. Unfortunately, not only were many of the beliefs I was raised with not true, in large part, they are utter nonsense! Worse yet, these philosophies are severely limiting! They kept me small, and it wasn't until I began learning from other tribes from other villages, in addition to my own, that I began to see additional light.

As a point of interest, I used to live in a bad part of town in Ft. Worth, Texas (that I lovingly referred to as "the ghetto"). Many of the people living there were impoverished. Were you to ask them to see their library, they might show you a CD library or perhaps a DVD library, but a library of books is not a common sight in homes in the ghetto. However, most educated, successful, accomplished, happy people have libraries—libraries of books on a myriad of different topics that have guided them along their path to a more fulfilling and meaningful life.

After creating the iPhone and the App Store, Apple Inc. trademarked the phrase, "There's an app for that." It was a simple phrase to suggest that no matter what we need, there's an app we can download onto our iPhones that will help us. Reading is no different. Regardless of what we want to learn, overcome, or make better in our lives, there's a book for that. The book has already been written, they are very inexpensive, and they just might be the missing link in our lives. As Mr. Rohn often said, "The book you don't read won't help." Reading good books every day is one of the most important disciplines we can implement in our lives. You may not observe a difference in your life after a day, a week, or even a month, but you will after a year! You've got absolutely nothing to lose and the entire world to gain.

The key is to read "good books." According to Google's advanced algorithms, there are currently 129,864,880 books that have been published in modern history. That's a lot of books! So, how do you find the "good ones"? You ask! Ask people who are living the life you aspire to have, what some of their favorite books are. Virtually all of the books I've read that have made the deepest impact in my life were books recommended to me by people I looked up to in some way. One of the things I love about my association with Pre-Paid Legal/LegalShield is the emphasis on personal development. All of the top money earners, and many of those who aspire to be, are always reading and recommending great books to one another.

Below is a short list of some of my favorite books that have made the most difference in my life. (I give away two of them on my website to those who join my email list. You can buy your own copy of these books at any bookstore, but if you want a free .pdf copy, you can download them now from my personal development website.) One of the two free books have the word "rich" in the title, but if wealth does not interest you, don't be put off. Substitute rich for whatever it is that you want. The principles work the same no matter what the objective.

Download, *The Science of Getting Rich and As a Man Thinketh* at www. ourfriendtravis.com/ebooks

People who want to be wealthy, study wealth. People who want wonderful relationships, study relationships. People who want to live long, healthy lives, study longevity and health. What do you want to know more about? I promise there's a book for that! These are some of my favorites.

- *The Bible*
- *The Book of Mormon*
- *The Science of Getting Rich*, Wallace Wattles
- *Power -vs- Force*, David R. Hawkins
- *As a Man Thinketh*, James Allen
- *Black Like Me*, John Howard Griffen
- *Richest Man in Babylon*, George Samuel Clason
- *Benjamin Franklin: An American Life*, Walter Isaacson
- *Habits of Highly Successful People*, Stephen Covey
- *Think and Grow Rich*, Napoleon Hill
- *You Were Born Rich*, Bob Proctor
- *The Success Principles*, Jack Canfield
- *The Narrative of the Life of Frederick Douglas*, Frederick Douglas
- *Rich Dad, Poor Dad*, Robert Kiyosaki
- *How to Win Friends and Influence People*, Dale Carnegie
- *The Power of Positive Thinking*, Dr. Norman Vincent Peale
- *10 Secrets for Success and Inner Peace*, Dr. Wayne Dyer
- *7 Spiritual Laws of Success*, Deepak Chopra
- *The Magic of Thinking Big*, David J. Schwartz
- *The Road Less Traveled*, Dr. M. Scott Peck
- *The Secret*, Rhonda Byrne
- *A Lifetime of Riches* (Biography of Napoleon Hill), Michael J. Ritt & Kirt Landers
- *The Greatest Salesman in the World*, Og Magdino

- *The Divine Center*, Stephen Covey
- *The Prayer of Jabez*, Bruce Wilkinson
- *The Slight Edge* by Jeff Olson
- *Man's Search for Meaning*, Victor Frankl
- *Coming out of the Ice*, Victor Herman
- *The Last Lecture*, Randy Pausch
- *The Power of Intention*, Wayne Dyer
- *Leadership and Self Deception*, The Arbinger Institute
- *Breaking the Habit of Being Yourself*, Dr. Joe Dispenza

## Positive, Educational, and Motivational Audios

The most memorable part of the movie *Superman*, for me, is the very beginning when Kal-El, baby Superman, was placed into that crazy little spaceship and sent billions of miles away to planet Earth, as his home planet, Krypton, explodes in the background. During his trip to Earth, the audio instruction played continuously in his vessel taught him much of what he needed to know, and gave him every possible advantage. There's a lesson in this.

Best selling author and business consultant, Brain Tracy, teaches to turn your car into a University on Wheels. The idea is to listen to educational audios any time you're in your car. According to the US Census Bureau's American Community Survey, the average person spends more than one hundred hours a year commuting to work and back. I've met people who commute more than five hundred hours a year. And this is just their commute. This doesn't include time spent in the car running errands or dropping off and picking up kids from school. Can you imagine what we could learn if we spent five hundred hours a year in a University on Wheels?

Years ago, I happened upon a story about a man who had worked on a car assembly line in Detroit for twenty-five years. When the Great Recession hit, he lost his job and didn't know what to do, saying, "All I've ever done is make cars. It's all I know how to do." I wonder, had he turned his own car into a mobile classroom, educating himself to and from work for twenty-five years, if he would not have felt so desperate by his sudden misfortune. Had he been learning sales, business, marketing, communication, real estate, leadership, or entrepreneurship while driving back and forth to work for twenty-five years, odds are that he would have never been laid off in the first place. He would have either risen to a position of prominence within the organization, giving himself a higher level of job security, or perhaps more realistically, as this man continued to learn and heighten his awareness and raise his level of consciousness, he would have become so enlightened and so motivated and enthusiastic about becoming his own man, he would have quit that job a decade or two previous and started his own enterprise.

Formal education, or one you might acquire in a college or university, can make you a living. But a self-education, such as one attained in a mobile classroom (or through a book, seminar, etc.) can make you a fortune. Rather than spend time or waste time commuting, why not make an investment into your mind and future by turning your car into a classroom? Much of my success in business can be attributed to listening to my favorite audio-learning programs over and over again.

One of my favorite audio programs is *The Challenge to Succeed,* by my mentor, Mr. Jim Rohn. I bought Jim's entire library many years ago, even before I could really afford it. I had a water-resistant CD player hanging in my shower, and every day for several years, I would start my day by turning on that CD player and listening to Mr. Rohn. I loved it! He got me fired up and motivated to conquer my day and my life! One day, Sky teased me because of my long showers, and I said, "Baby, you have no idea what it's like to take a shower with Jim Rohn!"

I really believe the practice of starting my day with inspiration instead of stress, compounded over time, has had an incalculable positive effect in my life. Think about it. Most people, just after rising for the day, especially if they had a short night, are upset in the morning. They are annoyed by the alarm clock and feeling groggy. Once the mind starts working correctly, they begin to stress and worry about the day, or perhaps about their personal, relational, financial, or health problems. This worry is wasteful. It serves no positive purpose. Rather than wallow in those issues, or others, I would immediately turn on the audio, and almost instantly, my emotional and mental state turned positive. I can remember many times having to discipline myself to stay present with the audio. It seemed like every day, after listening to this or another audio for fifteen or twenty minutes or so, my mind would start drifting . . . in a good way. I would have all kinds of creative ideas and get excited about different possibilities in my life. Again, think about these two different ways that we can start our day, and what the long-term effects would be with one compared to the other. Our results, one way or the other, will speak for themselves.

Listening to audios every day is yet another way to get outside of your own village and tribe. No village and no tribe has all the answers. Not mine and not yours. If you are someone who is looking for truth, for freedom, for fulfillment, for success, for happiness, or for anything else, you've got to get as close to others who are enjoying these things as you possibly can. And listening to their books or seminars on audio is a great way to do this.

Here's a tip. Go to your local library. Less than three percent of our population owns a library card, and yet they are free. Recently, I was in my local library browsing the audio section. I was astounded by the number of incredible educational audio programs sitting on the shelf just waiting to unleash their power onto and into an open mind willing to receive it. I like purchasing my audios because I value having my own library; however, if money is tight, or you don't care to have an audio library, you have a vast resource available to you in your local library. Another resource for you is YouTube.com or Ted.com. Just this morning while taking a shower and getting ready for the day, I listened to a one-hour seminar given by a man who lived on the streets and was homeless when he was seventeen years old. Today, he has become so incredibly wealthy that he has not driven a car in twenty-one years, because when he's not on his private yacht or his jet, he hires people to drive him from place to place. I was inspired and learned so much, and it cost me absolutely nothing! It didn't even take any time out of my already busy schedule. I listened to this seminar while I was doing things I was going to do anyway. Think about what you could be learning and how much your life could change if you listened to something motivational, educational, or inspirational while you are showering, bathing, cooking, going to the restroom, running, walking or exercising, doing house work or yard work, driving to work, or running errands. This is idle time and could be used to enhance your life.

Like the saying, there's a book for that, so too, there's an audio for that. If you don't read well, then double up on the audios. Someone once told me that if you listen to educational audios on one topic, every day during your commute to and from work, that in five years you will be in the top five percent of all people in the world who are knowledgeable on your chosen subject. For example, let's say you wanted to become an expert on elephants. If you simply listened to everything you could on and about elephants, in five years, you could be one of the top elephant experts in the world. So, what would you like to be an expert on? Relationships? Money? Love? Investing? Happiness? Real estate? Business? Fitness? Sales? Elephants? Pick a topic, grab some audios, and turn your car into a University on Wheels!

Before we move onto the next topic, I want to give you a gift: an audio you can start listening to right now. It's the digital version of one of my most popular personal development CDs, *Occupy Your Own Life: Achieving Success and Freedom Through Personal Responsibility.*

Download your free copy here: www.ourfriendtravis.com/occupy

## SEMINARS, WORKSHOPS, AND CLASSES

Many years ago on *Saturday Night Live*, the late Chris Farley played a character named Matt Foley. Matt was a broke, unemployed, overweight, sloppily dressed, out of style, thrice divorced, homeless, self-proclaimed motivational speaker who lived in a "van down by the river." In the skit, he was invited to speak at a "family communication session" to two wayward teenaged kids played by David Spade and Christina Applegate. During Matt's speech entitled, *Go For It!,* he yells, belittles, and berates the teens, saying they'd better shape up or they're going to wind up eating a steady diet of government cheese and living in a van down by the river. If you've not seen it, Google: Chris Farley Motivational Speaker. It's fantastic!

As funny as this skit is, it has cast a bit of a negative shadow on the profession of motivational speaking. Perhaps it was a meaningless skit meant only to entertain, or perhaps the writers' intention was to mock motivational speakers. Nevertheless, these professional speakers have played a very important role in my life, and in the lives of successful people around the globe.

One of the downfalls of the educational "system" in America is that when we get our degree, we think we are done. The fact is, if we want to thrive, we can never be "done." We must always be learning and growing and expanding in knowledge, skills, awareness, and consciousness. I heard a speaker once say that the Glory of God is intelligence, and that all we take with us from this life into the next life is the knowledge we acquire while we are here. I like that.

Think about this. How tall does a tree grow? As tall as it can! Have you ever heard of a full grown, three-foot oak tree? They don't exist. Trees don't just grow for a while and say, "I'm good," and then decide to stop growing. However, humans, God's greatest creation, do. The reason people don't, for the sake of learning and growing, read books, listen to audios, and attend seminars is because they have decided they are "good." They have, in essence, said to God and the Universe, "I'm good," and they stop growing. As a result, so much of the good ceases its flow into that person's life. Like water, if there is no source of new, useful, life- giving and life-enhancing information flowing into our lives, our lives become stagnant and stale.

Seminars, workshops, and classes are similar to books and audios in that, for what you get, the investment is negligible. Again, to be able to sit at the feet of someone who is further down the road than you are in one or more areas of life that are important to you, is a very special opportunity, one that too few people take advantage of. There have been so many instances where I have been sitting in a seminar, workshop, or other class and the speaker or teacher said something that forever transformed my life. I couldn't help but think, *What if I missed this?*

In this modern information and communication age, educational opportunities abound! They are everywhere you look! People who are considered gurus in a myriad of different fields give away some of their best material via video courses on the Internet. There was a time, not that long ago, where if you wanted to take a class you had to physically go somewhere to take it. Today, the Internet has changed all that. You could take thousands of classes and never leave your home! You can even take piano or guitar lessons online! That said, as a side note, classes where you are required to "go somewhere" are recommended. The face-to-face interaction, the socializing, networking, and relationship building of a live, in- person seminar, workshop, or class enriches the experience and deepens the impact of the information.

A success principle I've lived my life by for many years, is simply this: don't miss. Don't miss the book. Don't miss the audio. Don't miss the seminar. Don't miss the opportunity to grow. Again, these opportunities are everywhere, yet so few take advantage of them.

I've got a question for your consideration. If you *can* learn more, should you? What do you think? You get to decide the correct answer to that question for you. If you decide that, yes, you should learn more, now the question is, *will you?* If you will, I've given you a great place to start—reading books, listening to audios, and attending seminars, workshops, and classes.

## APPLY THE STRATEGIES, TECHNIQUES, AND PRINCIPLES YOU LEARN

Those who implement the things we've previously discussed will be immeasurably better off than those who don't. However, we can take it to yet another level by practicing and doing the things we learn in the books, audios, and seminars. This may seem like common sense, but it's not. I know many people who have spent a lifetime learning from the best materials available, who still aren't experiencing their desired results. Why? Because they are "learning" a lot, but they are doing little to nothing with it. To be ever learning and growing is good, so long as we are applying the things we learn in our lives. As Calvin Coolidge once said, "The world is full of educated derelicts." (Derelict: adjective – in a very poor condition as a result of disuse and neglect.)

Let me illustrate this concept by telling the story of Robin. Robin is a man I met about ten years ago in Park City, Utah. He was forty years old, never married, and worked as a graveyard shift security guard. We talked about his life and what events had brought him to where he was. It was evident to me that Robin needed some personal development in the area of financial success. So I suggested that he read *Think and Grow Rich*, but before I could even get the title of the book off my lips, he blurted out, "*Think and Grow Rich* by Napoleon Hill! I love that book!" I was surprised that he had heard of the book, and even more surprised that he had read it and loved it.

"You read the book?" I asked.

"Yeah!" he said. "I read it like twenty years ago when I was in college."

Now my surprise turned into confusion. Three years after reading *Think and Grow Rich*, I had exponentially multiplied my income, my free time, and my overall happiness in life. That's the purpose of the book! It teaches the reader how to, a) think, and b) grow rich! I couldn't understand how he could have read the same book I read, twenty years earlier, and not also had outrageous results. The confusion dissipated as I realized that Robin must have *read* the book, but not *applied* what he read or not believed what he read, or both. I was so naïve. I assumed that since I experienced such phenomenal results from the books I was reading, that everyone else would too. But as this story illustrates, that's not the case. Robin *read* the book, but didn't experience results. There are too many of these "educated" people in the world today, who talk a lot and accomplish little. They know it all, but get little to no results, again because they don't apply what they are learning.

Let me give you a simple example of what I mean. Let's say you read a book on goal setting, the best book ever written on the subject. And let's say the author gave you a promise and a guarantee that if you do what she outlined in the book that you would succeed in achieving all of your goals. Were you to read the book, you would have the knowledge and the information, but you would not have, nor get any of the promised results, unless and until you apply the principles, strategies, and techniques you learned in the book consistently over time. This is what separates the sheep from the goats in the pursuit of success in any endeavor. It's in the doing, not the learning alone. James of the New Testament summed this concept up as succinctly as it can be, when he taught: *Be ye doers of the word, and not hearers only, deceiving your own selves.*

## THE LAW OF ASSOCIATIONS

As a teenager, some of my friends were less than good influences. My dad would often say, "Son, if you dance around dog poop long enough, you're bound to step in it." He was right, and I stepped in it, a lot. This was my dad's mini-seminar on the power of associations. Associations are indeed powerful. The Law of Association states that we become like those we associate with, regardless of whether they have a positive or negative influence in our life. An interesting observation is how so many of us, as parents, are so concerned about our children's actions and associations, but care little about our own. For example, mom and dad both smoke and drink, but they don't want their kids to. The children can only watch G-rated shows and movies, meanwhile mom and dad are taking in good, quality movies full of blood, guts, and porn. The kids can't hang out with little Johnny because he's a bad influence, but it's okay for Mom and Dad to hang out with the Tenenbaums, who everyone knows have the worst attitude in the neighborhood.

As adults, we should be as concerned about our associations and environment as we are about those of our children. It's been said that if you hang around nine negative people, you are bound to be the tenth. Said another way, you become a combined total of the people you spend the most time with. If they cuss, you cuss. If they read good books, you read good books. If they are disrespectful, you are disrespectful. If they are successful, you are successful. If they are losers, the odds are . . . you know? This is what was meant by the old English proverb, "Birds of a feather, flock together." Like attracts like. That which is like you is attracted to you, and you are attracted to it. Additionally, we can also become like those we spend time with, even if we were not initially "birds of a feather." This is one of the meanings of the phrase, "Therefore shall a man leave his father and his mother and cleave unto his wife and the two shall become one flesh." There is a literal meshing and merging of those we surround ourselves with, especially our spouses.

There are two parts of the Law of Association. One is to associate with those who have your solutions, and the other is to disassociate from those who have your problems or create them in your life. Will Rogers said, "A man only learns in two ways, one is by reading, and the other is by association with smarter people." Charlie Tremendous Jones said it this way, "You are the same person today you'll be five years from now, except for two things; the people with whom you associate and the books you read." If you want to become successful, it doesn't make any sense at all to spend all of your discretionary time with people who are not successful, and/or who are negative and unsupportive. You must associate with those who have what you want, or who are at least loving and supportive. On the other side of the coin, you must disassociate with those who are negative, toxic, caustic, or otherwise bad influences. Have you ever known someone who was so negative and talking with them left you exhausted, or who you could physically feel enter the room?

One day, some friends and I went out to eat at a restaurant in town. Just as we were finishing our meals, someone came up behind me and put their hands over my eyes. They didn't say anything to me, they just covered my eyes, and my job apparently was to guess who it was. I didn't have to guess. I knew exactly who it was. This gal was so negative that I could literally feel her negativity pulsating into and through my body. I instantly recognized her energy and called out her name. She was dumbfounded. She said, "How in the world did you know it was me? There was no way you could have known I was here." She was beside herself, thinking I was a bit of a magician. I just chalked it up to a lucky guess.

If you know anyone like this, these people should be at the top of your list to disassociate with. They affect you, whether you think they do or not. Each of us has an energy about us that can be detected by others. And our energy affects those around us, and their energy affects us. It's been said that every person who enters a room either brightens the room or dims it. It's true.

When time permits, sometimes in my seminars, I do a powerful live demonstration of the power of our associations. Some chiropractors and other alternative health practitioners use what's called applied kinesiology as part of their diagnostic process. By testing certain muscles, in certain ways, these practitioners are able to get feedback about the functional status of the body. Others have used this technique as a no-tech lie detector test. Applied kinesiology teaches that when the body is compromised, the muscles will test weak. When a person lies, they are out of integrity and the whole body is compromised, resulting in a weak muscle response. But research has also determined that the body can be compromised by the negative energy of other people. To illustrate this in my live events, I'll ask for a volunteer to leave the room, while I give the audience the following instructions. "When our volunteer comes back into the room, I'll have her come up to the stage. I want you to begin thinking the most powerful, loving, and supportive thoughts about her as you are able. See your positive thoughts leaving your mind and gently wrapping themselves lovingly around our volunteer. Then I will muscle test her and you'll see that she tests strong. Then, as I prepare to test her again, I want you all to send terrible, angry, fearful thoughts to her. See your destructive thoughts wrap around her like chains, and you'll see that your influence, your thoughts, your energy will weaken her."

The volunteer is then escorted back into the room and onto the stage. Her first test she is strong. And her second test, she is so weakened that she can hardly hold her arm up. The volunteer often is in shock, confused about how they could have become so weak from one moment to the next. When we let them in on the secret, they can hardly believe it, but eventually accept it as they experienced it firsthand. Our associations absolutely have an effect on us, both good and bad. One guy said to me, "I'm a pretty tough nut, man. People don't have an effect on me." I don't know if this type of thinking is naiveté or ignorance or a combination of the two, but I know that it's wrong. Positive associations have a positive or strengthening affect on us. Negative associations have a negative or weakening effect on us, and we don't have a choice about it. You can choose who you hang out with, but you can't choose how you're affected by them. As much as you possibly can, associate with positive people, and disassociate with negative people.

## SUCCESS SYSTEM AT-A-GLANCE

If you want to succeed in any endeavor, here's what the recipe looks like at a glance:

1. Read books in the fields you want to succeed in.
2. Listen to audios in the fields you want to succeed in.
3. Attend seminars, workshops, and classes related to the fields you want to succeed in.
4. Consistently apply what you are learning from all of the above resources.
5. Associate with others who are positive and successful in the fields you want to succeed in.
6. Disassociate from negative influences.

This is what I did to walk away from poverty and enjoy a much better quality of life. It's what I taught Travis that allowed him to do the same. It worked for me. It worked for him, and it can work for you too. Travis and I both wanted to be financially successful. We used these principles to help us to do that. But not everyone cares about that, and I get it. As a reminder, these principles can help you succeed in any area you choose.

## TRAVIS'S FAVORITE PRINCIPLES
Travis was a gifted speaker and teacher. As we watched him grow and develop as a speaker, we observed that he gravitated to a handful of principles, which he taught often during his speeches and trainings. Those principles included personal development, which I have already touched upon, but Travis also loved to talk about matters of the heart: spiritual things. The following were some of his favorite principles.

## AN ATTITUDE OF GRATITUDE
The English author Aldous Huxley once wrote, "Most human beings have an almost infinite capacity for taking things for granted." Although we all take things for granted from time to time, there is little more repugnant than an ingrate.

One day after a business seminar, some of my Pre-Paid Legal colleagues and I went to have dinner. While walking in the parking lot toward the restaurant, a woman approached us telling us a sad story about not having money to buy diapers for her new baby. A little skeptical, I pulled out my money clip and handed her $20. She ripped the bill out of my hand, looked at me with utter disgust, and yelled at me, "Twenty dollars? Twenty dollars? Do you know how much diapers cost these days?" I was so stunned by her lack of gratitude and her despicable rudeness, I couldn't even respond to her. I just stood there in the middle of the parking lot in a stupor.

I'll never forget this experience. It's etched into my soul. After my emotions settled down from having been verbally pistol-whipped, I was left with compassion for her. I believe we reap what we sow, and this woman was sowing some really bad seeds. Unless she has changed since then, I have no doubt that this woman is reaping a harvest of devastation. She was the epitome of an ingrate. This is an example of someone who exhibits the furthest thing from an attitude of gratitude. I still can't believe she didn't even say thank you before she started scolding me.

That said, there is a big difference between saying "thank you," when someone does something nice for us, and *being* in the spirit of gratitude. Saying thank you is saying thank you, and gratitude is gratitude, and the two are not necessarily synonymous. Saying thank you for a kindness someone shows us is an expression of gratitude, but it is not in and of itself, gratitude. Gratitude, as I define it, is an attitude. It's a state of being. It's not a switch that gets flipped to the on position when good fortune comes our way and flipped off when nothing great is happening in our lives. It's a constant in our lives, no matter what perceived fortune or misfortune presents itself in our lives.

The Lord said, "Thank the Lord thy God in all things." If we are to thank the Lord in all things, I would think we should thank Him at all times. *This* is an attitude of gratitude; being in the spirit of gratitude for all things, all the time.

Cicero taught, "Gratitude is not only the greatest of all virtues, but the parent of all the others." Joseph F. Smith taught, "The grateful man sees so much in the world to be thankful for, and with him the good outweighs the evil. Love overpowers jealousy, and light drives darkness out of his life . . . Pride destroys our gratitude and sets up selfishness in its place. How much happier we are in the presence of a grateful and loving soul, and how careful we should be to cultivate, through the medium of a prayerful life, a thankful attitude toward God and man!"

Travis embodied this principle. He was someone who could find the light in the very darkest moments. It was his ability to focus on the good and the light that allowed him to escape the darkness of his childhood. Later, it was this same ability that allowed him to count his many blessings, even while experiencing financial hardship and emotional struggle.

Gratitude is a key to happiness and abundance. How can we be happy with more if we cannot be happy with what we currently have? I really do feel that sometimes God tests us. He keeps us in the wilderness, if you will, for as long as it takes for us to learn gratitude, for the wilderness. When we learn it and embody it, always and for all things and in all times, we are infused with new energy and power. It's that energy and power that attracts more good into our lives.

One of the hardest things in the world to do is to feel gratitude when there is seemingly nothing to be grateful for. I know. I've been there, and was there for too long. I believe this is a skill that must be mastered before a person can exchange a life of lack for a life of abundance. So how do you do it? It starts by taking time out of each day to be *in gratitude;* to feel it, and be it. Prayer, morning and night, is a good time and place to do this. While praying, just take time to think about, and *feel about* the things you are grateful for. If you can't think of anything, thank God for being God. Thank God for giving you the ability to pray. You can thank God for your life. If you ate or drank anything today, thank Him for that. If you have an income, be grateful for that.

If the sun is shining, be grateful for that. If it's raining, be grateful for the rain. If you are single, be grateful for this season of preparation, so when you do find that special someone you will be a much better mate. If you have lost a loved one, be grateful that you had them for the time that you had them. If you are unemployed, be grateful for the additional time you have to pray, meditate, journal, and hone your skills. Then, throughout the day, look for things to be grateful for. Beautiful flowers, birds, trees, architecture, furniture, automobiles, good teachers, books, family, technology, friends, laughter, your health, roads, food, etc. When you see someone cooing at a newborn baby and you catch yourself experiencing pure joy, be grateful for that. When you see an elderly couple holding hands on a park bench, be grateful for that. When good fortune comes into the life of a friend or a neighbor, be grateful for that. As my friend Darnell says, "If God is blessing your neighbor, don't be upset, because that simply means God is in your neighborhood!" Be grateful for that! Try your best to stay in this place of gratitude each day. This is the spirit of gratitude, an attitude of gratitude. Be grateful, always, for all things and in all times, no matter what.

## YOUR PAST DOES NOT HAVE TO EQUAL YOUR FUTURE

One day, as a teenager, I was talking to my dad about a mistake I had made. In an effort to console me, he said, "It doesn't matter how tattered your past is, your future is always perfect." This statement made an indelible mark on my memory. What a wonderful truth! Later, I would hear it said another way: Your past does not have to equal your future. Like my friend and mentor Jim Rohn said, "You can tear up the current script of your life and begin to write an entirely new one at any point. Just because life has been a certain way for many years doesn't mean it always has to be that way." Your life can be any way you choose! Isn't that incredible? So many of us let life happen to us rather than happening to our lives. Some see their life as if we are God's little rag dolls created only to endure His grand puppet show, as though we are tied to strings on his fingers and have no say over how the story unfolds. Not true!

God is our Creator, but as it says in Genesis, as His offspring, having been created in His image and in His likeness, we too are creators by default. We have the ability to create what we want in our lives. God gave us our higher faculties: reason, memory, perception, will, intuition, and imagination. He gave us the ability to aspire, and with it, the ability to achieve! Crocodiles don't have the innate ability to look upon a snow-capped mountaintop and be stirred with the desire to summit that mountain, and go after it. Archibald MacLeish wrote, "The only thing about a man, that is a man, is his mind. Everything else can be found in a pig and a horse." In other words, the only thing that differentiates us from a pig is our minds, and it's the proper use of our minds that will allow us to more fully differentiate ourselves from the animals.

It is true that you can have the good life, whatever that might mean to you. But you don't get it because you want it. Contrary to popular belief, you don't get what you want, you get what you are. If you don't like what you are getting, you must change what you are. As you intentionally and purposefully change who and what you have been in the past, your future will be different. Period.

In my seminars, I talk about something called a "default future." I introduce the term, and then ask the audience what they think it means. They often say something like, "The future you are going to experience by default," which is correct. The fact is, if you want to know what your future is going to look like, just look at your past. Your default future is more of the same. It's your past placed in your future. It is the future you are going to experience by default. It requires no effort on your part. If your past, however, is not something you want more of, there is a way to avoid experiencing more of it. Change. Again, when you change, things will change for you. The title of this section is, "Your past does not *have to* equal your future." For most people, their past *will* equal their future, but it doesn't *have* to. If you do nothing more than you have been doing in your life up to this point, you will experience more of the same. If you want to experience something different, then you must do and become something different. Again, in my seminars, I'll frame all of this in a question. "How many of you want your future to be significantly better than your past?" Of course, all hands go up. Then I'll say, "All of us want our futures to be significantly better than the past, so the million dollar question is, how? How do you make your future *significantly* better than the past?" If there are 300 people in attendance at the seminar, I might get as many different answers. But here's the correct answer. *If you want your future to be significantly better than your past, then you must get significantly better in the present.* That's it. How do you get better? Personal development.

What is personal development? I defined it in the previous pages. Personal development is engaging in activities that increase your knowledge and skills, improve your awareness and identity, develop your talents and potential, build human capital, facilitate employability, enhance your quality of life, and contribute to the realization of your dreams, goals, and aspirations. It's the practice of taking specific actions that will help you reach your goals, whatever your goals may be. What are those specific practices? Read good books, listen to positive, educational, and motivational audios, attend seminars, classes, and workshops, apply the strategies, techniques, and principles you learn, associate with positive, supportive, and successful people, and disassociate with people who are negative, toxic, caustic, or otherwise unsupportive.

As we do these things, we will get better. As we get better, our lives will get better. When our lives get better, our futures will be better. Your past does not have to equal your future. For most it does, but it does not have to for *you*. It's your choice.

## Eternal Progression

Millions of people around the world are deeply involved with personal development for a myriad of reasons. As I mentioned earlier, personal development/self-help is a $10 billion a year industry. Untold numbers of people and their families and others around them have been blessed by this industry of light and knowledge. I've been passionately pursuing personal development in my life for more than fifteen years. I love it. I love the changes I have experienced, and I love the fruits that have resulted from my dedication to my own personal development. But what's it all really about for me, and for Travis as well? Progress.

One of the many things I love and appreciate about the Mormon church, is it's position on the purpose of our existence, in this life and the next. It's about progress and fuller expression. In fact, the church refers to it as "eternal progression." Even though he was not Mormon, the late best-selling author, Jim Rohn, uses this same term in his book, *The Seasons of Life*, where he describes his belief that we came from somewhere, and that we can improve our situation in the next life by our choice to grow in this life. (Jim's chapter on eternal progression is so good, that alone is worth the price of the book, which I highly recommend.)

M. Scott Peck takes these ideas of growth, progress, and becoming more to an entirely new level. In his bestselling book, *The Road Less Traveled: A New Psychology of Love, Traditional Values and Spiritual Growth*, which has sold more than seven million copies around the world, Dr. Peck wrote:

> If we postulate that our capacity to love, this urge to grow and evolve, is somehow "breathed into" us by God, then we must ask to what end? *Why* does God want us to grow? What are we growing toward? Where is the end point, the goal of evolution? What is it that God wants of us? It is not my intention here to become involved in theological niceties, and I hope the scholarly will forgive me if I cut through all of the ifs, ands, and buts of proper speculative theology. For no matter how much we may like to pussyfoot around it, all of us who postulate a loving God and really think about it

eventually come to a single terrifying idea: God wants us to become Himself. We are growing toward godhood. God is the goal of evolution. It is God who is the evolutionary force and God who is the destination. That is what we mean when we say that He is the Alpha and the Omega, the beginning and the end.

When I said that this is a terrifying idea, I was speaking mildly. It is a very old idea, but, by the millions, we run away from it in sheer panic. For no idea ever came to the mind of man which places upon us such a burden. It is the single most demanding idea in the history of mankind. Not because it is difficult to conceive; to the contrary, it is the essence of simplicity. But because if we believe it, it then demands from us all that we can possibly give, and all that we have. It is one thing to believe in a nice old God who will take care of us from a lofty position of power which we ourselves could never begin to attain. It is quite another to believe in a God who has it in mind for us precisely that we should attain His position, His power, His wisdom, His identity. Were we to believe it possible for man to become God this belief by its very nature would place upon us an obligation to attempt to attain the possible. But we do not want this obligation. We don't want to have to work that hard. We don't want Gods responsibility. We don't want the responsibility of having to think all the time.

As long as we can believe that godhood is an impossible attainment for ourselves, we don't have to push ourselves to higher and higher levels of consciousness and loving activity; we can relax and just be human. If God is in heaven and we're down here and never the twain shall meet, we can let Him have all the responsibility for evolution and the directorship of the universe. We can do our bit toward assuring a comfortable old age, hopefully complete with healthy, happy and grateful children and grandchildren; but beyond that we need not bother ourselves. These goals are difficult enough, and hardly to be disparaged. Nonetheless, as soon as we believe it is possible for man to become God, we can really never rest for long, never say, "OK, my job is finished, my work is done." We must constantly push ourselves to greater and greater wisdom, greater and greater effectiveness. By this belief we will have trapped ourselves, at least until death, on an effortful treadmill of self-improvement and spiritual growth. Gods responsibility must be our own. It is no wonder that the belief in the possibility of Godhood is so repugnant. The idea that God is actively nurturing us so that we might grow up to be like Him brings us face to face with our own laziness. (*The Road Less Traveled: A New Psychology of Love, Traditional Values and Spiritual Growth*)

The first time I read these words, I lost my breath. I have always believed this (Travis did as well), and was shocked to have stumbled onto someone else who not only also believes it, but was able to so beautifully wrap words around this idea and make it so palatable and so easy to comprehend. I take the Bible literally when God said: "Let *us* make man in *our* image, after *our* likeness. So God created man *in His own image, in the image of God* created He Him; male and female created He them" (Genesis 1:26-27). I do not see myself as a mere creation, as one of God's playthings, but as the literal offspring . . . the child of a Deathless Soul, the Grand Architect of all that is, God the Eternal Father. Paul said it this way, "The Spirit itself beareth witness with our spirit, that we are the children of God. And if children, then heirs; heirs of God, and joint heirs with Christ" (Romans 8:16). I love that word, *heirs*. Paul used it for a reason. Defined, it means: a person who inherits or is entitled to inherit rank, title, position, and property of another.

Jesus commanded us to, "Be ye therefore perfect, even as your Father which is in heaven is perfect." (Matthew 5:48) But is perfection possible in this life? On our own, I think the answer is no. But when we add Jesus to the mix, the answer changes to yes. If my bank account is overdrawn and Jesus combines his account with mine, my account would go from a negative amount to an infinite amount in an instant. It's the opposite of multiplying by zero. Any number multiplied by zero is zero. No matter how big the number, when multiplied by zero, the sum is zero. With Jesus, no matter how negative the number, when multiplied by Jesus the sum is infinite, perfect, and whole. I want and need to be multiplied by Jesus. I know that He is willing to multiply me, anyway, no matter what. But, I want to do my part. I don't want to just have something. I want to become something. As my teacher and mentor always said, "Pity the man who inherits a million dollars and who isn't a millionaire. Here's what would be pitiful: If your income grew and you didn't." This man had something, but did not, through his own efforts, become something. Jesus said, "If ye love me, keep my commandments." (John 14:15) James taught the importance of doing our part when he said, "Be ye doers of the word, and not hearers only." (James 1:22-25) Paul said it another way, "For as the body without the spirit is dead, so faith without works is dead also." (James 2:26)

It's my opinion that we ought not be idle, waiting on God to do a miracle in our lives. He is indeed a God of miracles, but there is work that we can do. We need to be anxiously engaged in *that* work, focused on serving, growing, and becoming something better, something new. That's what personal development is all about. It's about taking what we've been given, and adding upon it through our own study and toil, over a lifetime. The coach to Kings and Queens, Tony Robbins, calls it CANI, Constant And Never-ending Improvement. I like that. In other words, eternal progression.

## Who Are You?

As Sky mentioned previously, Travis was in the process of writing a book when his life was taken. Had he known that his life was about to come to an end, and were he given an opportunity to complete his book, I believe it would have included the teachings from the previous pages. Were he alive to talk to you, only to you, as he was wrapping up his own book, I believe this is what he would say, to you, in conclusion (parts are taken from his blog).

Do you know who you are? Not who the world has made you, but who you really are, at your core, who you were before you came to this earth, who you are now, and who you will be when this life is over? Let me tell you. You are a child of the Most High God. You are His child, unique and special in every way. You are divine, and as such, you have limitless potential. You can do what you want to do, have what you want to have, experience what you want to experience, accomplish what you want to accomplish, and be what you want to be. Why not? You're God's precious child.

When I was a kid, I experienced extreme poverty, ignorance, neglect, and abuse. In many ways, life was very dark. But not always. My mother adored my great-grandfather Vic. He only lived about an hour away from where my family lived in Southern California, but it was rare that my mother was in any condition to be seen by Vic. About twice a year though, my mother would clean herself up enough as well as us kids for a visit with my grandfather in his home. He would take us out for pizza. We would go with him to walk his dogs. We played checkers and played with other toys he kept for us. He was the one who taught me the alphabet. I loved him! He was not only a bright spot in my life, he was my hero! Every time before leaving his home, I would go give him a hug. Without exception, my grandpa, whose demeanor was typically cheery and casual, would suddenly become very serious. He would grab me by my shoulders, shake me gently back and forth, while looking deeply into my eyes, penetrating my spirit, and would say the following words. "Travis, you need to know that you are special and that there isn't anything that you can't do. There's something great inside you. You're special, Travis, don't you ever forget it." He would then scoop me up into a tight embrace.

I didn't know it then, but I have since learned that grandpa knew what was going on in my mother's home and was doing what he could do to offset her negative influence. He knew how she treated us and what she would say to us when she was coming off a drug high—that we were miserable and worthless and that we ruined her life. Of course these words hurt me, but every time she screamed those words at me, I would hear Grandpa's words instead. Every time she punched me in the back, I'd feel Grandpa's hands on my shoulders instead. I'd think to myself, *This woman has no idea who I am. She has no clue that I am special.* There was something great inside of me, and try as she may, she couldn't get to it!

No matter what else was going on in my life, how could I lose with a grandpa like Vic? Anything good I have accomplished in my short thirty years on this planet can be attributed to Grandpa Vic. Each time I left his home, he would say those same words to me. He would say them with such conviction that I believed him, and it has impacted every aspect of my life.

Since then, I have come to realize two things. First, my great-grandfather was right, I am special. I took his advice. I never forgot it and I never will. Second, I have learned I am no better than anyone else. So as you read the conclusion of this book, I hope that you will let these pages grab you by the shoulders and gently shake you and tell you that *you* are special, that there is something great inside *you*. I pray that you will allow the words you read to stare deep into your eyes and instill in you that there isn't anything you can't do. My desire is that this book will do for you what Grandpa Vic did for me, that you will believe what is already true, that *you* are special.

My favorite quote is by author Maryanne Williamson.

Our deepest fear is not that we are inadequate. Our deepest fear is that we are powerful beyond measure. It is our light, not our darkness, that most frightens us. We ask ourselves, who am I to be brilliant, gorgeous, talented, fabulous? Actually, who are you not to be? You are a child of God. Your playing small doesn't serve the world. There's nothing enlightened about shrinking so that other people won't feel insecure around you. We are all meant to shine, as children do. We were born to make manifest the glory of God that is within us. It's not just in some of us; it's in everyone. And as we let our own light shine, we unconsciously give other people permission to do the same. As we're liberated from our own fear, our presence automatically liberates others. (*A Return to Love*)

Indeed, you are special. You are a child of God. You were born to make manifest the glory of God! So, are you? Are you making manifest the glory of God in your life? Are you that light on a hill that cannot be hidden? Do you let the light of your life shine, so that others see the good that you do and glorify God because of it, or do you hide under the proverbial bushel? If you were called home today, would you be happy about the life you lived? Have you created a legacy? Have you made your mark on this world? Have you planted something on this planet, either in the ground or in the heart of another human being that will outlive you? What will you be remembered for? Are you satisfied with that? If not, change that! Change that while you still can! Life is so short, and none of us have a guarantee that we will live to see another day! You only get one shot at this life, and the clock is ticking. If you're going to do anything, why not do something great? If you're going to live life anyway, why not live it in style? Carpe diem! Seize the day! Laugh a little longer. Hug a little harder. Forgive a little faster. Work a little smarter. Be a little kinder, and love! Love with reckless abandon! Finally, if no one has ever told you that you can, let me tell you. You can. If no one has ever told you that they do, let me tell you, that I do; that I love you. I. Love. You. Eternally . . . Travis.

# What Do Mormons Believe?

DURING THE TRIAL, CHRIS AND I and many of our LDS friends have had trial watchers and people interested in this case reach out to us in an effort to learn more about the Church of Jesus Christ of Latter-day Saints, otherwise known as the Mormon Church. Some have become deeply curious about why they have heard so many terrible things about the Mormons and their theology, but during the trial learned that much, if not all, they had learned was false. The Mormon Church is by far the most persecuted Christian sect in American history. In the early days of the church, Mormons were hunted like wild beasts. In fact, on October 27, 1838, the then Governor of Missouri, Lilburn Boggs, issued Executive Order 44, known as the Mormon Extermination Order. Boggs directed that "the Mormons must be treated as enemies, and must be exterminated or driven from the State if necessary for the public peace—their outrages are beyond all description." Men, women, and children were murdered in cold blood. Women were raped and otherwise violated, houses and lands were plundered, eventually forcing the Mormons out. They eventually landed in the area of the United States which today is the state of Utah. That "Extermination Order" remained on the books in Missouri until 1976 when Governor Kit Bond rescinded the law, citing the unconstitutional nature of Bogg's directive.

Personally, I find it interesting that the Mormons, who, as a whole are a really wonderful people, have had so much evil spoken about and done to them. I can't help but think of Jesus Christ. He was "despised and rejected of men; a man of sorrows, and acquainted with grief." (Isaiah 53:3) Men spoke all manner of evil about him . . . that he was a blasphemer . . . that he was possessed of devils (Mark 3:22–30). Men could say what they would, it did not change the fact that he was the very Son of God, the Savior of the World.

Throughout my life, I have learned that if I want to know what a Baptist believes, I should ask a Baptist. If I want to know what a Muslim believes, I should ask a Muslim. Chances are, if I ask someone of any religion other than Islam what the Quran teaches and what Muslims believe, there is a good chance that I will be told something about killing all the infidels (non-believers) and 72 Virgins for Islamic "martyrs." Anyone who has ever talked to a Muslim about their beliefs or read the Quran will find this to be absolutely false. We have several Qurans in our home. We have read the Quran. We have many Muslim friends, some of whom we have attended a Mosque (Islamic Center) with, and consider them to be among the kindest, most wonderful, God-fearing friends we are blessed to have in our lives. But, we would never have had this gift had we not gone to the source in an effort to further understand and love our Brothers and Sisters of Islam.

Growing up as a member of the Church of Jesus Christ of Latter-day Saints, I learned at a young age that people believe a lot of strange things about us; things that often defy all reason. It would seem that with many of these strange beliefs, common sense would kick in and the person would realize that it just wasn't true, but unfortunately, because their pastor or their parents told them something, common sense didn't kick in. A teenager wouldn't ride my friend's horse because it was a "Mormon horse" and had horns. I have heard more than once that Mormons have horns, worship the devil, ride bikes, and howl at the moon.

Travis was a Mormon, and he loved the gospel of Jesus Christ. He loved to share what he believed. We have included some information about what we believe. Hopefully, this will clear up any misconceptions and answer any questions that people may have. All of the information found below was taken directly from mormon.org, and you can find more information there, including many wonderful and inspirational videos. If you have any questions, or want a complimentary copy of the Book of Mormon, please call: 877-537-0003.

As a disclaimer, anything we have expressed up to this point in this book in relation to Mormonism or religious views are our opinions and understandings, and not the official view of the Church of Jesus Christ of Latter-day Saints. The following is directly from the LDS Church's website.

# JESUS CHRIST, OUR SAVIOR

Jesus Christ is the Savior of the world and the Son of God. He is our Redeemer. The Holy Bible teaches us that Jesus Christ's mother was Mary, His father on earth was Joseph, that He was born in Bethlehem and raised in Nazareth, and labored with Joseph as a carpenter. When he turned 30, He began a three-year ministry of teaching, blessing, and healing the people of the Holy Land. He also organized His Church and gave His apostles "power and authority" (Luke 9:1) to assist in His work.

But what do we mean when we say He is the Savior of the world? The Redeemer? Each of these titles point to the truth that Jesus Christ is the only way by which we can return to live with our Heavenly Father. Jesus suffered and was crucified for the sins of the world, giving each of God's children the gift of repentance and forgiveness. Only by His mercy and grace can anyone be saved. His subsequent resurrection prepared the way for every person to overcome physical death as well. These events are called the Atonement. In short, Jesus Christ saves us from sin and death. For that, he is very literally our Savior and Redeemer. In the future Jesus Christ will return to reign on earth in peace for a thousand years. Jesus Christ is the Son of God, and He will be our Lord forever.

# What Jesus Christ Means to Us

When we accept Jesus Christ's help we can feel peace in this life and return to Heavenly Father after we die. God is our Heavenly Father, and like any parent He wants us, His children, to be happy. In the scriptures, He teaches "my work and my glory [is] to bring to pass the immortality and eternal life of man" (Moses 1:39). Eternal life means to live in heaven, in His presence, with our families, forever. God has given us commandments, which teach us what is right and wrong and chart a way through life that will offer the greatest happiness. Jesus Christ taught, "If ye love me, keep my commandments" (John 14:15). But the scriptures also teach that "no unclean thing can dwell with God" (1 Nephi 10:21). As hard as we try to live good lives, we all sin, so how can we live in God's perfect kingdom if we are imperfect? God sent Jesus Christ to earth to give us a way to overcome our sins and imperfections. "For God so loved the world, that he gave his only begotten Son, that whosoever believeth in him should not perish, but have everlasting life." (John 3:16).

# Jesus Christ Suffered for Us

Without the grace and mercy made possible by His Atonement, we could not be saved from sin. Even before God created the world, He prepared a plan that allows us to learn and grow during this life. Jesus Christ is the center of this plan. Christ's mission was not only to teach us about God the Father and how we should live, but also to make a way for us to be forgiven after we sin. Sin is more than just making a mistake. When we sin we disobey God's commandments or fail to act correctly despite our knowledge of the truth (James 4:17). Before He was crucified, Jesus prayed to God in the Garden of Gethsemane on our behalf. Christ's suffering for our sins in Gethsemane and on the cross at Calvary is called the Atonement. He suffered for us so that we can be made clean and return to live with our Heavenly Father. The Gospel of Jesus Christ is the "good news" of Christ's sacrifice for us,

giving us a path back to the Father. "Wherefore, how great the importance to make these things known unto the inhabitants of the earth,
that they may know that there is no flesh that can dwell in the presence of God, save it be through the merits and mercy, and grace of the
Holy Messiah" (2 Nephi 2:8).

## "WHERE DID I COME FROM AND WHY?"

It's hard to move forward when you don't know where you're headed or
why. God's plan gives us the answers to life's most basic questions like,
"Where did I come from?" "What's my purpose here?" And, "What
happens when I die?" Knowing the answers gives us hope and helps us
find peace and joy. Your life didn't begin at birth and it won't end at
death. Before you came to earth, your spirit lived with Heavenly Father
who created you. You knew Him, and He knew and loved you. It was a
happy time during which you were taught God's plan of happiness and
the path to true joy. But just as most of us leave our home and parents
when we grow up, God knew you needed to do the same. He knew you
couldn't progress unless you left for a while. So he allowed you to come
to earth to experience the joy—as well as pain—of a physical body.

One thing that makes this life so hard sometimes is that we're out
of God's physical presence. Not only that, but we can't remember our
pre-earth life which means we have to operate by faith rather than
sight. God didn't say it would be easy, but He promised His spirit would
be there when we needed Him. Even though it feels like it sometimes,
we're not alone in our journey.

## WHEN BAD THINGS HAPPEN

Sometimes bad things happen—even when we make good choices. We
get sick. Loved ones die. We lose our job or home. Our spouse is unfaithful. It's hard not to ask why God allows us to suffer so much. Know
that while God takes no pleasure in your suffering, your difficulties,

regardless of their cause, can bring you closer to Him and even make you stronger if you endure faithfully (2 Nephi 2:2, Revelation 3:19). It's comforting to know that God's Son, Jesus Christ, suffered all things. He understands your pain and can help you through your trials. When you have faith in God and His plan, you can be assured that there's a purpose to all that happens to you here on earth. Our time here is short compared to our eternal life. As the Lord told Joseph Smith during a period of intense suffering:

"Know thou, my son, that all these things shall give thee experience, and shall be for thy good. The Son of Man hath descended below them all. Art thou greater than he?" (Doctrine and Covenants 122:7-8).

Coping with calamities can strengthen you and make you more compassionate. It can help you learn, grow and want to serve others. Dealing with adversity is one of the chief ways you're tested and tutored in your life here on Earth. Our loving Heavenly Father has the ability to compensate us for any injustices we may be called upon to endure in this mortal life. If we endure faithfully He will reward us beyond our ability to comprehend in the life to come (1 Corinthians 2:9). Amazingly, with God's help you can experience joy even in times of trial, and face life's challenges with a spirit of peace.

## GOD'S PLAN- WHAT JESUS CHRIST DID FOR US

Heavenly Father knew you would make mistakes in this mortal life. Your mistakes might be as simple as hurting your friend's feelings, or a sin far more serious. Seeing the pain we've caused and feeling the misery of remorse, shame and guilt can sometimes be overwhelming and devastating. We wonder if we can ever overcome our mistakes and feel the peace of being forgiven. We unequivocally can, because of the Atonement of Jesus Christ and the process of repentance. We can confess our sins to God and ask His forgiveness. And he's promised that He'll "remember them no more" (Doctrine and Covenants 58:42). It works because Heavenly Father sent his son, Jesus Christ, to voluntarily suffer and pay for our sins and sorrows by atoning for them Himself. We can't fully understand how Jesus suffered for our sins. But we know that in the Garden of Gethsemane, the weight of our sins caused Him such agony that He bled from every pore (Luke 22:39-44) . Later, as He hung upon the cross, Jesus willingly suffered painful death by one of the cruelest methods ever known (Alma 7:11).

However, His mental and spiritual anguish went well beyond the pains of the cross. The Savior tells us, "For behold, I . . . have suffered these things for all, that they might not suffer . . . even as I" (Doctrine and Covenants 19:16–17).

In addition to asking God's forgiveness, He also wants us to ask forgiveness of those we've harmed, see if we can repair the damage, and promise not to repeat the same mistakes. Then we can move forward feeling God's love and the incredible peace and joy that come from being fully forgiven.

To make His Atonement fully effective in your life, you need to:

* Exercise faith in Him.
* Repent.
* Be baptized.
* Receive the Holy Ghost.
* Choose to follow His teachings for the rest of your life.

## WHAT HAPPENS WHEN I DIE?

Picture your hand inside a glove. The glove moves only when your hand does. Take your hand out and the glove sits lifeless on the table. This is an easy way to visualize what happens when you die. Imagine your body is the glove being operated by who you really are—your spirit. When you die your body gets left behind, lifeless like a glove, but your spirit lives forever.

Countless scriptures and personal accounts by prophets throughout time have told us this is true.

Our physical death isn't the end, but rather is a step forward in Heavenly Father's plan and a time of indescribable joy for the person making the transition.

When you're the one left behind—the one losing a friend or loved one—the pain of that loss is very real. But there's a lot of comfort in knowing you'll see him or her again. And because of Christ's death, at some point our spirit and body will be reunited (resurrected) and made perfect never to be separated again.

## Immortality- One of God's Greatest Gifts

If you could have one wish, what would it be?

Most of us would probably say we want to live forever. That's exactly what God gave to each of us when He sent His son, Jesus Christ, to earth to die for us and to atone for our sins. It's called resurrection and everyone born on earth, even wicked people, will receive this gift of immortality (1 Corinthians 15:22).

On the third day after His Crucifixion, Jesus Christ became the first person to be resurrected. His spirit was reunited with His glorified, perfected body and He could no longer die. When Christ's friends went to visit His tomb, angels said, "He is not here: for he is risen, as he said" (Matthew 28:6).

## "Will I Go To Heaven?"

Yes! God will judge all men fairly and reward them appropriately with a place within His kingdom.

## Christ Organized His Church on Earth

"I am the way, the truth and the life" (John 14:6) Christ told his followers during his brief but powerful ministry on earth. It was a timely and needed message since a few hundred years before His birth many people had stopped living according to God's commandments. Christ brought light back into the world when He proclaimed His gospel just as he had to the prophets of old like Abraham, Isaac, and Moses. He chose twelve men to be His apostles—including Peter, James and John—and laid His hands on their heads to give them authority called the priesthood to perform baptisms, govern His church, and spread His word throughout the world.

In spite of His great influence and many miracles, He was ultimately rejected and crucified. After his death, His brave and faithful apostles carried on without Him, baptizing new members, and starting various congregations.

## THE DARK AGES OF CHRISTIANITY

Regardless of the valiant efforts of Christ's apostles and their faithful followers, the original church that Christ restored began to fade away. Members faced severe persecution and all but one of the apostles were martyred. This is a period called the Great Apostasy, when there was a "falling away" (2 Thessalonians 2:1-3) from the gospel Christ organized. The apostolic authority to bestow priesthood keys and to receive revelation for the Church was lost along with many precious teachings. Errors about His teachings crept into the church resulting in conflicting opinions and lost truths. This period is what we call the Great Apostasy.

## CHRISTIAN DARK AGES

Without authority or divine direction, Christianity struggled to survive with conflicting opinions on even the most basic teachings of the gospel. Without priesthood authority or the full gospel, people had to rely on human wisdom to interpret the scriptures, principles and ordinances. Many false ideas were taught as truth, and much of what we know about the true character and nature of God the Father, His

Son Jesus Christ, and the Holy Ghost was lost. Essential doctrines like faith, repentance, baptism, and the gift of the Holy Ghost became distorted and important doctrines were lost entirely.

Centuries later, inspired people, such as Martin Luther and John Calvin, recognized that practices and doctrines had been changed or lost and tried to reform the churches to which they belonged. But without the authority of the apostles of the Lord Jesus Christ, His gospel and Church could not be returned to their original form.

## GOD RESTORED CHRIST'S CHURCH THROUGH JOSEPH SMITH

If the boy next door told us he was called by God to restore His true church on earth, would we believe him? Probably not. Neither did many people in Nazareth believe their neighbor, Jesus Christ the carpenter, was the Messiah.

After centuries of spiritual confusion people were in desperate need of Jesus Christ's original truths. When God selected a 14-year-old boy in 1820 as His messenger, most people refused to listen. Joseph Smith lived in the United States, which was the only country to proclaim religious freedom at the time. His family was deeply religious and constantly sought the truth.

Joseph had to decide which of the many Christian denominations to join. After careful study, Joseph Smith still felt confused as to which Christian church he should join. He later wrote, "So great were the confusion and strife among the different denominations, that it was impossible for a person young as I was . . . to come to any certain conclusion who was right and who was wrong. . . . In the midst of this war of words and tumult of opinions, I often said to myself: What is to be done? Who of all these parties are right; or, are they all wrong together? If any one of them be right, which is it, and how shall I know it?" (Joseph Smith—History 1:8, 10).

He turned to the Bible for guidance. He read, "If any of you lack wisdom, let him ask of God, that giveth to all men liberally, and upbraideth not; and it shall be given him" (James 1:5). With simple faith he decided to do just that. In the spring of 1820 he went to a nearby grove of trees and knelt in prayer. He described his experience: "I saw a pillar of light exactly over my head, above the brightness of the sun, which descended gradually until it fell upon me. . . When the light rested upon me I saw two Personages, whose brightness and glory defy all description, standing above me in the air. One of them spake unto me, calling me by name and said, pointing to the other—This is My Beloved Son. Hear Him!" (Joseph Smith—History 1:16–17). In his vision God the Father and His Son, Jesus Christ, appeared. The Savior told Joseph not to join any of the churches. Although many good people at that time believed in Christ and tried to understand and teach His gospel, they didn't have the fullness of truth or the authority to baptize and perform other saving ordinances. This vision marked the beginning of the Restoration of the Church of Jesus Christ to the earth, which God authorized to be established 10-years later by a wiser, heaven-tutored Joseph Smith, once again allowing everyone to receive the joy and blessings that come from living it.

## THE BOOK OF MORMON

Since its publication in 1830, the Book of Mormon has blessed the lives of millions through its powerful message about Jesus Christ and His gospel.

The Book of Mormon testifies that Jesus Christ did indeed live on the earth and still lives today as our divine Savior. It's a second witness affirming the existence of Jesus Christ and the truth of the Bible. The account of its origin is as miraculous as the other events surrounding the restoration of the Church.

In 1823 Joseph Smith was visited by a heavenly messenger named Moroni just as angels often appeared to Apostles in the New Testament.

Moroni told Joseph about a record of the ancient inhabitants of the American continent that was buried in a nearby hill. He said it contained the fullness of the gospel of Jesus Christ and was written on thin metal sheets of gold. Joseph translated the book into English. The book was named the Book of Mormon after Mormon, the ancient prophet who compiled it.

Translated and written in the same scriptural style of the Holy Bible, the Book of Mormon tells us about the struggles of the righteous people of that time who were trying to live God's commandments. Just as sometimes happens today, they were often made fun of and persecuted for their beliefs. A particularly inspiring section of the book recounts Christ's visit to the American continent soon after His resurrection. He invited the people to feel the wound marks in his hands, feet and side. He blessed and healed them, performed miracles, and gave twelve men the same authority as His twelve apostles whose works are recorded in the Bible. The effect of His visit was so profound that for nearly 170 years the people lived in peace and righteousness.

## GOD IS YOUR LOVING HEAVENLY FATHER

The central truth of the restored church is that God is our Heavenly Father and we are his spirit children. He knows us personally and loves us more than we can comprehend. He wants us to be successful in this life and return to live with Him. Our life on earth is part of His plan for us to gain a body, learn, grow and find joy. Sometimes life is hard, lonely or frightening, but Heavenly Father is always concerned about you. In answer to your prayers, He is ready to give you comfort, peace and guidance.

He has prepared a path for us to follow that will bless our lives. This path is necessary for us to return to Him. This will enable us to receive the fullness of the effects of Christ's atoning sacrifice. As we do, we'll find greater peace and joy both in this life and in the life to come.

## FAMILIES ARE VITAL TO GOD'S PLAN

Maybe we were raised in a happy and secure family with two loving parents. Maybe we weren't, and growing up was tough without the love and support we longed for. Likely, as an adult we want a happy home.

Living peacefully in a family isn't always easy, but in God's restored church, marriage and families are believed to be the most important social unit now and in eternity. God wants us to do all we can now to prepare ourselves to live with our family forever. If we build our marriage and family around Christ's principles including faith, prayer, repentance, forgiveness, respect, love, compassion, work and wholesome fun, home can be a place of refuge, peace and immense joy.

We must not get discouraged. No matter how hard we try, our marriage and home won't be perfect. That's part of the growth process we're meant to experience. God wants us to learn how to be patient and loving when our spouse, toddler or teen is acting only too human. Our job is to serve them, which in turn will help us become more like God.

## HOW GOD TALKS TO US TODAY

One of the ways God talks to us is by answering our prayers.

He also gives us direction through his prophets who have the authority to speak and act in His name. Throughout history, brave prophets like Noah, Abraham, Moses, Peter, John the Baptist, Paul the Apostle and countless others bore fervent testimonies of Christ to help our own faith in Him grow.

When Joseph Smith was tragically martyred in Carthage, Illinois in 1844, the leadership of the restored Church was passed to Brigham Young who was the senior apostle at that time. He led the Church under Christ's direction for the next 33 years—leading the first group of pioneers across the plains to the Salt Lake Valley in 1847. He supervised the immigration of over 70,000 additional people from the U.S.

and Europe, and founded over 350 settlements in the Western U.S., Canada, and Mexico.

The succession of prophets continues today with our current prophet and President of the Church, Thomas S. Monson. He is assisted by two counselors, Henry B. Eyring and Dieter F. Uchtdorf. Together, they make up the First Presidency of The Church of Jesus Christ of Latter-day Saints (much like Peter, James, and John in Christ's time). Just as God led the Israelites out of slavery to a better place through His prophet Moses, He leads us into happier, more peaceful lives when we choose to follow Jesus Christ by following His living prophet. We are all invited to read or listen to the words of living prophets and consider how knowing God's will can benefit our lives.

## Divine Guidance

Remember how our parents would teach us rules when we were young? Rules like not playing in the street or not playing with matches. Remember how sometimes the rules seemed like a burden, like our parents must have invented them to keep us from doing the things we really wanted to do—the things we thought would make us happy? As we grow up we learn how important these rules are, how we could have been seriously injured or even killed if we had not obeyed.

Like our parents growing up, God gives us commandments to help keep us focused on what is most important and how to stay safe. All of His guidance is meant to keep us safe, help us stay close to Him and, in the end, to give us more freedom and happiness.

The word "commandment" might make us think of the Ten Commandments—a list of "Thou Shalt Nots"—God does not only tell us what we should not do, but He also tells us what we should do. His greatest hope is for our eternal happiness, so we can be sure that His commandments are not restrictive rules, but they are divine guidance meant to protect us from harm and lead us to better ways of living.

## THE TWO GREAT COMMANDMENTS

Our obedience to God's commandments comes from our desire to show our love for Him, for our fellow human beings, and for ourselves. While Jesus Christ was on earth, a man asked him, "Which is the great commandment in the law?" Jesus replied,

"Thou shalt love the Lord thy God with all thy heart, and with all thy soul, and with all thy mind. This is the first and great commandment. And the second is like unto it, Thou shalt love thy neighbour as thyself. On these two commandments hang all the law and the prophets" (Matthew 22:36-40).

Jesus Christ teaches us in these few lines that at the heart of all these "do's and don'ts" is a focus on loving God and loving the people around us. As we think about the commandments listed below, it helps to consider how each of them relates to these two foundational commandments.

## LAW OF CHASTITY

The power and holiness of sexual intimacy requires careful protection so it can be a source of joy and closeness. The power of procreation is a sacred part of God's plan. It's an expression of love and allows husband and wife to create life. God has commanded that this power and privilege of a sexual relationship only exist between a man and woman who are legally married. This commandment is called the law of chastity. It requires abstinence from sex before marriage and complete fidelity and loyalty to our spouses after marriage. God expects us to keep our thoughts clean and be modest in our dress, speech, and actions (Matthew 5:27–28). We must also avoid viewing pornography and engaging in homosexual relations.

We understand that the principles of the law of chastity set The Church of Jesus Christ of Latter-day Saints apart and may sound strict to the rest of the world, yet great blessings of peace, self-respect, and self-control come from obeying this commandment.

# THE CHURCH OF JESUS CHRIST

"Come unto me." Those three simple words spoken by Jesus Christ (Matthew 11:28) sum up the central purpose of His Church—to help all people come unto Christ, that they might receive salvation.

In return for following Jesus Christ's way, He promises us many things, two of which are answers to our prayers and rest to our souls. We can all use a little rest. We all struggle with something. To all of us He says: Lay down your burdens. Let me carry your load. Turn away from the darkness and into the light. He also promises peace. "Peace I leave with you, my peace I give unto you. . . . Let not your heart be troubled, neither let it be afraid" (John 14:27).

The roadmap to our Heavenly Father and His Son Jesus Christ is outlined in the restored gospel and taught by The Church of Jesus Christ of Latter-day Saints. It starts with being baptized into Christ's fold and participating in His sacred ordinances and the fellowship of His Church. The journey continues with a loving congregation whose purpose is to lift and be lifted—and ultimately be saved in the Kingdom of God.

# JOSEPH SMITH: A PROPHET OF GOD

The western part of New York State in the early 1800s was known as the "Burned Over District." The fervor over religion was intense. Many religions sent ministers seeking converts to their flock. So much so that no one, it was supposed, was left to convert. It was a time and a place of theological turmoil.

This is the setting into which Joseph Smith, Jr., son of Joseph and Lucy Mack Smith, was born. His large family found themselves in the heart of this religious revival, wanting to live good lives but not sure which of the competing churches was the right one to join. Members of Joseph's family leaned toward different religions, but none felt certain that theirs was the true Church of Christ.

Members of the Mormon Church share their feelings and testimonies about Joseph Smith, the Prophet.

Joseph heard so many competing versions of truth that he decided to turn to God for answers.

As a young man of fourteen years, Joseph already had a desire to find the truth. Like the rest of his family, he was deeply religious, and when the time came for him to be baptized, Joseph had to decide which of the many Christian denominations to join. After careful study, he still felt confused. He later wrote, "So great were the confusion and strife among the different denominations, that it was impossible for a person young as I was [ … ] to come to any certain conclusion who was right and who was wrong [ … ] In the midst of this war of words and tumult of opinions, I often said to myself: What is to be done? Who of all these parties are right; or, are they all wrong together? If any one of them be right, which is it, and how shall I know it?" (Joseph Smith-History 1:8, 10).

Joseph turned to the Bible for guidance. He read,

"If any of you lack wisdom, let him ask of God, that giveth to all men liberally, and upbraideth not; and it shall be given him" (James 1:5).

This verse deeply impressed him. He decided to pray about what he should do, with simple faith that God would hear and answer him.

## A PROPHET OF GOD

In response to a humble prayer, God called Joseph to re-establish the Church of Jesus Christ.

In the spring of 1820, Joseph went to a grove of trees near his home and knelt in prayer. He described his experience: "I saw a pillar of light exactly over my head, above the brightness of the sun, which descended gradually until it fell upon me [ … ] When the light rested upon me I saw two Personages, whose brightness and glory defy all description, standing above me in the air. One of them spake unto me, calling me by name and said, pointing to the other-This is My Beloved Son. Hear Him!" (Joseph Smith-History 1:16-17).

This vision of Heavenly Father and His Son Jesus Christ was the beginning of Joseph Smith's calling as a prophet of God. He was told that none of the churches on the earth had the fullness of truth. Over time, Joseph Smith was chosen to establish Christ's Church and restore the priesthood, or the authority to act in God's name. He was led by God to an ancient record and given the ability to translate it into English. This record is called the Book of Mormon. He continued to pray and receive revelation for the Church throughout his life. These revelations were compiled into a book of scriptures referred to as the Doctrine and Covenants and shows that God still leads His children today. Joseph Smith formally organized The Church of Jesus Christ of Latter-day Saints on April 6, 1830.

## A LEADER OF JESUS CHRIST'S CHURCH

On the morning of a beautiful, clear day, early in the spring of 1820, young Joseph went into these woods to pray, to a place where he had previously designed to go. Here, God the Father and His resurrected Son, Jesus Christ, appeared to Joseph Smith to commence the Restoration of the gospel in the latter days.

Joseph Smith led the expanding Church through physical, emotional, and spiritual adversity.

Sometimes, when we reach a position of responsibility, we feel like we don't need help anymore, but Joseph Smith relied on the Lord more and more after he was called as a prophet. He knew that his responsibility was not to spread his own teachings, but to pass along the things God revealed to him. Most of the text that makes up the Doctrine and Covenants is God's answers to Joseph Smith's prayers and questions. He asked God to clarify parts of the gospel and asked for guidance about how he should lead the Church and the growing number of Mormons. God told him to call apostles, prophets, and other leaders to oversee the Church.

Early Mormons endured serious persecution because of a perceived commercial, political and religious threat to their neighbors, so Joseph and the people he called to assist him had to lead multiple Mormon migrations to friendlier areas of the country. Despite all of the suffering they endured, early members of the Church built temples, did missionary work, built thriving cities and some served in the United States military as they migrated west. Years before Joseph died, the Lord directed him to organize the Quorum of Twelve Apostles and eventually he bestowed upon them all the keys, rights, and authority necessary to lead the Church. Following Joseph Smith's death, Brigham Young, then the senior Apostle on the earth succeeded him as the second prophet and president of the Church. The prophet today, Thomas S. Monson, is the authorized successor to Joseph Smith. He and the Church's other Apostles trace their priesthood authority back to Jesus Christ in an unbroken chain of ordinations through Joseph Smith.

## THE WORD OF GOD- THE BOOK OF MORMON

Missionaries are handing out copies of the Book of Mormon all over the world, even as you read this. So what is this book? If it's given out for free, why do so many members of The Church of Jesus Christ of Latter-day Saints count their Book of Mormon as one of their most valuable possessions? What kind of book can cause so many readers to change their lives, their minds and their hearts? What kind of book can answer life's seemingly unanswerable questions?

The Book of Mormon is the word of God, like the Bible. It is Holy Scripture, with form and content similar to that of the Bible. Both books contain God's guidance as revealed to prophets as well as religious histories of different civilizations. While the Bible is written by and about the people in the land of Israel and surrounding areas, and takes place from the creation of the world until shortly after the death of Jesus Christ, the Book of Mormon contains the history and God's dealings with the people who lived in the Americas between approximately 600 BC and 400 AD. The prophets in the Book of Mormon recorded God's dealings with His people, which were compiled by a prophet named Mormon onto gold plates.

Before these faithful Christians perished, their record was safely hidden away. Joseph Smith obtained these ancient records in 1827, and with the gift and power of God Joseph was able to translate the ancient writings into what we have today. The Book of Mormon, along with the Bible, testifies that Jesus Christ is our divine Redeemer and that by living according to His gospel we can find peace in this life and eternal happiness in the life to come.

God can give people special help when they need it for a righteous cause. He gave Joseph Smith the ability to translate an unfamiliar language in order to bring the Book of Mormon to each of us. When Joseph Smith was 21 years old, an angel named Moroni gave him the ancient records. Joseph had little formal education and was unfamiliar with the ancient language written on the metal sheets of gold, but he was able to translate them because God gave him the gift and power to do so. The translation took less than three months, and in 1830, 5,000 copies of the Book of Mormon were published in Palmyra, New York. God chose Joseph as a prophet, seer, revelator and translator to restore The Church of Jesus Christ in modern time, and the Book of Mormon was essential to this restoration. Joseph Smith was given an extraordinary calling, and because he kept himself worthy of the blessings of heaven, he was able to bring the Book of Mormon to the world. The focus of the Book of Mormon is Jesus Christ, His atoning sacrifice and His gospel.

We believe that having faith in Jesus Christ is the first step in understanding the gospel and receiving the eternal happiness that God our Heavenly Father wants for us. But where does that faith come from? How can we come to believe that Jesus Christ is our Savior if we don't know who He is or what He did? We can develop faith in Jesus Christ by reading about Him in the scriptures and praying to know if what we've read is true.

The title page states that the Book of Mormon's purpose is to convince all of us "that JESUS is the CHRIST, the ETERNAL GOD, manifesting himself unto all nations." It was written to help us develop a true knowledge of Jesus Christ and His mission on earth. The Book of Mormon reaffirms what we learn from the Bible, that Jesus Christ is the Son of God who came to earth to help us overcome our sins. The people in the Book of Mormon, the Nephites and the Lamanites, recorded their testimonies of Jesus Christ. Many of the prophets who wrote the records that make up the Book of Mormon saw Christ personally, just as happened with the Apostle Paul, which he recorded in the Bible (see Acts 9:3-6). The climax of the book is when Jesus appeared to all the Nephites soon after He was resurrected. He blessed them, taught them his gospel and said,

"Arise and come forth unto me, that ye may thrust your hands into my side, and also that ye may feel the prints of the nails in my hands and in my feet, that ye may know that I am the God of Israel, and the God of the whole earth, and have been slain for the sins of the world" (3 Nephi 11:14).

## THE BOOK OF MORMON AND THE BIBLE SUPPORT EACH OTHER

Like two eyewitnesses strengthen an argument in court, the Book of Mormon and the Bible both testify of Christ.

Some people think that because we read the Book of Mormon, we don't read the Bible. That's just not true. It's like saying that we don't eat oranges because we eat apples. Both are good fruit! The Book of Mormon is not a replacement for the Bible. In fact, because the Book of Mormon and the Bible both contain the gospel of Jesus Christ as it was revealed to different civilizations, studying them together can clarify some concepts that are difficult to understand. The Book of Mormon tells us to read the Bible and affirms that its message is true (Mormon 7:8-10). And in the Bible, Jesus told His apostles, "Other sheep I have, which are not of this fold: them also I must bring, and they shall hear my voice; and there shall be one fold, and one shepherd" (John 10:16). Christ visited these "other sheep" in the Americas after He was resurrected, teaching the same message to the Nephites that He taught to the people of Israel. The Book of Mormon makes it clear that Jesus Christ's message and His atonement are not for one group of people at one time. They are for everyone, everywhere, from the beginning of the earth to the end. Having the Book of Mormon as another testament of Jesus Christ reminds us that He is mindful of every one of us.

## THE BOOK OF MORMON ANSWERS QUESTIONS OF THE SOUL

Most of us have some hard questions in the back of our minds — the kind no one else can really answer for us. Some are far-reaching questions about the nature of our existence like the following:

Is there really a God?

MOSIAH 4:9

Believe in God; believe that he is, and that he created all things, both in heaven and in earth; believe that he has all wisdom, and all power, both in heaven and in earth; believe that man doth not comprehend all the things which the Lord can comprehend.

Does my life have a purpose?

2 NEPHI 2:25-27

25. Adam fell that men might be; and men are, that they might have joy.
26. And the Messiah cometh in the fulness of time, that he may redeem the children of men from the fall. And because that they are redeemed from the fall they have become free forever,

knowing good from evil; to act for themselves and not to be acted upon, save it be by the punishment of the law at the great and last day, according to the commandments which God hath given.

27. Wherefore, men are free according to the flesh; and all things are given them which are expedient unto man. And they are free to choose liberty and eternal life, through the great Mediator of all men, or to choose captivity and death, according to the captivity and power of the devil; for he seeketh that all men might be miserable like unto himself.

Did I exist before I was born?
ALMA 13:3
And this is the manner after which they were ordained—being called and prepared from the foundation of the world according to the foreknowledge of God, on account of their exceeding faith and good works; in the first place being left to choose good or evil; therefore they having chosen good, and exercising exceedingly great faith, are called with a holy calling, yea, with that holy calling which was prepared with, and according to, a preparatory redemption for such.
What happens after I die?
ALMA 40:11-13, 23

11. Now, concerning the state of the soul between death and the resurrection—Behold, it has been made known unto me by an angel, that the spirits of all men, as soon as they are departed from this mortal body, yea, the spirits of all men, whether they be good or evil, are taken home to that God who gave them life.

12. And then shall it come to pass, that the spirits of those who are righteous are received into a state of happiness, which is called paradise, a state of rest, a state of peace, where they shall rest from all their troubles and from all care, and sorrow.

13. And then shall it come to pass, that the spirits of the wicked, yea, who are evil—for behold, they have no part nor portion of the Spirit of the Lord; for behold, they chose evil works rather than good; therefore the spirit of the devil did enter into them, and take possession of their house—and these shall be cast out into outer darkness; there shall be weeping, and wailing, and gnashing of teeth, and this because of their own iniquity, being led captive by the will of the devil.

23. The soul shall be restored to the body, and the body to the soul; yea, and every limb and joint shall be restored to its body; yea, even a hair of the head shall not be lost; but all things shall be restored to their proper and perfect frame.

As we read the Book of Mormon, we learn about the gospel and God's Plan of Happiness. A knowledge of these things puts our questions in an eternal perspective. From the scripture that says this life is "a time to prepare to meet God," for example, we learn that we will continue to exist after we die, and that by keeping the commandments we can return to heaven (Alma 12:24). We also learn that repentance, forgiveness and the covenant to serve others are essential to our eternal salvation. Any of these questions of the soul can be answered by applying the gospel of Jesus Christ as it's written in the Book of Mormon.

## THE BOOK OF MORMON DRAWS PEOPLE CLOSER TO GOD

God is our loving Heavenly Father. We can get to know Him better by reading His words in the Book of Mormon.

Some descriptions of God make Him sound abstract and unapproachable, or angry and vengeful, but we learn in the Book of Mormon that "God is mindful of every people" (Alma 26:37) and that like the Book of Mormon prophet Lehi, we can be "encircled about eternally in the arms of his love" (2 Nephi 1:15).

Though we might not get to speak with God face-to-face in this life, He has given us the scriptures to help us draw closer to Him. Of the Book of Mormon, Joseph Smith said, "a man would get nearer to God by abiding by its precepts, than by any other book." We get nearer to God by building faith in Him, and we build faith in Him when we learn about His plan and keep His commandments.

The Book of Mormon teaches us God's plan and shows us how those who live according to His counsel are blessed in this life and the next. When we read prayerfully, the Holy Ghost can teach us, deep in our hearts, that the words in the Book of Mormon are a message to us from our Heavenly Father, sent to help us through this life.

## How To Know The Book of Mormon Is True

Through honest study and humble prayer, we can each know for ourselves that the Book of Mormon really is the word of God. Of course it's one thing to read the Book of Mormon and another to believe deep in our hearts that what it says is true. This sincere belief, or testimony, in the truth of the Book of Mormon comes when God sends His Spirit to confirm the truth of what we read. We can feel this confirmation when we study the Book of Mormon with diligence and faith, as we are promised in the following scripture:

"And when ye shall receive these things, I would exhort you that ye would ask God, the Eternal Father, in the name of Christ, if these things are not true; and if ye shall ask with a sincere heart, with real intent, having faith in Christ, he will manifest the truth of it unto you, by the power of the Holy Ghost. " (Moroni 10:4)

God's method is simple: we read the Book of Mormon; we pray and ask Him to tell us that what we've read is true and He answers us through feelings of peace and assurance given by the Holy Ghost. First of all, we have to study the Book of Mormon diligently, applying its principles to our own lives and doing our best to understand the lessons that God wants us to learn. Second, we have to pray "with a sincere heart, with real intent, having faith in Christ." We need to hope and believe that God will answer us, and we may have to pray more than once. Last, we need to be willing to accept the answer when it comes, however it may come. Believing that the Book of Mormon really contains the word of God means that we will be willing to live up to the standards of faith and obedience He describes in it. God has promised that He will bless us with much more than it takes to live up to His high standards.

One of the first things we're taught as children are the Articles of Faith — 13 statements that summarize our fundamental beliefs. Two years before he died, the Prophet Joseph Smith wrote them in a letter to a newspaper editor, John Wentworth, who had asked for information about the Church. Ever since the Articles of Faith were written, they've inspired and directed us in the basic principles of our gospel. They enhance our understanding of certain doctrines and help us commit to living them. They invite further thought. And they're a good tool for explaining our beliefs to people unfamiliar with them.

13 Articles of Faith

1. We believe in God, the Eternal Father, and in His Son, Jesus Christ, and in the Holy Ghost.
2. We believe that men will be punished for their own sins, and not for Adam's transgression.
3. We believe that through the Atonement of Christ, all mankind may be saved, by obedience to the laws and ordinances of the Gospel.
4. We believe that the first principles and ordinances of the Gospel are: first, Faith in the Lord Jesus Christ; second, Repentance; third, Baptism by immersion for the remission of sins; fourth, Laying on of hands for the gift of the Holy Ghost.

5. We believe that a man must be called of God, by prophecy, and by the laying on of hands by those who are in authority, to preach the Gospel and administer in the ordinances thereof.

6. We believe in the same organization that existed in the Primitive Church, namely, apostles, prophets, pastors, teachers, evangelists, and so forth.

7. We believe in the gift of tongues, prophecy, revelation, visions, healing, interpretation of tongues, and so forth.

8. We believe the Bible to be the word of God as far as it is translated correctly; we also believe the Book of Mormon to be the word of God.

9. We believe all that God has revealed, all that He does now reveal, and we believe that He will yet reveal many great and important things pertaining to the Kingdom of God.

10. We believe in the literal gathering of Israel and in the restoration of the Ten Tribes; that Zion (the New Jerusalem) will be built upon the American continent; that Christ will reign personally upon the earth; and, that the earth will be renewed and receive its paradisiacal glory.

11. We claim the privilege of worshiping Almighty God according to the dictates of our own conscience, and allow all men the same privilege, let them worship how, where, or what they may.

12. We believe in being subject to kings, presidents, rulers, and magistrates, in obeying, honoring, and sustaining the law.

13. We believe in being honest, true, chaste, benevolent, virtuous, and in doing good to all men; indeed, we may say that we follow the admonition of Paul-We believe all things, we hope all things, we have endured many things, and hope to be able to endure all things. If there is anything virtuous, lovely, or of good report or praiseworthy, we seek after these things.

Made in the USA
Columbia, SC
02 May 2019